EASTERN KARELIA

HELIGOLAND
SCHLESWIG
THE
DANZIG
CHANNEL
ISLANDS
ALLENSTEIN

TANNU TUVA

CARNARO
AND FIUME

SOUTH
RUSSIA

TRIESTE

BATUM
EASTERN RUMELIA

MANCHUKUO

CAPE
JUBY

THE TWO
SICILIES

SASENO   HATAY

ALWAR

KIAOCHOW

NANDGAON

RYUKYU

TANGIER
INTERNATIONAL
ZONE

TRIPOLITANIA

HEJAZ

SEDANG

BHOPAL

OBOCK   UPPER YAFA

LABUAN

THE CAROLINES

BIAFRA

PERAK

THE SOUTH MOLUCCAS

ELOBEY, ANNOBON
AND CORISCO

SOUTH
KASAI

ILE SAINTE-MARIE

MAFEKING

ORANGE
FREE STATE

VAN DIEMEN'S LAND

NOWHERELANDS

BJØRN BERGE

NOWHERELANDS

AN ATLAS OF
VANISHED COUNTRIES
1840–1975

Translated from the Norwegian *Landene som forsvant. 1840–1970*
by Lucy Moffatt

This translation has been published with the financial support of NORLA

NORLA
NORWEGIAN LITERATURE ABROAD

First published in the United Kingdom in 2017 by
Thames & Hudson Ltd, 181A High Holborn, London WC1V 7QX

www.thamesandhudson.com

First published in the United States of America in 2017 by
Thames & Hudson Inc., 500 Fifth Avenue, New York, New York 10110

www.thamesandhudsonusa.com

Norwegian edition published by Spartacus Forlag AS, Oslo
Published by agreement with Hagen Agency, Oslo

Original edition © 2016 Spartacus Forlag AS
This edition © 2017 Thames & Hudson Ltd, London

British Library Cataloguing-in-Publication Data
A catalogue record for this book is available from the British Library

Library of Congress Control Number 2017934857

ISBN   978-0-500-51990-5

Printed and bound in Hong Kong

CONTENTS

Foreword

*History as well as life itself is complicated –
neither life nor history is an enterprise for those
who seek simplicity and consistency.*

JARED DIAMOND[1]

For me, knowing where you are in the world has always
been the very meaning of life.

I show up wide open and wide-eyed every summer when
I take a week off to hike down along the coast of Europe.
I follow every cove and every quay systematically, walking
along sandy shores and over dikes, through storms and
searing sun. It has taken me eleven years to cover the
distance from Hirtshals in northern Denmark to Saint-
Valery-en-Caux near Le Havre in France, as the crow flies
a little over 1000 km (650 miles) to the southwest, and every
step of the way is imprinted on my body, complete with
smells, colours and noise, as if on a map where I myself
am the scale. Slowly but surely, I am conquering *the planet*.

With a touch of melancholy, I have gradually come to
realize that it will be difficult to make it the whole way
round. Of course, I could change tactics and walk every
day all year long for the rest of my life. But naturally
that's impossible, physically and otherwise. Prompted by
this realization, I have embarked on two supplementary
projects, the common trait of which is that they let the
world come to me instead.

The first is collecting flotsam washed up on the shingle
beach below the house where I live – plastic, wood, whatever. Quality and beauty are a secondary concern. The
most important consideration is that the objects have been
marked by their journey, preferably in such a way that I
can reconstruct it. The patterns thus created gradually
encompass more and more of the planet. One of the gems
in my collection is an algae- and barnacle-covered tin can
stamped with characters from the Hudum alphabet. It
may be from Mongolia or from the Republic of Tuva in the
Russian Federation. Either way, it originated in a country
that does not have its own coastline, and the first leg of its
journey must have been along the Yenisei River, through
Siberia to the Arctic Ocean. The icing on the cake is the
fact that the can is still unopened, although this is hardly
surprising. Thanks to the little air bubble secreted in most
of them, it isn't at all unusual for the beer and soft drink
cans we find along the seashore to be full. I don't know
what's inside my Hudum can but one thing's for certain:
it will be opened on my deathbed.

And then there's the stamp collection. I collect stamps
– but not just any old stamps. My aim is to collect a stamp
from every country and every regime that has ever been
active since the first Penny Black was issued in England
in 1840. For me, an unused stamp isn't especially exciting.
The more signs there are of handling and of life, the more
valuable it feels. I take out my stamps, sniff them and
stroke them, maybe lick them; the taste is of crumbling

gum arabic, vegetable starch and hide glue – and in the best of cases, an indefinable something that may go back to previous licks, many years ago in some remote corner of the world. Impressions that are not my own, but which I share in as they stream by.

Thus I conquer the planet and existence on three flanks in one big pincer movement.

The book you are holding right now takes as its starting point the increasingly important flank of stamp collecting, and it's about a group of countries that no longer exist. There's plenty of material here. Worldwide, more than a thousand regimes have considered themselves important enough to issue stamps. Some have mysterious names like Obock and Sedang and Cape Juby, which very few of us connect with anything at all. Others may stir up associations, such as Biafra and famine, Bhopal and environmental disaster – often altogether sorry affairs. Although many of the names may have an almost benign ring to them, behind each without exception lies a tale of manipulation and the exercise of might. After all, the main purpose of encircling a territory with borders has never been to increase the happiness of its people. Just how badly things can go wrong becomes clear if we look at Africa and the Middle East, where the colonial powers only rarely carved up territory along the lines of traditional tribal regions. And in the Balkans, political jockeying between the great powers of the East and the West led to the intermingling of different population groups. The consequences flare up continuously in the form of bloody conflicts.

The motifs on the postage stamps give a fairly clear indication of what it's all about: an almost monolithic masculine culture of monarchs in all their pomp and circumstance, monuments to military conquest and loyalist heroes of all stripes (preferably represented as strutting peacocks or puffed-up, chest-drumming gorillas). Behavioural ecologists would quickly pigeonhole the entire business as pure showing off, whose main purpose is the acquisition of power and the crucial ingredients of which are exaggeration and self-deception.[2]

This leaves us men looking like slaves to testosterone. Or, at any rate, it may often seem that way. But there are clearly other reasons for going to war. One of them is *boredom*, although we prefer to call it *adventurousness*. Now and then, we all need something extraordinary in our lives, something that will expand our existence, for better or for worse, win or lose. Those who happen to be emperors, presidents or charismatic prime ministers can set the ball rolling themselves. And its impetus can be transmitted through the ranks, all the way down to the humblest soldier. Women also throw themselves into things, hoping to experience the intoxicating sense of being at the mercy of savage powers, not for the benefit of humanity but for their own sake. Most often, people return home crestfallen, with the wretched feeling that they've been tricked into taking part in a tedious battle of egos, no more and no less.[3]

Of course, kings, leaders and powerful politicians cannot legitimately justify wars and conquests on the basis of testosterone or boredom. Instead, they talk in terms of covering material needs, securing markets and ensuring access to raw materials to maintain or increase their own consumption. Or they claim it's a question of saving a neighbouring population from a despot, or imposing a system of government or religion that will be better for the inhabitants. These aspects have a tendency to get entangled.

But irrespective of the reason for establishing a new country, the following always applies: the plan works for a while, for anything from a matter of days to over a hundred years, but after that, the *fall* always lies in wait – as inevitable as it is inexorable.

My investigation is based on three levels of documentation: the *stamps* themselves, *eye-witness accounts* and later *historical interpretations*.

The stamps serve as the core evidence, providing concrete proof that the countries did in fact exist. Just as certainly, though, they lie. Countries will forever try to present themselves exactly the way they want to be seen: as more dependable, more liberal, more merciful, more awe-inspiring or better at the business of government than they actually are. The stamps must therefore be viewed as propaganda, in which truth will always be of subordinate importance. Even so, we can still rely upon the ever-present consistencies, colours, textures, smells and tastes of the stamps.

Next come the eyewitness accounts. These are texts written in direct contact with events. I have therefore assigned them a special place, like the basic formulae in a maths textbook. They can be used to conjure up images that are as close as possible to the truth. But it's important to be on the alert: there is trickery here, too.

The third and most unreliable level is the second-hand knowledge conveyed by historians and novelists, with or without political agendas. These are the sources that deal in hindsight and analysis. I have tried to exercise my critical faculties when it comes to this material, although without always feeling that I am in control. Professional historians can easily become antiseptic and heavy on dates, while novelists generally strike out in totally the opposite direction and romanticize things.

To enable readers to check my interpretations and to broaden their experience, I have included suggestions for further reading. For several countries, I have also recommended music and films, and on some occasions there are recipes too. During the process of writing, I've eaten my way through a variety of local dishes as a way of *grounding* myself. The recipes included are some of the most effective ones.

Finally, I would like to thank everybody who has contributed to the work on this book. Of all the world's librarians, special mention must go to Sofia Lersol Lund, Lars Mogensen, Stian Tveiten, Anette Rosenberg, Anna Fara Berge, Marie Rosenberg, Svanhild Naterstad, Trond Berge, Dag Roalkvam, Julio Perez and Gerd Johnsen.

And before you read any further, I want to stress that this is absolutely not intended as a guidebook to send people off in search of the ruins of forgotten countries and kingdoms. Because usually we're not talking package tours here, but long, complex journeys involving multiple different means of transport, and the climate implications of which go far beyond respectable levels – probably without bringing the reader an inch closer to the adventure. You'd be much better off looking at this book as a collection of bedtime stories to feed your dreams and carry you off into sleep.

Bjørn Berge
Lista, Spring 2017

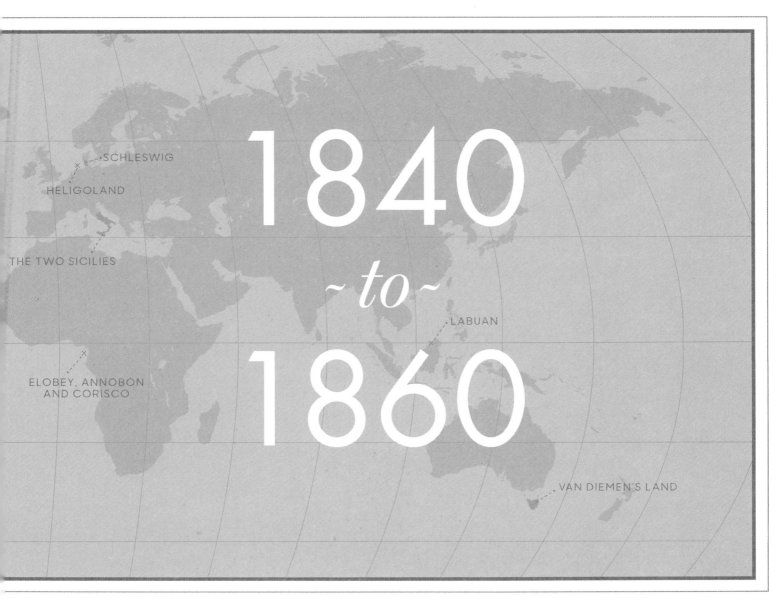

SCHLESWIG

HELIGOLAND

THE TWO SICILIES

ELOBEY, ANNOBON
AND CORISCO

LABUAN

VAN DIEMEN'S LAND

1840
~ to ~
1860

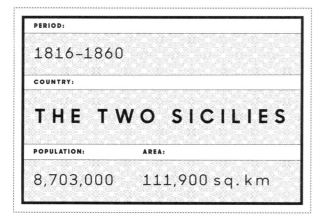

PERIOD:

1816–1860

COUNTRY:

THE TWO SICILIES

POPULATION: **AREA:**

8,703,000   111,900 sq. km

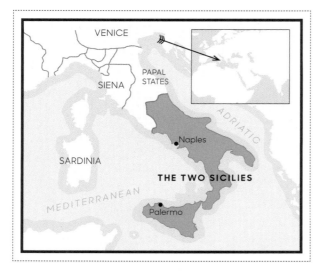

VENICE

PAPAL STATES

SIENA

ADRIATIC

SARDINIA

Naples

THE TWO SICILIES

MEDITERRANEAN

Palermo

Bottomless poverty and weary aristocrats

Meat, cakes, fruit and fist-sized balls of chalk-white mozzarella, all stuck together with minced sardines, tripe and olives to form a conical mountain of food – like a Vesuvius in miniature – that glitters juicily in the afternoon sun on the cobblestones in front of the castle in Naples. A cannon salute gives the ravenous mob its signal. A salvo of limp applause comes from the long-since overfed aristocrats on the balconies. The enormously fat king, Ferdinand I – far more eager than the rest – drums his fingers nervously on the parapet.[4]

The king had ascended to the throne in 1759 at the tender age of eight. Now in his early twenties, his main interest in life was hatching spectacular ideas for the next grand gala. Such occasions allowed a little of his wealth to trickle down directly to the common people – something that otherwise was a rare event.

The kingdoms of Naples and Sicily had already been ruled jointly, as the Kingdom of the Two Sicilies, on several previous occasions by the time Ferdinand I's father, Charles III of Spain, reinstated the system in 1735, with Naples as the capital. The country, which stretched as far north as the Papal States, was large by European standards.

Napoleon put a stop to the excesses in 1799 when he captured the Naples part of the kingdom. Ferdinand fled to Sicily, where he was protected by a strong British naval force.

Ferdinand returned to power following a peace congress in Vienna in 1816, although only after promising the British social reforms consistent with what had become the norm elsewhere in Europe by then. But he quickly forgot the agreement and carried on as before, heading a thoroughly aristocratic administration that had no interest whatsoever in anything but the well-being of the upper classes.

Dissatisfaction took root among the urban population and revolts broke out in both Sicily and Naples. Ferdinand responded with a reign of terror that involved spies, informers and random punishments. This pattern was steadfastly maintained by his descendants, especially Ferdinand II, who earned the nickname *Re'Bomba* – King Bomb – after putting down an 1849 revolt in Palermo by bombarding it with massive, poorly targeted cannon fire.

The British author Julia Kavanagh travelled the length and breadth of the country in the 1850s. Her ambition was to fulfil a childhood dream of climbing the volcanoes, Etna and Vesuvius, strolling in Mediterranean landscapes in airy muslin dresses, and visiting the churches and countless ruins left behind by previous conquerors. But the romance dwindled fast, and her travel journal is a litany of constant encounters with injustice, poverty, illiteracy and decline.

Before the ship that is due to take her over to Sicily sets out from Naples, some of the passengers gather on the aft deck to watch a boy who is rowing from boat to boat. He is perhaps nine years old, dressed in rags, but with 'a quick face', according to the journal. Balancing on the mid-thwart he performs a short play that opens with a tarantella. Then he acts the clown, sings a short aria and, finally, allows himself to be stabbed in the breast by an invisible enemy before falling on the deck, turning up the whites of his eyes. There he lies for a moment before leaping up again, this time with cap in hand. A few copper coins are thrown down to him.

Julia Kavanagh heaves a sigh of relief when at last the ship steams out of the Bay of Naples. 'Naples receded, and looked infinitely better for a little distance.'[5]

The desperation was most clearly reflected in the cities; out in the provinces, people were less liable to go to bed hungry. Here, life carried on as before, following a strictly feudal pattern that had been in place for hundreds of years.

In the district of Cilento just south of Naples, the landscape rose up from the cliffy coast with its wild olive trees, rubber trees and myrtle, through forests of oak and hawthorn, then beyond the treeline to the occasional, eternally snow-capped mountain. The villages were compact and yellowish-brown with red-tiled roofs. They clung fast to the mountainsides and hilltops, usually surrounded by precipitous fortified walls. Along with the church tower and the occasional dovecote, the nobleman's palace always held sway above the whole scene. The deeper one descended into the crooked alleyways and narrow cobbled streets, the more intense was the stink of the open sewers and the cellars where domestic animals were kept at night.

The villages of Cilento still stand. If you visit them today, you'll notice that the smell has gone. In terms of age they have the air of a no-man's-land – no ageing, no rejuvenation – like little kingdoms in a fairy tale. And that's what they probably were too. Although they all paid obeisance to the central power in Naples, they were eternally in conflict with one another.

The Kingdom of the Two Sicilies gets its own postage stamps in 1858. All of them are orange-brown, probably printed with cheap soil pigment, from the Siena region to the north, dissolved in linseed oil. The motif is the king's coat of arms, with a rearing horse and an apparently absurd figure formed of three symmetrical bent human legs: a triskelion. Just about visible on the right, beneath the seal, this symbol dates back to the time when Sicily was part of Magna Graecia (Great Greece). It is supposed to have been inspired by the triangular shape of the island. The *ANNULLATO* stamp tells us this was a test issue that has never been used on a letter. Consequently, some remnants of the glue remain. The taste has a hint of wheat.

The Two Sicilies survived until 1860, when Francis II, only installed as king in 1859, was overthrown by rebels led by Giuseppe Garibaldi. Supported by the Kingdom of Sardinia, the guerrilla leader landed on Sicily's west coast on 11 May 1860 with 1,000 men. Here, he picked up reinforcements in the form of 3,000 Sicilian volunteers and continued towards Palermo, after which he crossed the Strait of Messina en route to Naples.

1858: National coat of arms with lilies, a triskelion and a rearing horse.

The Italian writer, Giuseppe Tomasi de Lampedusa, had first-hand knowledge of the country through his own family. In his novel *The Leopard*, we follow the sometimes ambivalent nobleman Don Fabrizio Corbera during the final days before the fall of Palermo.[6] He and his family – like the rest of the town's aristocracy – lived with their servants and private priest in their own palace, with frescoes of Roman gods on the ceilings, all of it enclosed in a spacious garden with a wrought-iron fence. And it was in this garden that he noticed a repulsive stink one day, which proved to come from the corpse of a young soldier from the Fifth Regiment of Sharp-Shooters. He had been wounded in battle at San Lorenzo and had come into the garden to die, alone, beneath a lemon tree.

Over the nights that followed, the Corbera family watched as Garibaldi's army lit up more and more bonfires on the mountaintops to the south and west: silent threats to the city, which was still loyal to the king. Then Don Fabrizio's nephew Tancredi abruptly left to join the rebels, but only after going into the library where his uncle was sitting with his bulldog, Bendico. He tried to justify his position. 'Unless we ourselves take a hand now, they'll foist a republic on us. If we want things to stay as they are, things will have to change. D'you understand?' Don Fabrizio didn't answer, but squeezed one of the dog's ears so hard between his fingers that the poor creature whined, honoured doubtless but in pain.[7]

Tancredi's farewell created a stir at the dinner table that evening. Don Fabrizio tried to soothe everybody. He explained how useless the muskets of the royal army were; how the barrels of those enormous firearms had no rifling, how little force there was in the bullets they fired. Tancredi and the rest of the family survive the tumult and live to see Italy united in a single kingdom under King Victor Emmanuel II of Sardinia.

At once, reforms are set in motion, such as universal education, social security and health services. Even so, southern Italy remains poorer than the north, and many people soon emigrate to the USA, where the Mafia is waiting with open arms for the most ferocious of them.

BOOKS

Julia Kavanagh (1858)
A Summer and Winter in the Two Sicilies

Giuseppe Tomasi di Lampedusa (1958)
The Leopard

Susan Sontag (1995)
Volcano Lover

FILM

Il Gattopardo / The Leopard (1963)
Directed by Luchino Visconti

///

Naples receded, and looked infinitely better for a little distance

JULIA KAVANAGH

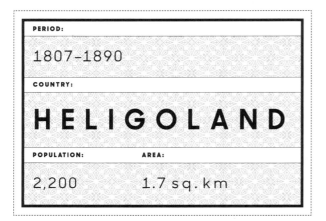

PERIOD:	
1807–1890	
COUNTRY:	
HELIGOLAND	
POPULATION:	AREA:
2,200	1.7 sq. km

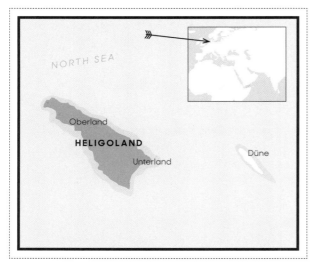

NORTH SEA

Oberland

HELIGOLAND

Unterland

Düne

From island realm to bombing target

The two small islands that form Heligoland (or 'holy land') lie 70 km (45 miles) off the western coast of Germany and are probably the remains of a larger archipelago. According to *Germania*, the ethnographic work from around AD 98 by the Roman historian Tacitus, it stretched right across the mouth of the Elba, with just a narrow passage on either side.[8] And legend has it that even in Christian times Heligoland had nine parishes and two monasteries.

The North Sea has perpetually gnawed away small pieces, now and then entire mouthfuls – as in 1720, when a severe storm split Heligoland in two for good. The smaller half ended up no more than a bank of sand and crushed seashells. The other half staggered on as an upright crust of sandstone facing off the breakers from the northwest: 1 sq. km (less than ¼ sq. mile) in area, 60 m (200 ft) at its highest point, and topped by a few sparse tufts of grass.

At first glance, Heligoland looks fairly worthless. But owing to its placement on the seaward approach to the powerful Hansa cities and several of Germany's large rivers, the tiny archipelago has always been coveted. First it was used as a pirate base, then for piloting and fishing.

And after being owned in turn by Denmark and different German coalitions for several hundred years, Heligoland was conquered without resistance by England in 1807, after Denmark allied itself with Napoleon. The important thing for the British was to maintain contact and trading links with the European continent.

At the same time, the island was a centre for espionage against Napoleon's forces, which had gradually gained control of the whole of the mainland coastline. The piloting business had ground to a halt and several of the pilots started to work as guides for the English. Many of them could have navigated the coast blindfold. They were familiar with every sandbank, and knew how they constantly shifted and changed shape. Brunsbüttel, Cuxhaven or even right inside the mouth of the Elba to Glückstadt – *Geen problem*!

In 1850, M. L'Estrange, the daughter of an English officer, publishes a book called *Heligoland*, based on her childhood experiences on the island in around 1820.[9] She must have been a particularly retiring woman because her full name does not appear either on the cover or elsewhere.

The book mainly tells the painful story of how she and her sister lose their parents to pneumonia, and includes an especially striking description of their last couple of days. But it also describes the girls' secure childhood on the island, where living conditions were good for the families of officers, who were given their own small house, complete with servant and cook. The mail boat brought two meals' worth of fresh meat every week, together with more flour, oatmeal, peas, rice and rum than a 'moderate' family could consume. What's more, exotic wares were available in abundance. Many of the former pilots had started to smuggle items from the British colonies into Germany, and to smuggle even more attractive German products out.

She goes on to talk about the two villages on the main island: Oberland on the higher land to the west and Unterland on the sand flats down towards the harbour in the southeast. The quays in Unterland were reserved for large ships, while the fishing boats were hauled up directly onto the beach after use. The buildings were compact: narrow, three- or four-storey houses with steep window gables that looked out onto the narrow streets. Whereas traditional Frisian buildings were made of red brick, many of the houses here were wooden. This was because there were few material resources in the area, other than somewhat dubious sandstone. Everything had to be shipped over from the mainland, and brick was heavy.

Much of the life on the island takes place on a steep stairway between the two villages, where the men laze about smoking cigarettes and chatting, while the women run up and down with bread baskets and heavy buckets of water, or go to milk the goats and sheep that are grazing on the ridge to the west. The women wear long scarlet skirts, supplemented in winter by cloaks tied so tightly over their foreheads that only their eyes and the tips of their noses are visible. 'The men dress in very coarse cloth made so wide that their trousers look like petticoats, enormous wooden buttons, their throats much exposed, and little tight caps upon the very top of their heads.'[10]

When people meet on the street, they first exchange a 'Good evening' and then – as they pass one another – 'Forget me not', often in the local dialect, Halunder, which is a version of Frisian. Women's names are also special in that they consistently end in 'o', as in Katherino, Anno and Mario.

One of the few events that can disturb the calm daily routine is the migration of thrushes, starlings and woodcock that stop off en route in spring and autumn. Then people drop whatever they're carrying to go hunting. Old and young, men and women, seize yarn, pickaxes and spades, and storm off. Up to the ridge or across the sand dunes.

The Napoleonic Wars were a time of prosperity for the inhabitants of the island. But after the Treaty of Kiel was signed in 1814, smuggling came to a halt. And when the last British soldiers left the island in 1821, trading activity also stopped abruptly. The warehouses fell empty and the merchants left.

There were now 2,200 people living on Heligoland and none of them wanted to move. That was when somebody came up with the apparently crazy idea of going in for tourism, but this wasn't something they'd pulled out of thin air. Just a few years earlier, in fact, British doctors had declared that saltwater baths were among the most health-giving activities imaginable. And the water should be cold. If there was one thing Heligoland had in abundance it was cold salt water, all year round. The inhabitants took a gamble on it. And by as early as 1826, the island was in full swing as a spa and bathing resort for wealthy burghers from England, Prussia, Poland and Russia.

1869–71: Embossed silhouette of Queen Victoria of England.

The island gradually lost its strategic significance for the British, but it did eventually launch its own stamps. As usual in British possessions, the then queen, Victoria, provided the motif. The stamps' most notable feature is that they use two colours (necessitating extra steps in the production process as well as exceptional precision): always red and green on white paper. 'Green is the land. Red are the cliffs. White is the sand. These are the colours of Heligoland.'[11] In addition, Victoria's white head is embossed. My specimen is torn and greasy from a great deal of finger contact. I can just about detect a rancid odour when I warm it between my hands and gently scrape the surface. It is one of the first issues from 1867, with the postage given in English shillings. After 1875, this will be changed to the German pfennig, reflecting a gradual rapprochement with the German mainland.

And in 1890, as if in a game of Monopoly, the English decided to offer Heligoland to Germany in exchange for the island of Zanzibar off the coast of East Africa. The Germans agreed and immediately simplified the name to Helgoland, without the 'i'. Eventually they set up a naval base, which would have great significance in both the First and Second World Wars. At the same time, tourism continued to thrive. It is said that the nuclear researcher, Werner Heisenberg, who was terribly troubled by pollen allergies and hay fever, only managed to formulate his quantum theory after a long stay on this island for the benefit of his health.[12]

In the final phase of the Second World War, the island is bombed to oblivion in British air raids. And after the war, the British take it over again. By then, the landscape is almost lunar, greenish-yellow and totally lifeless, useful at most as a practice target for planes and warships.

In 1952, the islands are handed back to Germany again. By that time, they are utterly lacking in any traces of history other than the occasional bomb crater. And it seems to me that the smell from my stamp – be it from fish entrails or rancid oil – must be one of the last concrete traces of the civilization that was once to be found there.

BOOKS

M. L'Estrange & Anna Maria Wells (1850)
*Heligoland or Reminiscences of Childhood:
A Genuine Narrative of Facts*

Alex Ritsema (2007)
Heligoland, Past and Present

//

The men dress in very coarse cloth made so wide that their trousers look like petticoats, enormous wooden buttons, their throats much exposed, and little tight caps upon the very top of their heads

M. L'ESTRANGE

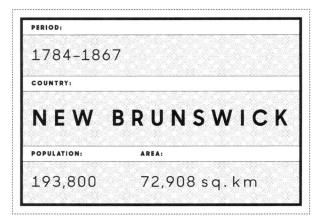

PERIOD:

1784–1867

COUNTRY:

NEW BRUNSWICK

POPULATION: | AREA:

193,800 | **72,908 sq. km**

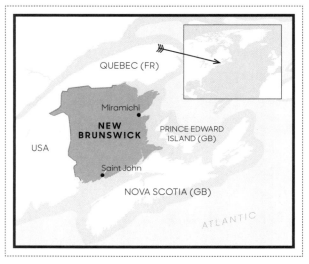

QUEBEC (FR)

Miramichi

NEW BRUNSWICK

PRINCE EDWARD ISLAND (GB)

USA

Saint John

NOVA SCOTIA (GB)

ATLANTIC

Immigrants with the wool pulled over their eyes

One of the eleven postage stamps that were issued in the British colony of New Brunswick bears the image of a steamship, for the first time ever in the history of stamps. The stamp was issued in 1860 and the ship appears to be the SS *Hungarian*, a transatlantic passenger vessel owned by Britain's Allan Line. It had been launched the year before and immediately started to transport immigrants across the Atlantic Ocean. This kind of travel picked up after Ireland's potato harvest was repeatedly blighted by a parasitic disease. The trip usually took 36 days, but the ships were required to have food and water rations for double that time in case of storms. The journey generally took place in late spring, which was thought to be a favourable time to travel.

So the SS *Hungarian* is out rather early in the year when it approaches the coast one stormy evening in mid-February 1860 after crossing the Atlantic Ocean. Visibility is poor and, like so many other ships before, it runs aground on the treacherous sandbanks of Cape Sable Island, south of Nova Scotia. The survivors of the shipwreck are visible from land, clinging onto the capsized hull, but strong winds and high waves prevent any rescue attempts. All 205 people on board die.[13]

For immigrants who had previously arrived in calmer waters, the first impression offered meagre consolation. The arms of the fjord were generally cloaked in thick sea mist and the tidal range could be as much as 16 m (52 ft). The shoreline had a barren, brutal look, not unlike the western coast of Norway, according to M. H. Perley. He describes the despair an immigrant might well feel:

The naked cliffs or shelving shores, of granite or other hardened rocks, and the unvarying pine forests, awaken in his mind ideas of hopeless desolation, and poverty and barrenness appear necessarily to dwell within the iron-bound shores.[14]

But in the next breath, Perley – who was, in fact, a propagandist for the British immigration authorities – draws the sting from this terror. Because just a short distance from the coast, with its Atlantic Ocean climate, a transformation takes place. He cites a report prepared for the British parliament: 'Of the climate, soil, and capabilities of New-Brunswick it is impossible to speak too highly. There is not a country in the world so beautifully wooded and watered.'[15] And Perley's colleague, surveyor Alexander Monro, follows up with:

... a healthy climate; an excellent soil for agricultural purposes; inexhaustible forests of valuable timber, accessible by an extensive sea-board and by navigable rivers; immense mineral resources, and oft-unparalleled coast and river fishery.[16]

The idea that life in the colony might nonetheless have its downside can be glimpsed when, to keep the record straight, Monro mentions that snowstorms rarely occur more than four times a year. He adds the cold comfort that the low temperature has the advantage of making the snow only half as heavy as at home in England. He also touches upon the dangers posed by wolves and bears. And in passing he mentions the Mi'kmaq – the indigenous population. Although they have been subdued, they are still embittered and disillusioned after their crushing military defeat at the hands of the French in the 1700s.

The Mi'kmaq were nomads. They spent the summer by the sea, where they fished, collected eggs and trapped geese. In the winter, they hunted for moose inland. The moose meat was dried and the skins used to make clothes and tools, and as underlay for their tents, known as wigwams. Wigwams were conical constructions built from fir poles the thickness of an arm and thatched with flakes of birch bark sewn together with thin root suckers. To cope with the harsh winters, they were further insulated with an inner layer of grass matting.

This is how most of the Mi'kmaq are living as boatload after boatload of immigrants arrives in the area. They keep their distance, but can't help being affected by the presence of the newcomers. Their hunting areas shrink and alcohol – firewater – becomes all too readily available.

The immigrant ships dock in the harbour at Saint John, an improvised settlement of smallish wooden houses that has rapidly become the most important town in the area. The passengers must remain on the ships for at least forty-eight hours after their arrival to prevent the introduction of infectious diseases. Those who still have symptoms after that are detained at the town's quarantine station.

If any 'lunatic, idiot, maimed, blind, or infirm person not belonging to an emigrant family' is found, the captain must pay a fine of seventy-five pounds. This is intended to cover the expenses of the person concerned for the first three years. The other immigrants pass through the controls quickly and look for lodgings.

On their first evenings, people step-dance at the hall up by the church. Some of them get jobs in the shipyards at Saint John and Miramichi, while others decide to wait for the wagon trains heading further inland. And then they jump on any old one that comes along – to Northumberland, Gloucester or Kent. Everywhere, land is being sold off in monthly auctions. The going price is three shillings an acre, which can be paid for with labour on the public roads.[17]

Leif Erikson's Vinland expedition almost certainly made it to this area in around AD 1000, but the French explorer Jacques Cartier stands as the official discoverer of Canada, on France's behalf, in 1534. While the French were expending their energy on subduing the Native Americans in the interior of the continent, the British occupied parts of the outer archipelago, establishing the colony of Nova Scotia – New Scotland. The territory was gradually extended towards the mainland to the west and in 1784 New Brunswick was partitioned off as a separate colony. It was named after the Duchy of Braunschweig in northern Germany, the childhood home of the British king, George I. The border

1860: Transatlantic steamer, probably the SS Hungarian, *of the British Allan Line.*

with the American state of Maine in the south was a long time coming, and was not defined until some way into the 1800s, during the so-called Aroostook War – which, despite its awe-inspiring name, was a purely legal conflict.

New Brunswick was incorporated as a Canadian province in 1867. Many people protested and, initially at least, proved justified in thinking this would cause it to be assigned lesser priority in relation to central Canada. But the situation changed towards the turn of the century, when the forestry industry took off, supplying raw material for an ever-hungrier paper industry.

New Brunswick is now Canada's only bilingual province, with both English and French mother-tongue teaching in the schools. Thousands of Mi'kmaq people still live in the area too. Forestry-related businesses remain important, but in the sea to the east, the ecological cycle has broken down and the fish have vanished.

BOOKS

Alexander Monro (1855)
New Brunswick: With a Brief Outline of Nova Scotia and Prince Edward Island. Their History, Civil Division, Geography and Productions

M. H. Perley (1857)
A Hand-Book of Information for Emigrants to New-Brunswick

Wilson D. Wallis & Ruth Sawtell Wallis (1955)
The Micmac Indians of Eastern Canada

///

The naked cliffs or shelving shores, of granite or other hardened rocks, and the unvarying pine forests, awaken in his mind ideas of hopeless desolation, and poverty and barrenness appear necessarily to dwell within the iron-bound shores

M. H. PERLEY

PERIOD:

1856–1875

COUNTRY:

CORRIENTES

POPULATION: 6,000   AREA: 88,199 sq. km

PARAGUAY

ARGENTINA

BRAZIL

Paraná

ARGENTINA

• City of Corrientes

CORRIENTES

URUGUAY

Stamps from the bakery

The Norwegian author and journalist Øvre Richter Frich travelled through the Province of Corrientes in Argentina at the beginning of the 1900s, and later used it as a setting for several of his thrillers. In *The Condor*, he describes the rippling, flowery carpet of grass on the pampas, overshadowed here and there by thistles:

> They grew like small trees, and could be several metres high, advancing across the lush, uncultivated land like armoured warriors that nothing can harm... and the *viscacha*, the prairie dog, burrows its pitfalls beneath the earth. And the apes, the vampire bats and the small tropical crocodiles that prefer not to grapple with anything but the very smallest Indian children roam the vast swamps of Corrientes.[18]

A suitable backdrop for a thriller, then, but also the atmosphere that fellow Norwegian Georg Wedel-Jarlsberg experiences after being robbed in the region ten years later. When he goes to report the incident, he is discreetly taken aside by the governor who admits, forehead beading with sweat: 'The inhabitants of Corrientes are the worst in the republic. Most of them belong to the Roman race: they are cowardly but treacherous and vengeful.'[19]

Local rebellions and wars of emancipation in the early 1800s left Argentina close to independence after 300 years as a Spanish colony. The period that followed was anything but harmonious, though, with major internal clashes and civil war.

The provinces of the interior and those along the coast had come into particularly severe conflict over the exploitation of the rivers and the distribution of the lush, bright-green pastures of the pampas. These clashes continued even after the Argentine constitution was signed in 1854, ultimately resulting in a loose conglomeration of relatively autonomous provincial states.

One of these was Corrientes, inland and in the far northeast. Here the landscape formed gently sloping terraces suitable for the cultivation of tobacco and cotton, but not so suitable for cattle farming owing to the high temperatures and copious rain. Corrientes was named for the largest city in the area, founded as far back as 1588 on a ridge on the eastern bank of the Paraná River. The name was short for *San Juan de Vera de las Siete Corrientes* ('San Juan de Vera of the Seven Currents'), so called for the severe currents around the seven small peninsulas that projected there.

At one time, the city thrived on the traffic created by Jesuits travelling to and from the mission fields towards the Andes in the West and the sources of the Amazon in the north. Over the course of the 1800s, it grew to a respectable size, with a couple of churches and several blocks of pastel-painted brick houses, which were rarely more than one storey high – all in the familiar Spanish colonial style. The sole remarkable feature must have been the abundance of trees, mainly jacarandas and orange: a matchless sight when they came into bloom.

As early as 1856, Corrientes issued its own postage stamps – the first Argentine province to do so. A fresh feud had blown up with the coastal province of Buenos Aires over trading rights on the rivers, and Corrientes wanted to demonstrate its integrity by having its own postal system. At the same time, there was a shortage of paper money and coins with values of under eight centavos. So the decision was taken to issue stamps that could be used for two purposes: both as postage and as a means of payment.

The task was assigned to Pablo Emilio Coni, who had taken over as the director of the provincial printing press a couple of years earlier, but he had no experience producing printing plates. And that is when the bright baker's assistant, Matías Pipet, comes forward and announces that he served as apprentice to an engraver in Italy.[20] A glance at the results suggests it is just as likely that he was simply sick and tired of baking *empanadas* from cassava flour.

It isn't entirely clear what prompted the decision to copy the first French stamp from 1849, bearing the profile of Ceres, the Roman goddess of agriculture and fertility. But there is reason to believe that the provincial government wanted to underscore its kinship with the enlightened French Republic. At any rate, the resemblance was a very rough one: the clusters of grapes in her hair are largely simplified away, the goddess's nose runs in a straight line from her forehead, and her gaze gives the impression of an acute headache rather than divinity. It is true that the quality improves somewhat from one engraving to the next on the hardwood printing plate, which is divided into eight. Pablo Emilio Coni is reluctant to approve the work, but the pressure of time means that he has no choice.

There is also a severe paper shortage in Corrientes, and the stamps are printed on small sheets in pale variants of blue, grey-blue and greenish-blue – cut out of packaging paper. Made from sugar cane, this paper was originally used for shipments of imported goods.

On the first issues, the value is printed in a field at the bottom of the stamp, but this will be roughly scraped off the printing plates later, in 1860. At the same time, it is decided that the colour will now indicate the value, and the choice is expanded to include pink and pale yellow. My stamp is one of these types, and its pink colour probably represents a value of three centavos.

Stamp production continues until 1878, when the Argentine postal system is nationalized. Both before and after this time, many counterfeits are produced, all of which share the common trait that they are almost always of higher quality than the original. So it is definitely not beyond the bounds of possibility that my stamp is genuine.

Over the course of the 20th century, the province of Corrientes became an increasingly important agricultural region. Nonetheless, it was considered one of the poorest areas in Argentina, in which two per cent of the population owned fifty per cent of the land area. This was because several large land-owning families had always fought to

1860: Ceres, the Roman goddess of agriculture and fertility, copied from France's first postage stamp, from 1849.

block even the most modest land reforms. The most powerful was the Romero Feris family, which had controlled most of the tobacco industry since the end of the 1800s, and had managed the province almost like a private business.[21]

After a series of disputed election results in 1991, both the local population and more central politicians in Argentina had had enough. The then governor, 'Tato' Romero Feris, accused of embezzling public funds, was removed and sent to prison.

BEEF AND CASSAVA FLOUR EMPANADAS (MAKES 10)

Dough:
500 g (18 oz) cassava root
180 g (6 oz) corn flour
Salt

Filling:
50 g (2 oz) green pepper
100 g (4 oz) onion
1 clove of garlic
25 g (1 oz) butter
250 g (9 oz) minced beef
1 hard-boiled egg
½ tsp cumin
Salt and pepper

Preparation of the dough:
Peel the cassava root, cook it in salted water and mash into a puree. Knead in the corn flour and a little salt until you have a firm dough.

Preparation of the filling:
Lightly fry the green pepper, onion and garlic in butter. Add the mince. Season with salt, pepper and cumin.

Empanadas:
Mould the dough into circles with a diameter of around 13 cm (5 in.). Add the filling and top it off with the chopped egg. Fold into a half-moon and seal, then fry in oil until golden brown.

BOOKS

Joseph Criscenti (1993)
Sarmiento and his Argentina

Øvre Richter Frich (1912)
Kondoren
('The Condor')

Georg Wedel-Jarlsberg (1913)
Da jeg var cowboy
('When I was a Cowboy')

///

The inhabitants of Corrientes are the worst in the republic. Most of them belong to the Roman race: they are cowardly but treacherous and vengeful

GEORG WEDEL-JARLSBERG

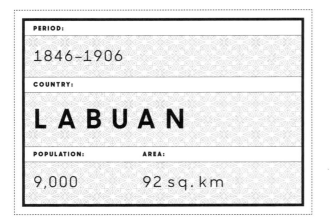

PERIOD:	
1846–1906	
COUNTRY:	
LABUAN	
POPULATION:	AREA:
9,000	92 sq. km

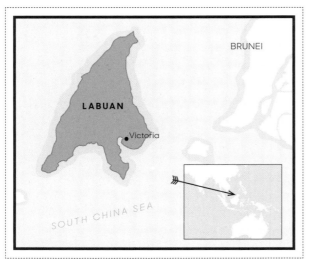

Binge drinking in a seedy South Sea paradise

Some 8 km (5 miles) off the northwest coast of Borneo lies the island of Labuan. Apart from Bukit Kubong, a hill that creeps up to a modest height of 148 m (486 ft) in the north, Labuan is quite flat.

When the British were sniffing out the possibility of taking possession of this almost uninhabited island, it was overgrown with rainforest and practically impenetrable – unless one could find some route through the labyrinth of swamps. But it had good harbour conditions and its location in the South China Sea offered a good base from which to challenge the many pirates who were causing havoc in the area. And once coal deposits were found on the surface near Bukit Kubong, the British ceased to doubt.

Just before Christmas 1846, Sultan Omar Ali Saifuddin II of Brunei signed a treaty granting the British dominion over Labuan and the adjoining small islands. Although the otherwise mighty sultan did not consider Labuan an especially great loss, we may assume he came under a certain amount of pressure. It is later claimed that British men-of-war threatened to bombard the sultan's palace if he refused to sign. The correct version is probably that this was an advance payment of 'protection money' – the same as in your average Mafia story.

An administrative town was rapidly established on the east coast. It was given the fairly unimaginative name of Victoria, already in use in countless other places in the British Empire. From here, you could just about see the waves breaking on the coast of Brunei and make out the mountaintops even further inland, rising to heights of 4,000 m (13,000 ft). Settlers were invited and came – some admittedly less willingly than others, such as convicts from Hong Kong and Singapore. Soon there were more than 9,000 inhabitants on the island.

It rapidly transpired that Labuan had some weak points. Many of the buildings in Victoria had to be relocated after the monsoon repeatedly sent tidal waves through the residential districts. The climate was unexpectedly humid and unalleviated by drier periods. And it was, above all, hot. During the summer months, the temperature held steady at over 30 °C (85 °F).

The whole thing was tailor-made for malaria-carrying mosquitoes. Many people fell ill and died. The only effective cure was quinine, made from the bark of the cinchona tree diluted in bitter tonic water. And the stuff was much easier to wash down mixed with gin.

Unsurprisingly, Labuan was never popular in the British navy, which opted to find other places to stock up on coal and take shore leave. The island fell off the beaten track.

If there are tigers on Labuan at this time, they belong to the now-extinct species of Java tigers. And they almost certainly roam at the edge of the forest, watching the colonial administration slowly succumb to inner decay.

Those who are not entirely debilitated by alcohol or illness argue about everything from membership of the English Club to improbable strategies for enabling local businesses to make inroads into Borneo. And the first English governor, James Brooke, is as active in this respect as he is talentless, according to colleagues: 'My friend Brooke has as much idea of business as a cow has of a clean shirt.'[22]

But as is so often the case, the English still manage to keep up appearances when a Swedish expedition led by Adolf Erik Nordenskiöld, an aristocratic scientist and explorer, docks at the harbour in the converted whaler, the *Vega*, in 1879. It is on its way home after becoming the first ship to navigate the Northeast Passage.

And Nordenskiöld finds everything in perfect order. He is enthusiastic about the coal-mining operation and believes the island is perfect as a base for closer investigation of Borneo's geology. He travels along the coast and on a couple of occasions finds abandoned fishermen's houses on stilts out in the water:

> They were surrounded at flood tide by water, at ebb by the dry beach, bare of all vegetation. In order to get inside these huts, one must climb a ladder two to two-and-a-half metres high [6–8 ft], standing towards the sea. The houses have the same appearance as a warehouse by the seaside at home, and are built very slightly. The floor consisted of a few rattling bamboo splints lying loose, and so thin that I feared they would give way when I stepped upon them.[23]

He is surprised by their location, but has some theories: 'It is probable also that the mosquitoes are less troublesome along the sea-shore than farther into the interior of the country.'[24]

If Nordenskiöld was seduced by the Englishmen, the Italian writer Emilio Salgari went much further beyond reality a few years later in his well-known pirate adventure, *Sandokan: The Tigers of Mompracem*. It evolved into a blockbuster of a series that sold millions of copies, and there is little doubt that it greatly contributed to European perceptions of the South China Sea towards the turn of the century.

Salgari, who can, at his best, be seen as an Italian Jules Verne, used detailed maps and had built up a solid knowledge of the region. However, his writing tends to be sprinkled with overly large doses of drama, set in stormy seas and awe-inspiring jungles, where, among other things, we are taken along on an improbable tiger hunt in the interior of Labuan. But the central theme of the series is love.

Early in book three, we meet the Pearl of Labuan. She is described as follows:

Petite, slender and elegant, with a superb build, and a waist so slim that a single hand would have sufficed to encircle it. Her complexion was as rosy and fresh as a newly bloomed flower. Her little head was admirable, her eyes were blue as sea water, her forehead was incomparably pure and, below this, stood out the sharp outline of two gently arched brows that almost touched.[25]

1894: Overprint on a stamp from North Borneo from the same year, depicting a saltwater crocodile.

The pirate king of British lineage falls head over heels in love, of course. And even though the Pearl of Labuan has already started to waste away after a couple of chapters, he battles with more or less unrequited love for the rest of the series.

According to the novelist and philosopher Umberto Eco, Emilio Salgari wasn't trying to create great literature. All he wanted to do was give his public a dream to escape into. The whole thing was almost too heartfelt to be classified as kitsch.[26]

Many of the stamps issued on Labuan from 1864 onwards help to reinforce the romantic preconceptions Salgari had planted in the minds of the European public. They are produced and printed in London, and bear delightful images of awe-inspiring animals, like the slithering fresh-water crocodile on my stamp.

Subsequent developments in real-life Labuan are anything but romantic, though. The buildings decay, the coal company closes down and soon only three people are left serving in the colonial administration, including the governor himself. On 1 January 1907, the end comes and Labuan is placed under the authority of the much larger British colonial region, the Straits Settlements. This regime lasts until 1963, when the island is finally handed over to Malaysia and made part of the state of Sabah.

BOOKS

Stephen R. Evans, Abdul Rahman Zainal &
Rod Wong Khet Ngee (1996)
The History of Labuan Island

Emilio Salgari (1900)
Sandokan: The Tigers of Mompracem

///

My friend Brooke has as much idea of business as a cow has of a clean shirt

CAPTAIN KEPPEL, OF THE BRITISH GOVERNOR

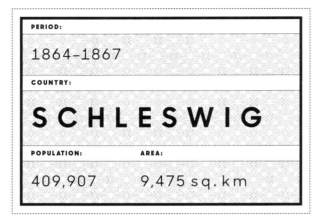

PERIOD:

1864–1867

COUNTRY:

SCHLESWIG

POPULATION: | AREA:

409,907 | 9,475 sq. km

Jutland
DENMARK

Funen

Düppel •

Flensburg •

SCHLESWIG

NORTH SEA

BALTIC SEA

HOLSTEIN

GERMAN STATES

Scandinavianism and martial music

Just before Christmas 1863, Norwegian playwright Henrik Ibsen wrote the poem 'A Brother in Need': 'A people doomed, whose knell is rung / Betrayed by every friend / Is the book closed and the song sung? / Is this our Denmark's end?'[27] He wanted to fire his countrymen up in support of Denmark, which risked losing part of its realm to the German Confederation. The area in question was Slesvig (now Schleswig), the country between the seas, with its lush meadows and sheltered bays in the east, across wide-open heaths and marshes to the windswept mudflats of the North Sea coast in the west; a landscape the artist Emil Nolde portrayed again and again in the years that followed, in rough horizontal strokes of blue, pink, red and dark green: no people, always desolate.

Like many other Nordic intellectuals of his day, Ibsen was a Scandinavianist, alongside writer Bjørnstjerne Bjørnson in Norway. And in Denmark, Scandinavianism was led by the poets N. F. S. Grundtvig and Adam Gottlob Oehlenschläger. The movement emerged in the 1840s as a national romantic homage to shared historical heritage, languages and ethnicity. The goal was for the Scandinavian countries to be joined in a common union. The poet Johan Welhaven had formulated the essence of this in a speech to the students of Christiania (Oslo) in 1846: 'We recall the image of ancient times, because there we are closer to the life source of our people.'[28]

The landscape in Slesvig was open and ideally suited to warfare. Over a couple of thousand years, it had vegetated, a kind of political no-man's-land and a buffer zone between the Danes and whatever might come from the south: Germans, Franks, Saxons or the Holy Roman Empire. At some points, the region seemed like a patchwork quilt of Danish-, Frisian- and German-speaking zones.

Nonetheless, during the Great Nordic War at the beginning of the 1700s, the Danish managed to conquer the area as far south as the Elbe. In addition to Slesvig, this also included the province of Holstein. Both would remain duchies, but now under Danish rule. This resulted in that rarest of things: a period of peace that would last more than a hundred years.

In the meantime, a liberal and national movement was growing in Europe that culminated in the February Revolution in Paris in 1848. It also kindled the hopes of the German-speaking inhabitants of Slesvig and Holstein. They assembled in ever-growing numbers, firing themselves up with polyphonic renditions of their anthem: 'Schleswig-Holstein, embraced by the sea, guard of German custom.' And soon the States Generals in Slesvig and Holstein sent delegations to the king in Copenhagen, demanding full autonomy.

Their demands were rejected by an otherwise indifferent Frederick VII, who opted instead to tighten the reins through measures that included imposing Danish as the language of instruction in schools throughout the area. This resulted in the First Schleswig War, which lasted from 1848 to 1850. Large Prussian forces marched in on the German side, but had to call a halt when the Russians threatened to take Denmark's side. Tsar Nicholas didn't want to risk the possibility of the Prussians increasing their influence around the Baltic Sea and, in the worst of cases, growing into a major power.

To cool tempers, Frederick agreed to slightly more autonomy in both Slesvig and Holstein. But his heir, Christian IX, who had been born at Gottorf Castle in Slesvig, abruptly went back on this and decided, in late autumn 1863, that Slesvig should be fully integrated into Denmark through a common constitution – the November Constitution. That prompted the Prussians to declare war again, this time with mighty Austria as their ally. The Second Schleswig War was under way.

In Norway, Ibsen's initiative met with a positive response, and many people started speaking out in support of Denmark, but this didn't alter parliament's decision to stay out of the conflict. Even so, some volunteers left. One of them was Christopher Bruun, a young theologian.

The Prussians were many, and they were better equipped than the Danish. And they advanced fast, helped by an extra-cold winter that had frozen large stretches of marshes, making it easier for them to press forward. When Christopher Bruun reached the battlefield at Düppel halfway through April 1864, the Danes had recently retreated from the Viking Danevirke, a 30-km- (19-mile-) long earthwork fortification that crosses Jutland at its narrowest point. In Düppel, the defences were more modern.

Barely a day goes by without Bruun sitting down to write a letter to his mother in Lillehammer. But he keeps quiet about the fact that the battlefield around Düppel is soon drenched in blood. He assumes a humorous tone:

> When I sought cover from a shell or the fragments of a shell that had exploded, I usually did so with a feeling no different from when I duck to avoid a snowball.... We hurled ourselves down behind an earth embankment and once it was all over, we often couldn't help laughing at each other.[29]

After bombarding the entrenchments continually for several weeks, the Germans launch an assault on the morning of 18 April. The advance is accompanied by a large Janissary band led by the composer Gottfried Piefke. They perform the specially composed *Düppel Storm March* continuously throughout the battle. When a shell lands close by them, there is a little pause during which only a flute and a snare drum keep going. This is later included as an effect in the reworking of the piece, which goes on to become a staple at every conceivable German military parade.[30]

The bulk of the action lasts only a few hours before the Danes admit defeat and flee the battlefield. Christopher Bruun is so frustrated that he immediately writes to his mother after arriving at a provisional camp on one of the Danish islands: 'Is this a people "battling for its existence", as we are told in all the speeches?'[31]

1865–1867: Stamp with oval motif inscribed with the value, from the Duchy of Schleswig.

He travels back home to Norway, where he takes up his priestly duties. He eventually becomes one of the more liberal theologians and is instrumental in establishing Norway's Folk High School movement.

The fact that the Prussians advanced northwards until the whole of Jutland was occupied was primarily a demonstration of might. They soon withdrew to the borders of the old Slesvig, just south of Kolding. The duchy was declared free and sovereign, and the spelling was changed to Schleswig.

Shortly afterwards, the duchy issues its own stamps. The Danes have already issued two generations of stamps in the region, the first a shared issue for Slesvig and Holstein and the second, regular Danish stamps. The new series bears simple coin-like motifs, with the value given in schillings. Archetypically German, they are uncluttered and unfussy, containing no more than is absolutely necessary. There's no need for bombast. Nobody is posing a threat. Denmark has been beaten once and for all.

My crimson stamp is postmarked 1867. Later in the same year, the postal services in Holstein and Schleswig are merged and switch to shared stamps. These are only valid for a year before the two duchies become part of the North German Confederation, requiring yet another new generation of stamps. And after the formation of the German Empire in 1871, regular German stamps come into use.

The seventh generation of stamps comes in 1920. These are issued ahead of a plebiscite on allegiance after Germany loses the First World War. The Danes set the terms. In Holstein and South Slesvig, both with German-dominated populations, their chances are small. The Danes choose to divide rest of the voting area in two: Central Slesvig and North Slesvig. In Central Slesvig, eighty per cent of the inhabitants vote to remain in Germany. In North Slesvig, seventy-five per cent vote to become part of Denmark. As a result, the southern part of Jutland, down to Flensburg, returns to Denmark. If the voting areas had been counted as a single unit, Denmark would have lost the entire region.

BOOK

Christopher Bruun (1964)
Soldat for sanning og rett.
Brev frå den dansk-tyske krigen 1864
('Soldiers for Truth and Justice.
Letters from the Danish–Prussian War, 1864')

MUSIC

Gottfried Piefke (1864)
Düppel Storm March

///

When I sought cover from a shell
or the fragments of a shell that
had exploded, I often did so with
a feeling no different from
when I duck to avoid a snowball....
once it was all over, we often
couldn't help laughing at each other

CHRISTOPHER BRUUN

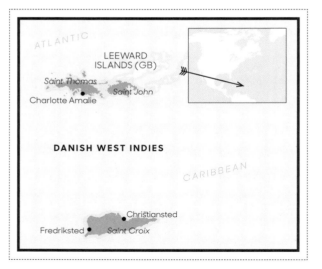

ATLANTIC

LEEWARD
ISLANDS (GB)

Saint Thomas

Saint John

Charlotte Amalie

DANISH WEST INDIES

CARIBBEAN

Christiansted

Fredriksted   *Saint Croix*

Panic sale of slave islands

They only saw that here, out in the middle of an ocean so enormous that they couldn't have dreamt it up in their wildest nightmares, and on which they had, besides, been sailing for month after month, there were some small islands with houses so smart and elegant that they had never seen anything like them in Africa…. The crooked, busy narrow streets of Charlotte Amalie. The long, straight, bright streets of Christiansted, which crossed one another at right angles, the arcades and paved squares. Noble mansions, several storeys high, churches with towers and spires, horse-drawn coaches. And everywhere, these slight creatures clad in silk and muslin that only a very few people had seen in Africa: the white women. But even so, most of the inhabitants on these distant islands were black, just like at home.[32]

It all started when the Danish West India–Guinea Company staked a claim on a group of islands just east of Haiti over a period from the middle of the 1600s. The three islands in question were unusually fertile: Saint Thomas and Saint John were volcanic in origin, with mountains and hilly terrain, while Saint Croix was formed by a coral reef and was fairly flat in appearance. They had a combined area of close to 350 sq. km (135 sq. miles) and the Indian population had already vanished: the Spanish had transported them all as slaves to their colonies further into the Caribbean.

On board the first ship were 190 voluntary settlers. They were men and women from Denmark and Norway, the latter taken on board in Bergen. After six months, 161 of them had died, mainly of various tropical diseases. Even so, some small family farms gradually took shape, but more hands were needed to set up profitable plantations and exploit the islands' full potential. An interim solution was to use prison inmates and convicts from Denmark, who were promised freedom in return for a few years' work on the islands. But few lived long enough to claim their reward.

The first boatload of more robust manpower arrived from Guinea in Africa in 1673. They were slaves bought from local chiefs who had captured them in tribal wars. The project proved a success and, after just a few years, the slave trade really took off. To facilitate the export of slaves, a couple of forts were established on the western coast of Africa. From here, frigates were loaded with up to 500 slaves and sent across the sea to Saint Thomas, which rapidly became one of the most important slave-trading centres in the whole of the Caribbean.

Many of the slaves remained on the islands, and soon they accounted for such a large share of the population that the whites felt threatened. Consequently, strict and detailed regulations were introduced whereby participation in rebellions was punishable by death, while escape and theft resulted in a brand on the forehead or the amputation of a limb the absence of which would not restrict the person's ability to work. And 'should anybody tire of working, a whip will soon cure him of this sickness'.[33]

The West India–Guinea Company had been quick to see the potential of what was termed triangular trade. Put briefly, this involved exporting weapons and other industrial goods to Africa in exchange for slaves, who were then shipped to the West Indies to provide manpower for the sugar plantations. The third and last stage was the transport of sugar, rum and other plantation products back home to Europe. It was a brilliant concept.

Nonetheless, the company did poorly and was teetering on the edge of bankruptcy when the Danish state bought up the entire group of islands in 1754, and turned it into a colony. There were 208 free whites and just over 1,000 slaves on the islands. The ruthlessness of the Danish state is evidenced by a census at the turn of the century, which shows that the number of slaves had risen to 35,000; the white population was around 3,500.

Private traders were still running the whole business. The state was merely the administrator, although it took care to collect the property tax on slaves in the same way as it did on animals and equipment. And the governor, Erich Bredal, complained about the large number of tax evaders who hid their slaves when census time came round.[34]

Until the end of the 1700s, the colony brought great prosperity to Denmark–Norway, but its commercial success was entirely dependent on slavery, which had already involved 100,000 slaves by then. When Denmark–Norway became the first country in Europe to prohibit the import of slaves in 1803, things looked bad. But slave trading was still permitted internally among the islands, as was some transport of slaves to other islands in the Caribbean. Here, Danish ships played a significant role. Only after a large group of slaves threatened a rebellion in 1848 was all slavery officially abolished.

That made the colony unprofitable overnight and the Danish parliament quickly started to discuss its sale. The pressure was exacerbated by domestic problems in Slesvig (Schleswig), which were taking up a steadily increasing share of the national treasury.

The USA was poised to buy in 1867, but the islands were struck by a severe hurricane halfway through the bargaining, rapidly followed by a series of earthquakes and fires. The USA lost interest at once.

A few years earlier, the archipelago has begun to issue its own stamps. They are printed in Denmark and a couple of local pharmacists are responsible for the gum. My stamp shows the schooner *Ingolf* outside the harbour of Saint Thomas, with smoke coming from its galley, and has Danish post horns in the corners. The postmark tells us it was sent from Christiansted on Saint Croix. This must have happened some time after 1905, since this type is one of the colony's last issues. The sailing ship motif looks old-fashioned and is difficult to interpret as anything but pure nostalgia.

In the meantime, the colony slowly wastes away. The government officials take corruption and alcohol abuse

1905: The schooner Ingolf, outside Saint Thomas harbour.

to new heights. Things aren't much better for the freed slaves either. Once they've become simple wage earners, it's no longer so important for the plantation owners to keep them in good health, or even alive.

It all culminates in a spontaneous uprising in 1878. We can picture for ourselves the landlady at one of the local taverns lying prostrate on her bed after yet another late night among boorish sailors and world-weary bureaucrats. She has just had a tray of tea and cakes brought in by the maid. Her lace curtains slowly waft to and fro in the breeze. Through the open window she sees the ocean. The seabed of white coral sand makes the water seem as clear as the air. It winks in the sunlight, sometimes with blue and sometimes with green eyes.'[35] She is woken by raised voices down below, but only realizes how serious things are when she smells smoke. In a matter of hours, swathes of Fredriksted are plundered and set on fire. Many plantation owners are lynched.

The uprising prompted the colonial administration to clean up its act, and the plantation owners slackened the reins a bit. Some years of calm followed until, in 1915, the land workers formed their own union. They announced at once that they were prepared to strike for higher wages and better working conditions. This sent Denmark off in search of buyers once again.

In 1917, the USA finally agreed to buy, for 25 million dollars. Since the previous negotiations, a new argument in favour of the purchase had emerged: Germany was still enjoying tailwinds on the European battlefields, and it was vital to prevent it from gaining a foothold in the seaward approach to the newly opened Panama Canal. A U-boat base here could have been fatal.

The USA rechristened the islands the Virgin Islands, but retained the Danish street names. The Danish holidays were also preserved, so that the inhabitants now observe both these and those of the USA – highly appropriate, seeing as the islands have since become a veritable tourist ghetto.

Meanwhile, a mere stone's throw from the hotels and beaches, the last remnants of the plantation buildings are being slowly but surely swallowed up by the increasingly impenetrable rainforest.

BOOKS

Henrik Cavling (1984)
Det Danske Vestindien
('The Danish West Indies')

Thorkild Hansen (1990)
Slavenes øyer
('Slave Islands')

//

Should anybody tire of working, a whip will soon cure him of this sickness

ANONYMOUS,
ABOUT LIFE ON THE PLANTATIONS

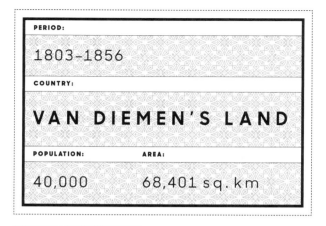

PERIOD:

1803–1856

COUNTRY:

VAN DIEMEN'S LAND

POPULATION:

40,000

AREA:

68,401 sq. km

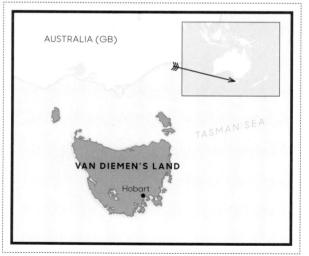

AUSTRALIA (GB)

TASMAN SEA

VAN DIEMEN'S LAND

Hobart

Penal colony with fearful stamps

'We were driven by a violent storm to the northwest of Van Diemen's Land. By an observation, we found ourselves in the latitude of 30 degrees 2 minutes south. Twelve of our crew were dead by immoderate labour and ill food; the rest were in a very weak condition,' writes Jonathan Swift in *Gulliver's Travels*.[36] A few paragraphs later, the ship is wrecked and the hero, Gulliver, manages to save himself, making his way to a shallow shoreline in the country of Lilliput, which is populated by people who are only 15 cm (6 in.) tall.

The northwest coast of Van Diemen's Land was both unknown and mysterious enough to provide the setting for Swift's book when it came out in 1726. At that time, people didn't even realize it was an island. Until the end of the 1700s, only a handful of European ships had visited the place – and then only far to the southeast. With cold polar winds blowing on the back of their necks, the crews had peered at its rugged landscape, which ended in mountaintops towering to heights of over 1,600 m (5,250 ft). Between them lay a network of river valleys, overgrown with sombre and impenetrable forest. It was hardly a cheerful sight.

After sailing around the island and confirming that it was roughly the size of Ireland, the British decided to colonize. It offered a favourable location on one of the busiest shipping routes to and from the southern Pacific Ocean, and the inlets to the south offered good harbour conditions. The first expeditions inland from the coast revealed that the island was fertile, with excellent soil. But it needed to be cleared.

This is how Van Diemen's Land became one of Britain's largest penal colonies. Many of the convicts had been sentenced for rebellion against the British authorities in Ireland, Wales and Scotland. Others were ordinary criminals. The worst were placed in closed institutions, while the rest were set to work in road-gangs or loaned out as manpower to a growing group of English settlers.

Of the 12,000 people on the island in 1822, sixty per cent were prisoners. To secure law and order, the entire place was organized as a police state, divided into nine police districts. A general prohibition on public assembly was in force throughout the island, and travel between the districts required a special pass. And an energetic pack of spies worked hand in glove with the governor, sticking their noses in everywhere.

Port Arthur quickly became the most notorious of the institutions. It stood on a forested peninsula in the inlet outside the capital of Hobart to the southeast, and was connected to the main island by a sandy isthmus known as Eaglehawk Neck. The penal settlement was built on a grassy hill that ran down towards a sandy beach, and was made of natural stone and reddish-yellow bricks. Inside the walls lay quays, administrative buildings, a hospital, a church and a grain mill, in addition to a huge four-storey penitentiary building. This was organized as a form of Panopticon, in which a single centrally placed guard post sufficed to monitor four prison wings laid out in a cross shape.

Although Eaglehawk Neck was regularly patrolled by soldiers and dogs, escape attempts still took place. The former actor George 'Billy' Hunt tried to make a break for it disguised as a kangaroo. Just a few steps short of freedom he was discovered by the guards who set off in hot pursuit, hoping for fresh meat – until Hunt fell to the ground, shouting out, 'Don't shoot! I'm only Billy Hunt.'[37]

His attempt earned him 150 lashes. And not with any old whip either. According to John Frost, who was imprisoned for leading a miners' rebellion in Wales in 1840:

> The knot was made of the hardest whipcord, of an unusual size. The cord was put into salt water till it was saturated, it was then put in the sun to dry; by this process it became like wire, the eighty-one knots cutting the flesh as if a saw had been used.[38]

Those who were serving their sentences at the homes of the settlers had an easier time of it. Most were treated well and with a degree of respect. And in what little free time they had, many would go out kangaroo hunting. The meat was lean, with the consistency of pork, and tasted like an unusual but subtle blend of chicken and fish. The kangaroo rapidly became extinct in large areas around Hobart, and eventually further inland too.

Up until then, the British had not been especially bothered about the small group of Aboriginal people who had been living on the island for several thousand years. They pursued a nomadic existence as hunter-gatherers in groups of fifty to sixty people and generally remained inland. Here they lived in simple huts made of branches thatched with flakes of bark. The kangaroo was an absolutely crucial part of their basic diet and was not just used for food. Every part of the animal had a purpose: the skin for clothes, and the bones for tools and hunting weapons.

In 1820, there were between 3,000 and 7,000 Aboriginal people. And they were in a state of panic. Out of sheer self-defence, a number of farms were set on fire and the occupants murdered. The British responded in a forthright manner: a huge human chain conducted a drive the length and breadth of the island. The Aboriginal people who survived were imprisoned in concentration camps where they soon wasted away. By the beginning of the 1850s, only sixteen remained.

It is also at this time that the colony gets its first stamps. The colonial secretary in Hobart sends his order to the central authorities in London on 9 May 1853:

> Dear Sirs.... Request that you will have the goodness to procure from Messrs Perkins and Bacon the requisite Plates for Stamps of the Value of 1d, 2d, 3d, 4d, 8d, 1s and to forward them with a supply of paper, and ink or inks for printing, together with the materials for making the adhesive paste.[39]

1855: Queen Victoria of England, based on a painting of 1837 by Swiss artist Alfred Edward Chalon.

Perkins & Bacon were respected engravers whose portfolio already included the world's first stamp, the Penny Black. And the order was efficiently executed and dispatched: the first stamps were in circulation just a few months later.

Naturally, they involved yet another portrayal of Queen Victoria. She has already turned thirty, but for some reason or another, the engraving is based on a portrait painted nearly twenty years before by the Swiss artist Alfred Edward Chalon. The painting is a full-figure portrait of the queen on the uppermost step of a white marble staircase. She is wearing the George IV State Diadem and has a beautiful, shy smile on her face. Although the diadem is still there on the stamp, she is no longer smiling but cowering. Her gaze is frightened and shifty – perfectly consistent with the island's increasingly fiendish reputation.

The governor, William Denison, is frustrated: 'There is a feeling here that to the name Van Diemen's Land a certain stigma attaches.'[40] And he proposes a solution: a name change. Van Diemen's Land is renamed Tasmania in 1856. The last Aboriginal inhabitant, a woman called Truganini, dies in 1876. The next year, the penal settlement is closed down, and in 1901 the island ceases to be a separate colony and is placed under Australian rule.

Today, the prison in Port Arthur is Tasmania's leading tourist attraction.

BOOKS

Sidsel Wold (1999)
Warra! Warra! Da de hvite kom til Australia
('Warra! Warra! When the Whites Came to Australia')

James Boyce (2010)
Van Diemen's Land

FILM

Van Diemen's Land (2009)
Directed by Jonathan auf der Heide

ART

Alfred Edward Chalon (1837)
Queen Victoria

//

The cord was put into salt water till it was saturated, it was then put in the sun to dry; by this process it became like wire, the eight-one knots cutting the flesh as if a saw had been used

JOHN FROST

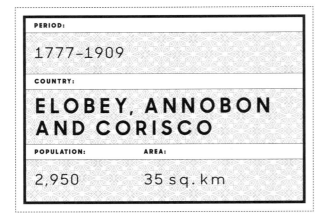

PERIOD:
1777–1909

COUNTRY:
ELOBEY, ANNOBON AND CORISCO

POPULATION:	AREA:
2,950	35 sq. km

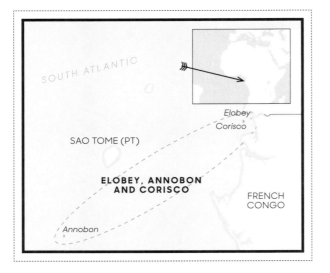

SOUTH ATLANTIC

SAO TOME (PT)

Elobey
Corisco

ELOBEY, ANNOBON AND CORISCO

FRENCH CONGO

Annobon

Anti-imperialism and nervous missionaries

In contrast to the green-black forest bordering it, the little sandy beach looks as white as chalk, with just a hint of a pinkish dove colour in the curving strip dampened by the waves that roll in continuously from the South Atlantic.

We are on the island of Corisco, where British traveller Mary Kingsley alights from the cutter *Lafayette* in 1895. She is wearing light men's clothes: elegant, slim and stately. Although her gaze is clear, her face is marred by a touch of severity around her thin lips. Along with a couple of local men from the crew, she sets off through the trees, then over a grassy plain and into another forest – this time of wild fig, the bark of which is grey-white like the beech trees at home – which climbs sharply upwards until they reach a plateau. Here a little village stands in front of a cluster of coconut palms. The bamboo huts would blend in with their surroundings if it weren't for the doors. They are painted cobalt blue and white, in chequered patterns and horizontal or diagonal stripes. All of them are different. The village is empty but for an elderly woman who asks for tobacco.[41]

Corisco lies in the southern part of the Gulf of Guinea, just off the western coast of Africa. Portugal had already laid claim to the island by the end of the 1400s, and retained possession until 1777, when it was exchanged, along with some neighbouring islands, for a collection of islands off the coast of Brazil belonging to Spain. This resulted in the Spanish colony of Elobey, Annobon and Corisco.

Furthest out to sea lies Annobon. Although it is the largest of the three islands, it is still only around 7 km (4 miles) long north to south, and 4 km (a little over 2 miles) wide at most. It is very hilly, with extinct volcanoes encircled by dense forests and undergrowth that extend all the way down to the seashore. The Creole population is descended from slaves and Portuguese settlers. At the beginning of the 1500s, they chopped down the best timber, so there is little of value here. The Spanish aren't impressed.

And Corisco is not much better. The Elobey Islands were the main attraction for the Spanish, or, more precisely, just Little Elobey. This tiny islet lies very close to the coast, and offers good harbour conditions. A trading station is quickly established there to handle exports of ivory, palm oil, rubber, mahogany and ebony from the mainland around the Gulf of Guinea. At the same time, weapons, ammunition, textiles and liquor are brought in.

So it is not by chance that my stamp bears a well-used postmark from Elobey. The other islands barely had any mail delivery at all. The motif is the child king Alfonso XIII of Spain – strong-willed but angelic nonetheless, to judge by his expression. He was monarch from his birth in 1886: his father, Alfonso XII, had only just managed to impregnate his mother, Maria Christina, before keeling over from tuberculosis.

Little Elobey was also on the route the missionaries took on their way over to the mainland. Many died after a short time, mostly of sleeping sickness, which is caused by a parasite transmitted by the tsetse fly. Gradually, the perception emerged that the risk must be lower in the fresh sea air out on the islands.

The American Presbyterian mission moved its base to Corisco in 1850. From here, the missionaries could still make shorter trips into the mainland, but they were mostly interested in training and equipping the locals to take over the longer evangelizing expeditions.[42] The move proved to be a mistake. The tsetse fly was just as aggressive on Corisco and, after a few years, the Presbyterians gave up.

When Mary Kingsley comes to Corisco in 1895, there are two Catholic priests and three nuns on the island. They live in the Misión Claretiana, a short walk from the village with the colourful doors. In a neat avenue of mango trees, she is met by a group of children in school uniform. For a moment, it feels as if she's in an English park. The cluster of houses wouldn't look out of place in Europe either. There is a little church, a shop and a school, as well as a large mission building. Everything is painted white, but like in the village the doors and windows are cobalt blue. She is served tea and avocadoes in the drawing room. The furnishings are unexpectedly elegant: nine chairs around a dining table, scent bottles laid out, and lithographs of English landscapes on the walls.

Mary Kingsley, who has already spent long periods with the indigenous tribes in the jungle on the mainland, is feeling a dawning sense of disdain for all this. After returning home to England in November 1895, she writes a book about her experiences.[43] She addresses herself directly to the reader:

> In reading this you must make allowances for my love of this sort of country, with its great forests and rivers and its animistic-minded inhabitants, and for my ability to be more comfortable there than in England. Your superior culture-instincts may militate against your enjoying West Africa, but if you go there you will find things as I have said.... The worst enemy to the existence of the African tribe, is the one who comes to it and says: Now you must civilize, and come to school, and leave off all those awful goings-on of yours, and settle down quietly.[44]

This wouldn't be an especially controversial thought nowadays, but at the time it caused an outcry. The Anglican Church was in despair and the larger newspapers refused to review Kingsley's book, which they saw as undermining British interests.

In 1909, Elobey, Annobon and Corisco was merged with the other Spanish territories around the Gulf of Guinea and eventually renamed Spanish Guinea. By the time the region gained its independence in 1968 as Equatorial Guinea, the mission station on Corisco had already been left in ruins by a fire. This was started by Father Andreas Bravo when he set a pile of coconut bark on fire while he was clearing

1905: Alfonso XIII, crowned king of Spain at birth in 1886.

the English garden in preparation for the Easter festivities. The priest left the same night, never to return.[45]

Even Little Elobey became irrelevant long ago. After nearly half a century as an administrative centre, all business there was discontinued in 1927. Today, the island is one great ruin. Beneath the canopies of the trees – which look almost like one continuous mass from the air – lie the remains of various buildings, trading houses and factories, all crowded together. Closer examination shows that all the organic material has long since crumbled to dust, but here and there, you may stumble across rusty Singer sewing machines and children's cribs in what used to be homes. In the ruins of the more elegant residences there are misshapen fountains, Art Deco windows, wrought-iron staircases and banisters, and everywhere masses of tableware and empty bottles of liquor of European origin.[46]

On Annobon, time has stood still. The population, which totalled 20,000 in 2013, is still poor. In the 1990s and 2000s, British and American companies dumped large quantities of poisonous and radioactive waste on the island. All the compensation paid out for this ended up in the pockets of the ruling elite on the mainland.[47]

BOOKS

Robert Hamill Nassau (1910)
Corisco Days. The First Thirty Years of the West African Mission

Mary Kingsley (1897)
Travels in West Africa. Congo Français, Corisco and Cameroons

///

The worst enemy to the existence of the African tribe, is the one who comes to it and says: Now you must civilize, and come to school, and leave off all those awful goings-on of yours

MARY KINGSLEY

PERIOD:	
1849–1866	

COUNTRY:	
VANCOUVER ISLAND	

POPULATION:	AREA:
30,000	31,285 sq. km

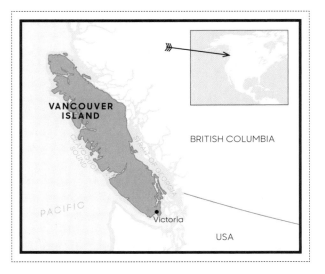

Wooden temples

He takes out a cigarette, slips the case into his blazer pocket and leans back in his deck chair. He is astonished. The island really does look like one great rock, and from south to north it is covered in an enormous forest. Through his Zeiss binoculars, the young aristocrat, Charles Barrett-Lennard, has spied Vancouver Island – the largest Pacific island east of New Zealand.

Along with his fellow-officer, Napoleon Fitzstubbs, he has set out on a pleasure trip after an arduous stint as a dragoon in the Crimean War. They have brought along a spacious cutter as deck cargo, together with their dogs, including a pure-breed bulldog. It is late in the summer of 1860 and they are planning to sail around Vancouver Island, where Captain James Cook was the first European to set foot in 1778.

After rigging up the cutter outside the little collection of wooden houses that form the administrative centre of Victoria at the southernmost point of the island, they set out in an eastward direction. They plan to sail along the mainland side of the island first, through the Strait of Georgia. There is a tailwind and blazing sunshine, and the ensign of the Royal Thames Yacht Club flutters on the stern. Soon they meet their first Native Americans, black-eyed and copper-skinned with broad faces, high cheekbones and smooth black hair that is never cut. And without exception they are dressed in 'bizarre, party-coloured garments'.[48] One chief wants to barter for the bulldog, a trade Barrett-Lennard refuses in no uncertain terms. Instead, he offers him a pair of trousers, for which the chief shows little enthusiasm even though they were cut by Hills of Bond Street.

In the Clayoquot Sound, they quickly spy a number of Native American villages in clearings along the shoreline. And they are amazed by the building traditions: 'The sight of these buildings produced the same effect of wonder on my mind as did the first visit to Stonehenge.'[49]

The houses are as large as railway stations and consist of coarse frameworks formed by posts measuring over a meter in diameter. The saddle roofs and walls are clad with broad planks split with wedges. And, unbelievably enough, the inhabitants are nomads. A tribe will generally make use of two or three villages, travelling between them. Each time they leave, they take the planking with them and leave the framework standing.

More than 30,000 Native Americans were living on Vancouver Island in the mid-1800s: the Kwakiutl, Nuu-chah-nulth and various Salish peoples. They lived as hunter-gatherers, also supplying the British Hudson Bay Company with the skins of otters, elks, beavers and squirrels. They were paid in knives, saucepans, needles and thread, but first and foremost in woollen blankets, which virtually served as the island's currency. The blankets were specially produced by the Hudson Bay Company and their value was reflected in their size and the amount of coloured strips woven into them.

The Hudson Bay Company was founded in 1670 and had since built up a monopoly on all fur-trading in the north of the American continent as far as the Arctic. The company had established the trading station of Victoria on Vancouver Island in 1846 and immediately secured a ten-year contract to handle all local exports and imports. The company's local director, James Douglas, had worked his way up from the bottom. His powerful build, bushy eyebrows and long whiskers gave him the air of a man of authority. And he got on well with the Native Americans.

News that the company was scooping up massive profits soon made its way across the sea and, in 1849, the British decided to formally designate the island a British colony. The 32-year-old aristocrat Richard Blanshard was sent over as the colony's first governor. He was well educated and considerably more cultured than Douglas – in his own eyes at least. His mission was to establish an efficient administration. In addition, he was to pave the way for immigration from Great Britain. But the whole project was beset with major problems. The Hudson Bay Company didn't want any changes. It didn't want the island to be flooded with settlers, but preferred to preserve the huge, impenetrable forests and the hunting opportunities they offered. And it wanted to maintain its good relationship with the Native Americans who provided it with furs.

The stage was set for a classic feud between Douglas and Blanshard, between raw strength and formal power.

Blanshard quickly came to understand that the company's initials, HBC, could also be read as meaning *Here Before Christ*.[50] He was ill equipped to combat the unanimous opposition he met at all levels, from the civilian population to government officials, and gave up in the first round.

It would seem that Blanshard then took his frustration out on the Native Americans. He had never attempted to conceal his disdain for their culture. He thought they were undisciplined and irrational, and had to be kept under control to prevent 'a sudden outburst of fury to which all savages are liable'.[51] After a couple of minor episodes of violence involving Native Americans, he arranged a punitive expedition. And he didn't waste any resources attempting to identify the actual culprits but instead subjected the tribes to collective punishment, burning down several of their villages. The result was fatal. For a while, all cooperation between the indigenous people and the whites on the island – including the Hudson Bay Company – hung in the balance.

We do not know whether Blanshard was ultimately pressured to leave or whether he simply got sick and tired of it all. But after less than two years as governor he resigned and went back to England. And in the years that followed, he never wasted an opportunity to sulk and whine about the colony: 'Nothing more than a fur trading post.'[52]

Unsurprisingly, James Douglas then took over as governor, while also remaining in charge of the Hudson Bay Company. He urged for renewed collaboration with the Native Americans, and continued develop his friendship with these 'children of the forest'.[53] The few new settlers who

1860: Bust of Queen Victoria of England.

had come in the meantime despaired, and vanished over to the mainland. The atmosphere was much improved and the district recorded many fewer confrontations between Native Americans and whites than was usual elsewhere in North America in those days.

It was also James Douglas who wrote a letter to the colonial administration in London raising the need for stamps. To save money, he suggested a joint issue with the neighbouring colony on the mainland, British Columbia. One type would suffice, he thought, and he enclosed his own sketch of what he thought was required. A hundred sheets of 240 stamps should meet the demand.

In 1860, the stamps are printed by De La Rue in London. They are bright red, have a face value of 2.5 pence and bear a portrait of Queen Victoria – anything else would have been unthinkable. This time, however, she is portrayed as much more mature and professional than on the stamp from Van Diemen's Land. Her white eyeballs and heavy eyelids give her the look of a Greek bust, making her appear haughty, unapproachable and cold: just the way we expect a monarch to be. Even so, I feel that my stamp may have lost a bit of its fire. It is much paler than it should be and may have spent a long time lying in the sunlight.

After gold was found on the mainland, all interest shifted there. And when Vancouver Island's budget failed in 1865, the decision was taken to merge the colony with British Columbia from the following year, under the name of British Columbia. In 1871, the whole region was converted into a unified Canadian province.

BOOKS

Matthew Macfie (1865)
Vancouver Island and British Columbia:
Their History, Resources and Prospects

Charles Barrett-Lennard (1862)
Travels in British Columbia: With a Narrative
of a Yacht Voyage Round Vancouver's Island

Margaret Horsfield & Ian Kennedy (2014)
Tofino and Clayoquot Sound: A History

//

The sight of these buildings produced the same effect of wonder on my mind as did the first visit to Stonehenge

CHARLES BARRETT-LENNARD

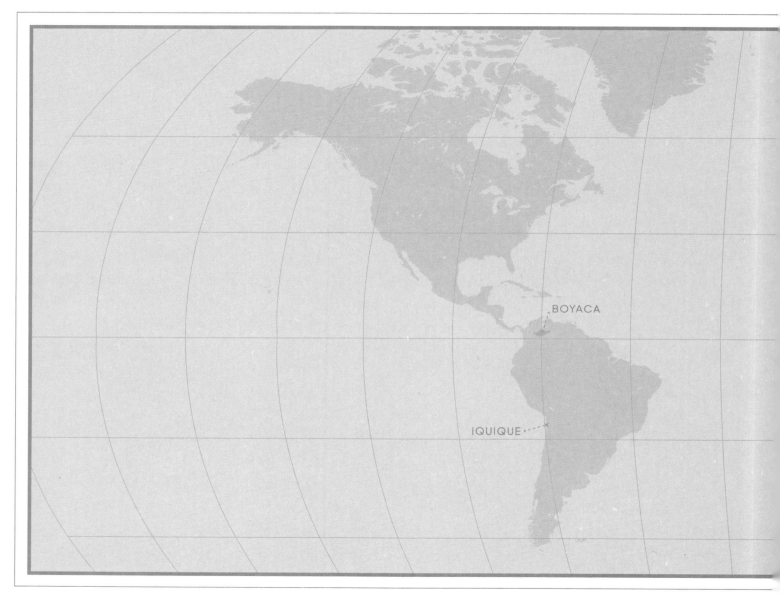

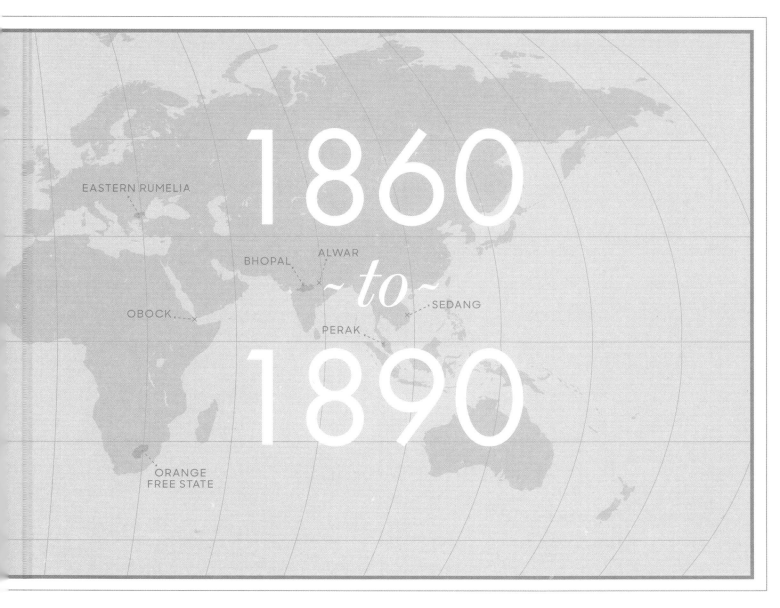

EASTERN RUMELIA

BHOPAL   ALWAR

OBOCK

PERAK

SEDANG

ORANGE
FREE STATE

1860
~ to ~
1890

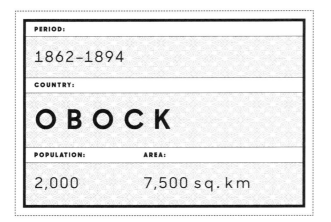

PERIOD:

1862–1894

COUNTRY:

OBOCK

POPULATION: 2,000 **AREA:** 7,500 sq. km

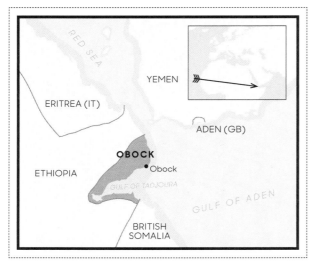

RED SEA

YEMEN

ERITREA (IT)

ADEN (GB)

OBOCK
• Obock

ETHIOPIA

GULF OF TADJOURA

GULF OF ADEN

BRITISH SOMALIA

Arms dealing and goat soup

When Obock was bought by France in 1862, the area was little more than a desolate fishing village surrounded by an olive-green desert the sand of which was somewhat coarser than in other deserts.

The atmosphere feels uninhibited and it is all too easy for a newly arrived colonial official to get caught up in the social excesses of the place. Partway through the welcome party, he wanders off drunkenly and finds himself lost on the rugged, crooked paths beyond the orderly colonial administration quarter, with its single-storey whitewashed brick buildings. Out here, the local population lives in simple huts made of twigs, straw and clay. It is a clear, starry night but dark nonetheless, with just the flicker of an occasional oil lamp. He stumbles, his bottle of liquorice liquor smashes and his mouth is filled with sand. Dogs bark. Somebody takes him in their arms. He wakes up early next morning, leaning against a bundle of furs. His head is swimming. Looking up, he can see daylight coming through the roof of woven grass matting. A woman serves him goat soup and bread, but he can't bring himself to eat it. He feels dreadful. But in the midst of it all, he feels a rush of relief at the thought that the rest of his family stayed behind in France.

Obock was the first French colony in the Red Sea region. Following the murder of the French consul to Aden during a tour of the area a couple of years before, the local sultans of Tadjoura, Gobaad and Rheita accepted all the terms. The price was a modest 10,000 Maria Theresa thalers,[54] coins named after a long-dead Austrian empress that were still in circulation in most of the region.

Work on the Suez Canal to the north had already been under way for some years. Both Italy and England were established in the area, and France wanted to set up its own base to secure coal supplies for its modernized navy and a steady stream of heavily laden merchant ships heading back home from the colonies in Southeast Asia.

But Obock soon proved to be a poor choice. Although it was surrounded by coral reefs, the harbour offered little protection against the heavy swells rolling into the Gulf of Aden from the annual storms out on the Indian Ocean. Nevertheless, they kept it going until 1894, when the whole business was moved across the Gulf of Tadjoura to Djibouti, where harbour conditions were much more favourable.

In its heyday, between 1884 and 1885, Obock was home to around 2,000 people. Other than the colonial administration and some semi-official tradesmen, many of them were adventurers and petty criminals, drawn there by the local king, Menelik, who had boasted of his massive stores of ivory and other riches.

One of the fortune hunters is the French poet, Arthur Rimbaud. At home, he has become famous for his boundless desire for freedom, as well as his groundbreaking experiments in intoxication and sexuality, but at twenty-one years of age he feels he's all written out. After wandering the length and breadth of Europe and then getting lost without trace in the jungle on Java, he turns up in Obock.

Disillusioned, full of regrets, exhausted and broke after many years of excess, he is trying to bring more order into his life, and above all to secure himself an income. He can no longer bear to live from hand to mouth. The solution is arms dealing.

He rents a simple brick house a little further west in the Gulf of Tadjoura to avoid attracting the attention of the other colonials:

> It is a little Danakil[55] village with a few mosques and a few palm trees. There is an old fort the Egyptians built where six French soldiers are now sleeping under the orders of a sergeant who is commander of the post.[56]

He regards Obock society with barely concealed scorn: 'The little French Administration is preoccupied with the throwing of banquets and drinking of government money, which won't end up netting a penny from that horrible colony, colonized by nothing more than a dozen freeloaders.[57]

He believes himself to be above it all, and is therefore content to collect substantial sums in return for providing Menelik with large numbers of obsolete French flintlocks at forty francs apiece. It proves easier than he had expected, spurring him to megalomania; he enters into a insistent correspondence with the French foreign minister, lobbying for support to establish a local arms industry in the country, although of course the endeavour never gets beyond the ideas stage.

Predictably, Rimbaud also becomes embroiled in a complicated romance, probably with a French woman. This goes awry too. We can picture it for ourselves: an unkempt, stoop-shouldered man of indeterminate age drifting constantly back and forth along the desolate shore, steeped in self-pity and despondency. He is impervious to impressions from the outside world, be it the sour stench of a beached school of sardines or the shimmer of sunlight on the bright blue water outside: 'I have seen too much of this masquerade.... I must therefore spend my remaining days wandering, in exhaustion and hardship, with nothing to look forward to but death and suffering.'[58]

In the end, he manages to pull himself together enough to flee over to the British territory of Aden, on the other side of the mouth of the Red Sea. Shortly afterwards, when he falls gravely ill, he is quickly bundled on a steamer called *L'Amazone* and dispatched to France, where he dies.

Menilek is the one who does best out of the whole business. He wins himself the throne to the Ethiopian empire, eventually to be succeeded by his grandson, daughter and then a cousin, the even more legendary Haile Selassie.

The motif on my stamp shows a group of native warriors with standard-issue shields and spears. This more than underscores the significance of the decrepit weapons Rimbaud had procured.

1894: Native warriors gathered for a council of war.

The stamp is postmarked 9 March 1894, in other words just before the colony is dissolved, and perhaps it was used to send news of an imminent reunion to those back home. Note the fake perforation teeth. The point of perforations was to make it easier to tear the stamps off by hand, and they had already been in use in most countries for a long time. Not in Obock, though.

France retained its position around the Gulf of Tadjoura, which was first renamed French Somaliland and later the Territory of the Afars and the Issas, after the two dominant tribes living there.

Only after a referendum and massive pressure from neighbouring countries was the Free Republic of Djibouti declared in 1977. Today, it is the smallest country on the Horn of Africa, although it still suffers severe internal conflict, which has repeatedly led to bloody clashes. The small city of Obock – which lies in the area traditionally belonging to the Afar tribe – has so far been spared.

///

The little French Administration is preoccupied with the throwing of banquets and drinking of government money, which won't end up netting a penny from that horrible colony, colonized by nothing more than a dozen freeloaders

ARTHUR RIMBAUD

BOOKS

Wyatt Mason (2003)
I Promise to Be Good:
The Letters of Arthur Rimbaud

Richard Alan Caulk (2002)
Between the Jaws of Hyenas:
A Diplomatic History of Ethiopia

FAH-FAH SOUP (FIVE PORTIONS)

500 g (18 oz) goat meat
250 g (9 oz) potatoes
¼ kale or cabbage
1 leek
1 tomato
1 clove of garlic
½ green chilli
1 onion
Salt, pepper and coriander

Preparation:
Chop up the vegetables and meat and add to a saucepan of water. Simmer on a low heat for twenty minutes. Add the coriander and crushed garlic. Add more water and simmer for another hour. Season with salt and pepper.

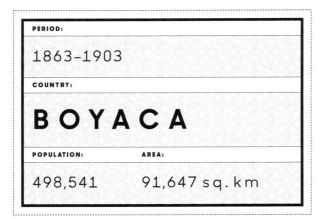

PERIOD:	
1863–1903	
COUNTRY:	
BOYACA	
POPULATION:	AREA:
498,541	91,647 sq. km

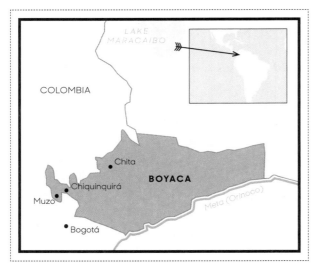

Decadents at war

The poet Julio Flórez never collected stamps. His interests lay in quite different directions. In photographs taken shortly before the turn of the century, he exudes an almost narcissistic dignity: hair swept back in greasy, oil-black waves, the tips of his moustache like panther tails and eyebrows so arched they would have done Salvador Dalí proud. All this arranged carefully around eyes that were slightly protuberant, as if subject to some pressure from within – the way you often see with poets. He has recently published a collection of erotic poems, to widespread moral outrage – which must have elevated him to a state of almost provocative ecstasy: against his father, against his mother, against the rest of his family.

Julio Flórez was born into the liberal aristocracy in the small town of Chiquinquirá in 1867. It was the administrative centre of the Estado Soberano Boyacá (the Sovereign State of Boyacá) in the coffee belt in the far north of the Andes. The town clings to the western face of the steep mountains of the Cordilla Oriental, which tower more than 5,000 m (16,500 ft) in the east before descending via the tropical high plateau, the Llanos, to the source of the Orinoco water system and the border with Venezuela in the north.

Until 1863, Boyacá was part of Colombia, which became South America's first constitutional republic in 1819. After a bloody civil war, the republic dissolved into a fairly unstable collection of more or less autonomous states. Boyacá was by far the poorest. This was not primarily because it lacked resources: Boyacá had large salt mines in Chita and emerald deposits near Muzo. There were also fertile agricultural areas, especially in the many long valleys to the west. But the road networks were very poor and all transport of goods had to be suspended during the two rainy seasons – with the exception, at best, of a couple of llama-loads of the locally produced hemp sandals known as *alpargatas*, which might find their way to the market in Bogotá.

After yet another civil war in 1885, Boyacá's sovereignty came to an end and the Republic of Colombia re-established. Boyacá was downgraded to a province, although it continued to have broad authority. In 1899, it saw a chance to issue its own stamps, one of which depicted a bald-headed Andean condor with a white collar and outspread wings reposing on a slightly indistinct coat of arms. The poor-quality paper used was easily torn and the printing quality is nothing to write home about either; a lick of the tongue shows that these are very dry goods indeed.

Julio Flórez's poetry collection was published in 1899. This was the same year that the future fabulist and surrealist, Jorge Luis Borges, first saw the light of day in Buenos Aires, around 4,700 km (2,900 miles) further south on the continent. And in the same year the last stamp from Boyacá was issued, 1904, the painter and poseur Salvador Dalí was born in Figueres, Spain. Julio Flórez, who had already been active for some years by then, was, in many ways, the ideological precursor of his better-known successors.

It is at this time that Flórez moves to Bogotá and forms *La Gruta Simbólica* ('The Symbolic Grotto') with a group of like-minded fellow-artists. The idea arose, he said, after they had a narrow escape from a battalion of government soldiers one night after curfew. The conversations and rum drinking that followed resulted, the next morning, in a pamphlet entitled 'Of Decadence and Symbolism'. It is strongly inspired by the French poets, Charles Baudelaire and Arthur Rimbaud.

The end of the 1800s was a period of prosperity, full of belief in the future; but many people, particularly artists and philosophers, did not share this optimism. The term *fin de siècle* was coined, describing with a certain melancholy a period on the wane. The most tenacious called themselves decadents. The term 'decadence' signified a phenomenon in absolute decline, and was part of a conscious strategy of provocation. The decadent artists did not, themselves, wish to appear decadent. Their intention was rather to reveal the decadence they believed they saw in their age. At the same time, they claimed the right to freedom of artistic development, independent of shallow and authoritarian influences. In poetry's 'supernatural' realm of beauty, declared Baudelaire, desire is 'pure', melancholy is 'gracious' and desperation is 'noble'.[59]

The Symbolic Grotto consists of seventy painters, musicians and poets, some of whom are women. They hold secret salons at restaurants near the Cathedral in Bogotá with names like The Greedy Cat and The Cradle of Venus. On warm evenings, they break into nearby graveyards:

> Melancholy music from stringed instruments issues from the crypt. Birds ruffle their wings in the cypresses, fireflies swarm about and the moon lights up the marble gravestones. Confidences are shared with the graves! Serenades are delivered to the dead! Some rest their foreheads on the tree trunks and meditate.[60]

At that time, Colombia was embroiled in the Thousand Days War, a liberal rebellion against a strict, conservative regime. It erupted after the conservatives were caught out in election fraud in 1899, and was intensified by an economic crisis that followed a fall in coffee prices. More than 100,000 were wounded or killed during the conflict, including a large group of child soldiers who were forcibly conscripted on the conservative side.

Little changed after a peace treaty was signed in 1902, under heavy pressure from the USA, which feared that the disturbances might delay the start of construction on the Panama Canal.

And in 1905, Julio Flórez was exiled for blasphemy. For reasons that are unclear, he returned to favour a couple of years later and was appointed secretary to the embassy in Spain, where he died in 1923, probably of cancer. Today he is largely unknown, but in Colombia, his poem 'Mis flores

1903: Coat of arms with an Andean condor and flag.

negras' ('My black flowers') still lives on: 'Listen: beneath the ruins of my passions / in the depths of this soul that you will no longer delight / amid the dust of dreams and illusions / my black flowers bloom benumbed'.[61] The poem, the title of which is probably a paraphrase of the title of Baudelaire's poetry collection, *Les fleurs du mal* ('The flowers of evil'), has been set to music and performed by numerous Latin American tango musicians.[62]

The original province of Boyacá is now divided into Boyacá, Arauca and Casanare. The new Boyacá Department mainly covers the mountainous areas to the west. The city of Tunja, 2,820 m (9,250 ft) above sea level with 180,000 inhabitants, is the capital of the province. The road networks are much improved, and the coffee, tobacco, fruit and grain production can now reach the markets.

In the background, the ghost of the political rivalry between liberals and conservatives still lingers, locking Bocayá into a persistent and sometimes extremely violent culture. But if nothing else, at least Julio Flórez has had a park named after him in his birthplace of Chiquinquirá.

BOOKS

Julio Flórez (1988)
Poesía escogida ('Selected Poetry'; new edition)

José Vicente Ortega Ricaurte & Antonio Ferro (1981)
La Gruta Simbólica ('The Symbolic Grotto')

Per Buvik (2001)
Dekadanse ('Decadence')

MUSIC

Carlos Gardel
Mis flores negras ('My black flowers')

//

> **Melancholy music from string instruments issues from the crypt. Birds ruffle their wings in the cypresses, fireflies swarm about and the moon lights up the marble gravestones**
>
> LUIS MARIA MORA

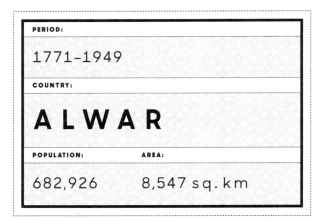

PERIOD:
1771–1949

COUNTRY:
ALWAR

POPULATION:	AREA:
682,926	8,547 sq. km

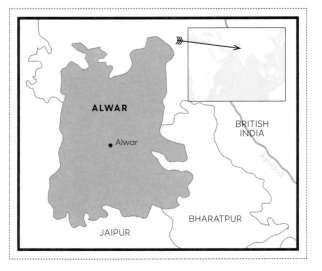

Potty princes and sweet dessert

The text on my stamp, from 1877, is in the Indian script called *devanagari*. At the top, it tells us we are in Alwar, a princely state roughly the size of North Yorkshire. At the bottom, the value is given, followed by the figure 31, which is a mystery. It probably relates to the die having been made in 1931 according to the Hindu calendar, equivalent to 1875 in the Gregorian calendar. The stamp itelf is not printed until two years later.

The motif is a traditional push dagger known as a *katar*, with an H-shaped hand-grip and a triangular blade, forged into a single piece. This is a reference to the legend of a prince who escaped from four assassins by seizing a *katar* from the belt of their leader using only his toes and then stabbing him in the stomach. This captures the essence of Alwar: its deeply ingrained traditions of treachery and arrogant violence make the adventures in the Arabian Nights look like non-fiction.

The backdrop to all this was the emergence of India's so-called princely states. Once again, it was the British who were pulling the strings.

The East India Company was the East's answer to the Hudson Bay Company in North America. It was a purely commercial concern set up in the 1600s by the British aristocracy and wealthy merchants. Its aim was to bring goods such as cotton, silk, indigo dye, spices, tea and opium home from the East. The British state was scarcely involved and the company had plenty of leeway to maximize exploitation without any ethical or diplomatic restrictions. It set up private armies and an administration that kept whatever remained of local autonomy in check. In India, the East India Company governed over sixty per cent of the area on its own, while the rest was organized into princely states.

The first princely state to sign a treaty of cooperation was Alwar – then called Ulwar – in 1803. Its maharaja, Bakhtawar Singh, led a dynasty descended from the Rajput warrior caste. The treaty secured him a large income while placing him beyond the reach of possible challengers to the throne. The company had his back.

Even so, the maharaja felt insecure enough to opt to settle scores with all the Muslims in the area in 1811. He burned their mosques and systematically chopped off noses and ears, which were then sent by the crate-load to Muslim princes elsewhere in the region. The bones of those he killed were also dispatched out of the country.[63]

The East India Company became uneasy, foreseeing prolonged problems with the Muslims, who made up a large share of the population in many Indian states. After threats from the company army, Bakhtawar Singh gave in and agreed that there would be no repeat. By way of consolation he was permitted to rename Ulwar Alwar, thereby advancing the princely state's position not just in the alphabet but also in the queue for many of the bureaucratic processes then under way in India.

Despite increased demand for colonial goods throughout Europe, the management of the East India Company eventually ran into major financial problems over the course of the 1800s. And after a series of catastrophic famines caused by the company's insistence on switching from grain to opium crops, a rebellion flared up in 1857, rapidly spreading to large areas of the Indian continent. The 280,000-strong company army found itself in trouble and the turbulence died down only in 1858 after the British government stepped in and nationalized the company. The fact that the hegemony thereby shifted from corporate imperialism to state imperialism meant little to the maharajas in Alwar and the other princely states. They may have had to quieten down a bit, but the power structures remained the same as before.

Towards the end of the 1800s, an American called Eliza Ruhamah Scidmore travels through Alwar. And like so many other foreign tourists, what she's interested in is the fairy-tale culture of the princes, with all its excesses of wealth and splendour.

In 1892, Jai Singh Prabhakar Bahadur had inherited the throne. In contrast to his predecessors, all of whom sported luxuriant, dyed beards, he looks more like a European: he has only a thin moustache and is otherwise clean-shaven. But his eyes glow with exoticism and he is dressed up in full regalia of silk, gold and diamonds, far outshining his peers in other princely states. The tourists are overwhelmed.

Eliza Ruhamah Scidmore tells of processions of 300 singers who follow the prince's elephant wherever it should roam. She tells of castles with huge chambers made of solid marble and furnishings of pure silver; of landscape gardens overgrown with rare orchids. She tells of tame tigers and blue parrots that recite full sentences in Rajput, of stables with 500 horses and forty elephants, 'tramping and swinging their trunks in idleness for the honour and glory of the raja'.[64]

Back at her hotel, she takes tea with her travelling companions. And she orders *kalakand*, a local cake made by warming up milk in a large pan and then adding sugar and dried fruit. In her room, she finds a sign that spells out the dark side of the princely state: 'Visitors will please not beat the servants, but report them to the manager, who will punish them.'[65] She is introduced to the so-called *begar* system, whereby anybody who is not a member of the aristocracy must contribute their unpaid labour for at least a month of every year. The prince himself decides when the work will be done. Women are summoned to the palace with no regard for their own domestic duties, and men must leave their own crops to rot in the fields while they harvest the prince's opium plantations. At the same time, taxation is heavy, and extraordinary taxes may be imposed without warning if, for example, a princess is to marry.

Jai Singh Prabhakar Bhadur buys a great many cars on his constant trips to Europe, and they are always luxury cars. After being insulted at a Rolls Royce showroom in London, he buys six of the company's most expensive models and, on returning home, has them refitted to serve

1877: Stamp with a katar dagger and text in *devanagari* script.

as rubbish trucks – to the despair of the car company, which rapidly loses contracts throughout the region.

On one occasion when he was dissatisfied with the horses during a local polo tournament, he had them soaked in petrol and burnt alive on the field. This tests the British officers among the public to their very limits,[66] and when it later transpires that he has used small children as live bait during his regular tiger hunts, this is the last straw. The maharaja is removed from office in 1933 and moves to Paris, where he spends his last years wearing gloves to avoid coming into physical contact with white people.

He was replaced by Tej Singh Prabhakar Bahadur, his cousin, who was not as savage, but his arrogance was intact, as was his absolute lack of interest in social improvements: 'We are the sons of the Sun God. The people are our children. The relationship is that of father and son. There is no mention of reforms in the Holy Book.'[67]

It all came to an end in 1949 anyway, when Alwar was incorporated into the far more democratic Indian Union. But Tej Singh Prabhakar Bahadur didn't give up without a struggle, largely at the expense of the democratically inclined Muslims in the area. Over the course of six months, almost all of them were thrown out.

Tej Singh Prabhakar Bahadur himself went back to Delhi, where he lived comfortably on his savings until his death in 2009.

//

We are the sons of the Sun God. The people are our children. The relationship is that of father and son. There is no mention of reforms in the Holy Book

TEJ SINGH PRABHAKAR BAHADUR

BOOK

Eliza Ruhamah Scidmore (1903)
Winter India

KALAKAND

1.5 l (50 fl. oz) milk
100 g (4 oz) sugar
1 tsp saffron
2 tbsp vinegar
Dried fruit (to garnish)

Preparation:
Boil the milk and stir in the sugar and saffron. Keep boiling until the milk has halved in volume. Set aside 150 ml (5 fl. oz) and add the vinegar to the rest, cooking it for a few more minutes while stirring slowly until the milk curdles. Set the pan to one side and let it rest for fifteen minutes. Drain off the liquid and carefully knead the curd that has formed.

Warm up about two-thirds of the milk you set aside and add the curd. Once the milk has been soaked up and the mixture has thickened, pour it into a bowl and put it in a cool place. Before serving, pour the last of the milk over the top, then sprinkle with chopped dried fruit.

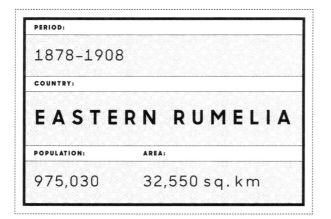

PERIOD:	
1878–1908	
COUNTRY:	
EASTERN RUMELIA	
POPULATION:	AREA:
975,030	32,550 sq. km

RUSSIA

BULGARIA

EASTERN RUMELIA

• Plovdiv

BLACK SEA

MACEDONIA

Drawing-board country

The Balkans have always been an unsettled region. At the end of the 1870s, conflict breaks out again, this time in the areas down towards the Black Sea in the east. International diplomacy proves all but useless and several of the great powers in the West send in agents, partly to try and influence the situation and partly to get some idea of what's actually going on there.

The same setting – if a little closer to our own times – is used in Francis Van Wyck Mason's novel, *Dardanelles Derelict*. It opens with two American agents parachuting into a snowbound mountain landscape: one is Hugh North, a James Bond-style character who appears in several of Wyck Mason's action novels, and the other is a beautiful newspaperwoman, Jingles Lawson. They have disguised themselves in advance as farmers, and North has to wear a wig because the men in the area never cut their hair. Meanwhile, all other bodily hair is shaven off, also in accordance with local tradition, 'apparently to ward off vermin', says a blushing Jingles. In addition, the agents have rubbed snuff into the corners of their eyes to make them look inflamed, and they have been given clear orders never to blow their noses on anything but their fingers. Although Wyck Mason's training as a historian probably guarantees the authenticity of these details to some extent, you get the sneaking feeling that the dramatics have got a bit out of hand here.

In the 1870s – as so often both before and since – it was all a matter of the great powers jockeying for position, far above the heads of the local populace. Russia had set itself the goal of conquering the territory it needed to secure its access to the Mediterranean. To achieve this, it had to drive out the Ottomans.

The Ottoman Empire was established by a clan of Oghuz Turks and passed its zenith in the 1600s, when it ruled over an empire that encompassed the Mediterranean in both south and east, and stretched across Asia Minor as far as the Indian Ocean. After a couple of centuries of stagnation, the empire was beginning to fall apart. Russia saw its chance in 1877: it intervened and easily won the area it had been eyeing. The Treaty of San Stefano a year later established the creation of a Russian-dominated Greater Bulgaria, which would stretch as far as the harbour town of Thessaloniki by the Aegean Sea.

The other great European powers, which had stayed on the sidelines until then, became increasingly uneasy about Russia's influence in the area. Great Britain, France, Italy and Austria-Hungary therefore refused to accept the treaty. The German chancellor, Otto von Bismarck, took it upon himself to serve as arbitrator and during the summer of 1878 the Treaty of Berlin was drawn up. In this treaty, Russia's spoils of war were drastically reduced. After stern threats, the Russians signed anyway.

Bismarck noted the solid contribution of the British Prime Minister, Benjamin Disraeli: 'That old Jew. What a man.'[68] Admittedly the Russians retained a certain influence over part of Bulgaria in the north, while Macedonia in the south would remain under Ottoman rule. In order to secure a peaceful coexistence, a separate autonomous zone was to be established between the two. On the suggestion of the British, it was called Eastern Rumelia. It would cover the area between the Black Sea in the east, the Balkan Mountains in the north and the Strandzha Massif in the south. The Ottomans would retain a kind of administrative authority, but only on condition that the new country had a Christian governor.

Absolutely no effort was made to take into account ethnic and political relations in the affected areas. The whole thing was nothing but a drawing-board plan, and even the British Foreign Secretary Robert A. T. Gascoyne-Cecil admitted it had some shortcomings: 'We shall set up a rickety sort of Turkish rule again south of the Balkans. But it is a mere respite. There is no vitality left in them.'[69]

The Ottomans nevertheless were satisfied and gave Great Britain the island of Cyprus as thanks for its support. Austria-Hungary, meanwhile, received the whole of Bosnia and Herzegovina.

Naturally enough, Russia was not as happy with the result, although it had at least managed to ensure that the new prince of what was left of Bulgaria in the north would be selected by Tsar Alexander II. He chose a nephew of his German wife, also called Alexander. When he went on to appoint a Russia-friendly minister of war as well, it was the last straw for the Bulgarians. Quite unexpectedly, the new prince took the side of the people, but was at once kidnapped by Russian agents. He relinquished the throne without a squeak. The Bulgarians took advantage of the sudden political vacuum to choose their own prince who, unbelievably enough, managed to stay on the throne in Sofia right up until 1918, to the great despair of the Russians.

In the newly established country of Eastern Rumelia, the Ottomans had in the meantime managed to find themselves a Christian Bulgarian prince with Ottoman sympathies, Alexander Bogoridi, whom they appointed governor general. The 975,000 inhabitants, most of whom were Bulgarian, responded with apparent apathy, but something had begun to smoulder at the grass-roots level.

Eastern Rumelia's first stamps are issued in 1881, perhaps as an attempt to inject a touch of national feeling. They are printed in Constantinople, and include clear design elements from existing Ottoman stamps, along with the fairly unambiguous inscription: 'Post from the Ottoman Empire' in Arabic. They also bear the same phrase in Greek, Bulgarian and French, which only serves to underscore the prevailing confusion.

My stamp is postmarked Philippopolis, which is the Greek name for the city of Plovdiv in the middle of the Thracian Plain in the east. It lies amid a rolling landscape of low hills on the shores of the Maritsa River and its history goes back more than 6,000 years. As this makes it one of the oldest cities in Europe, it is difficult to avoid adopting it as the new country's capital city.

1881: Crescent moon with the text 'Post from the Ottoman Empire' in Turkish, Greek, Bulgarian and French.

In the whole region, popular opinion is shifting ever more clearly in favour of a united Bulgaria. And the view is that it should not just include Eastern Rumelia and the remainder of Bulgaria in the north but also Macedonia. The tone is so aggressive that the Ottoman government gives up its right to keep troops in Eastern Rumelia, and withdraws them to Macedonia. When the Kresna–Razlog uprising breaks out in Macedonia shortly afterwards, hundreds of volunteers pour over the border from the north. The Ottoman forces only manage to quell the turbulence by the skin of their teeth.

Various activities in support of a united Bulgaria continue, and the Bulgarian Secret Central Revolutionary Committee is formed. They decide to gamble on an uprising in Eastern Rumelia, since there are no longer any Ottoman troops there. On 6 September 1885, the rebels seize power in the fledgling country, ably assisted by regular Bulgarian forces and without spilling a drop of blood. The inhabitants immediately take to the streets, intoxicated with freedom; they snatch up anything that can be used to make a noise, from washboards and pans to horns and trumpets. Soon the streets echo with a deafening racket and the air is filled with flying hats.

Eastern Rumelia is dissolved overnight and reunited with the rest of Bulgaria. But the goal of incorporating Macedonia to form a Greater Bulgaria is never achieved. The great powers are too sceptical and the Ottomans still too strong for this to happen. Eastern Rumelia continues to be run as a province with a certain degree of autonomous rule up until 1908, and it is accepted that the Ottomans retain a certain amount of influence in the area, at least on paper.

The stamps, large stocks of which still exist, remain valid until the revolutionary year of 1885 (after being overprinted with the Bulgarian lion, which is on my stamp). From 1886, only Bulgarian stamps are used.

BOOKS

R. J. Crampton (1997)
A Concise History of Bulgaria

Francis Van Wyck Mason (1950)
Dardanelles Derelict

//

> We shall set up a rickety sort of Turkish rule again south of the Balkans. But it is a mere respite. There is no vitality left in them
>
> ROBERT A.T. GASCOYNE-CECIL

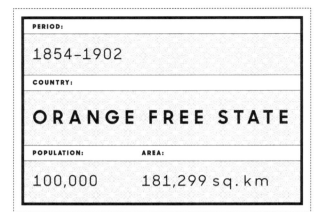

PERIOD:
1854–1902

COUNTRY:
ORANGE FREE STATE

POPULATION:	AREA:
100,000	181,299 sq. km

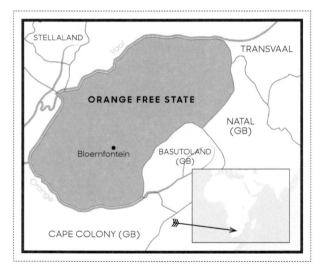

STELLALAND

TRANSVAAL

ORANGE FREE STATE

NATAL (GB)

Bloemfontein

BASUTOLAND (GB)

CAPE COLONY (GB)

Hymn-singing and racism

'What particularities might lie right in front of my nose, I do not know.'[70] Ingvald Schrøder-Nilsen, from Trøndelag in central Norway, sighs deeply as he leans over his drawing board in his tent on the highland plains of South Africa. He has been employed as a surveyor. It is evening and he is struggling to produce a fair copy of his day's work. The dip pen must be held steady throughout the whole line to avoid blotching, a task rendered almost impossible by all the flies.

It is 1898 and the Orange Free State, between the Vaal and Orange rivers in the South African highlands, has existed for nearly fifty years. The Orange, the larger of the two rivers, has its source in the Drakensberg Mountains, which soar to heights of more than 3,000 m (10,000 ft) in the east. This area sees 2 m (6 ft) of precipitation each year and in winter it falls as snow, decking the sharp mountaintops with white caps. On its way west towards the Atlantic Ocean, the Orange River changes character, becoming a dirty orange stream that teems with birds, crocodiles, hippopotamuses and elephants in its calmer stretches. It is hedged about on both sides by thorny acacia bushes, although these are still sparse enough for the sun to scorch the earth brown through the dry summers.

This was originally the tribal region of the Tswana, the Khoikhoi and the San Bushmen. But in the first half of the 1800s the area had almost been cleared by aggressive Zulu tribes from the east. The way was thus clear for the white settlers who arrived from the south towards the end of this period. They were descendants of Dutch and French Huguenots who had settled in the hills inland from the Cape of Good Hope several hundred years earlier, unhappy about the British colonization of the coastal area in 1795.

They called themselves Boers – Dutch for farmers – and were tall, sturdy people, good at riding and shooting. Above all, though, they were dogmatic Calvinists, believing that God predetermined whether an individual sinner was saved or damned. In line with this religion, the family system was patriarchal, and the Boers lived simple, frugal lives on small, scattered farmsteads.

On his surveying trip, Ingvald Schrøder-Nilsen experiences Boer culture at close quarters. And, being young, the first people to attract his attention are the girls:

> ...with peculiar headgear, a *kappie*, the brim of which extends so far forward that their faces sit in deep shadow. It completely protects them from sunburn, of which they appear to be most fearful. But as a result, the young women's complexions are the colour of milk and blood, just like in the fairy tales.... They are often pretty and plump in their early years, although one seldom sees what one might call a beauty.... And all the slightly older mothers are so corpulent that one would rather not think of one's wife-to-be like that.[71]

He is often invited in for coffee or supper, usually slow-cooked beef with sweet potato mash, pumpkin and mashed corn. It is served indoors in single-storey houses built of sun-dried mud bricks with roofing of corrugated iron or straw:

> They are divided into four or five rooms with earthen or plank flooring.... The only concession to comfort is the *rustbank*, or resting bench, a primitive sofa with a seat and back-rest of interwoven ox-hide thongs. The earthen floor, where present, is made very hard and smooth by using a mixture of clay and cow dung.[72]

And he accompanies them to church:

> Everybody coughed and cleared their throats good and long until the priest, who also led the singing, intoned a particularly prolonged and shrill note. It ended with some frightful trills, and immediately afterwards, everybody else joined in as loudly as they could – I have never heard music like it before![73]

Covering an area four times larger than the Netherlands, the Orange Free State was established as an independent republic in 1854, a couple of years after the neighbouring republic of Transvaal, which was also set up by the Boers. The administrative centre was Bloemfontein, a collection of rectangular blocks of low houses, interspersed with a few unusually broad streets of brown gravel. The official language was Dutch and all white men over eighteen had the right to vote in the *Volksraad* or 'people's council'. The notion that the few remaining indigenous people in the area should be viewed as subordinate was established in the constitution: 'The people desire to permit no equality between coloured people and the white inhabitants of the country, either in church or state.'[74]

All the same, many years passed in peace and calm, and the white population increased from 15,000 to 75,000 by 1875. But as many of the farms grew in size, the need for manpower increased. Gradually, the locals – whom the Boers called *kaffirs* – were incorporated into a kind of crofter system. Ingvald Schrøder-Nilsen noted that this made the business of running a farm in the region seem much less arduous than in Norway:

> The farmer lends them oxen and plough in the ploughing season, but in return, the *kaffir* is obliged to carry out all the agricultural work on the farm, while the women help the housewife with the laundry and slaughtering, as well as work in the house and garden, and the children herd the cattle and drive them home at night.[75]

In parallel, a slavery system was gradually developed, with slaves imported from Madagascar, Mozambique and Malaya. The British, who had in the meantime passed anti-slavery laws, claimed this was the main reason why they invaded the Orange Free State in 1898. There is much to indicate that they were, in fact, more interested in the neighbouring state of Transvaal, owing to the recent

1869: Standard issue with orange tree.

discovery of large deposits of gold and diamonds there.[76] The Orange Free State was dragged into the turbulence as a result of its mutual defence pact with Transvaal.

In any event, the Boer War was under way. The Boers were individualists and experts in guerrilla warfare, and the many, scattered farmsteads secured them reliable supplies. To break the resistance, the British adopted scorched-earth tactics, burning farms and crops, slaughtering domestic animals and salting the soil. Numerous concentration camps were also set up, where 30,000 women and children soon died of hunger, sickness and exhaustion.

My stamp bears an 1899 Bloemfontein postmark, made just before the British occupy the city. The Orange Free State issued its first stamps in 1868, and all the values and colours printed bear the same image of a neatly trimmed orange tree surrounded by three post horns. The motif is totally lacking in chauvinism and has a down-to-earth, honest, almost naive appearance. After taking Bloemfontein, the British find large unsold stocks of the stamps, which are immediately hand-stamped with the initials V.R.I. (for Victoria Regina Imperatrix or Victoria Queen and Empress) before being put back into circulation.

The Peace of Vereeniging is signed in 1902. Both the Orange Free State and Transvaal become British colonies. The Orange Free State is renamed Orange River Colony. In 1910, it is incorporated into the South African Union as the Free State Province.

Ingvald Schrøder-Nilsen had fought for the Boers. After being released from prison, he returned to Norway, where he eventually became a telegraph office manager in Molde.

Many of the Boers also left, but the majority remained. Their attitudes soon calcified into the South African constitution and the so-called Master and Servant Laws. This stripped the indigenous people of any right to land ownership and obliged them to place their labour at the disposal of farmers and mining companies. This was followed up with the apartheid policy pursued by every government until Nelson Mandela became president in 1994.

BOOKS

Anonymous (1875)
Sketch of the Orange Free State

Ingvald Schrøder-Nilsen (1925)
Blant boerne i fred og krig
('Among the Boers in Peace and War')

Everybody coughed and cleared their throats good and long until the priest, who was also the choirmaster, intoned a particularly prolonged and shrill note. It ended in some frightful vibrato, and immediately afterwards, everybody else joined in as loudly as they could – I have never heard music like it before!

INGVALD SCHRØDER-NILSEN

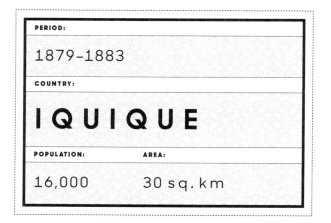

PERIOD:

1879–1883

COUNTRY:

IQUIQUE

POPULATION: | AREA:

16,000 | 30 sq. km

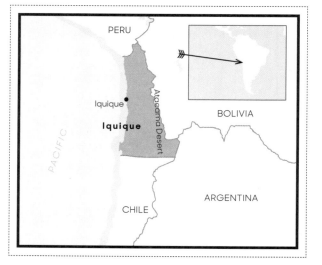

PERU

Iquique

Iquique

Atacama Desert

PACIFIC

BOLIVIA

ARGENTINA

CHILE

Saltpetre war in a dusty landscape

The mineral saltpetre is produced when the decomposed remains of plants and animals react with saline soil, for example in land that was once ocean bed but has since risen above sea level. The substance has been sought after since the early Middle Ages, when the Chinese invented gunpowder, which begins life as a finely ground blend of seventy-five per cent saltpetre, ten per cent sulphur and fifteen per cent charcoal. Spirits were then added to the mixture, which was kneaded into a dough and rolled out into sheets, then dried and broken up into the precious shiny black powder. Initially, it was mostly used for fireworks; after a gradual process of trial and error, gunpowder eventually became a crucial ingredient in wars all over the world.

Through the 1800s, the applications of saltpetre became broader. The substance is almost pure nitrogen, so it could easily replace compost and natural fertilizer in the large-scale agriculture that was developing in Europe and the USA. Technological developments in the explosives industry were heading off in new directions, and agriculture soon took over as the most important use for saltpetre.

The planet's largest saltpetre deposits were to be found in the Atacama Desert. Here it lay in metre-thick strata on a 1000-m- (3,300-ft-) high plateau that stretched 600 km (375 miles) along the Pacific Coast of South America. The deposits spanned across Peru, Bolivia and Chile, but Chilean companies were the only ones involved in the mining, and were raking in all the profits. This irritated both of Chile's northern neighbours, who warned that they would increase taxation and nationalize the business. Chile was provoked, and in spring 1879 it declared what would later be referred to as the Saltpetre War. With their old-fashioned flintlocks and muskets, Peru and Bolivia were ill equipped to combat Chile's modern army. Things were further complicated by the fact that the Chileans also systematically drugged their troops with *chupilca del diablo*, a mixture of gunpowder and strong spirits that transformed the foot soldiers into berserkers bereft of fear or regret.

As the Chilean forces stormed onwards, we can assume they underscored their victories with rape and plunder, as in most wars. But they also used stamps. In all the towns they conquered, they immediately started to produce postmarks for use on the large stocks of Chilean stamps the army had brought with them. All bore the portrait of Christopher Columbus in his customary sailor's hat, with peak and earflaps, and with an almost exasperatingly visionary expression on his face. For the people back home, keeping track of the advance, every new postmark that arrived was a cause for jubilation.

My stamp is postmarked Iquique, a town in Peru that was already conquered by November 1879. It lies on a narrow strip of coastal plain between the sea and the steep slopes up to the Atacama Desert. This is one of the world's driest regions and several years may go by without a single drop of rain.[77] Absolutely nothing grows here and, with the exception of the main streets, which are regularly sprayed with salt water, the buildings, roads and dockyards are covered in a thick layer of grey-white dust. Everything revolves around saltpetre and the only reason anybody has come here is to work and earn money, whether they are Croatian, Scottish, Chinese or Pakistani.

Many of the directors of the big saltpetre companies also live in Iquique. One of them is a Briton called John Thomas North. He hadn't seemed so upbeat when he landed at Valparaíso in 1866 with £10 in his pocket and dressed in a musty old suit. But he has gradually worked his way up and now runs his own company, which has a monopoly on the town's water supply.

New opportunities are now emerging. The outbreak of war has caused the value of the saltpetre mines to sink like a stone. And in the chaos that follows, North stakes a claim to most of the businesses – whether mining, shipping or transport. He is blessed with success because once the Chileans have conquered the Atacama Desert, prices return to their earlier levels and beyond.[78]

We can just about see the year on my stamp: 1882. By then, Iquique has been under Chilean occupation for three years, and it is also the year that John Thomas North returns to England, this time as one of the world's richest men. He has earned the nickname The Nitrate King, and quickly begins to throw his money about. A lot of it is invested in splendid properties, racehorses and greyhounds. He also arranges extravagant parties, where he dresses up as Henry VIII and surrounds himself with a growing crowd of notables from the British elite, such as Lord Randolph Churchill and the Prince of Wales, later King Edward VII.[79] He is made an honorary colonel and the papers soon give him as much coverage as the royal family. And the rumours run rife. Under the headline 'North Denials', the *Hampshire Telegraph* publishes an exaggerated account of the whole business in the form of a series of denials.

> Colonel North has not offered the Government a cool three millions sterling for the contents of the National Gallery, and he has no intention of covering the walls of his dining-room with Old Masters obtained from such a source. The 'Nitrate King' does not propose to wear a dress coat embroidered with the Koh-i-noor and other Crown jewels at his next private hop. The Colonel has not purchased the Great Eastern, nor does he intend to fit it up as a floating palace and invite the Prince of Wales to go 'yotting' with him in it. The 'Nitrate King' invariably uses a gold toothpick after dinner; but he is not in the habit of shaving with a diamond razor and he doesn't encourage Miss North to curl her fringe with brand-new Bank of England notes.[80]

Eventually the Saltpetre War fizzled out, and a peace treaty of late autumn 1883 stated that Peru must relinquish large areas of land to Chile, including Iquique. The year after

1878: Chilean stamp featuring Christopher Columbus, postmarked Iquique 1882.

that, it became clear that Bolivia had lost the whole of its coastline for good.

As a result, Chile gains geographic dominion over the saltpetre deposits. But most of the profit from the business still goes to foreign investors, mainly John Thomas North. This prompts the Chilean president, José Manuel Balmaceda, to propose the nationalization of the saltpetre mines in 1888. However, he meets with unanimous opposition from conservative politicians, who are heavily subsidized by North.

A civil war breaks out in which the conservative side is reinforced by the British navy, which blockades the harbour. The British press follow up by describing Balmaceda as a 'dictator of the worst stripe' and a 'butcher'.[81] After being defeated, Balmaceda commits suicide.

John Thomas North dies of oyster poisoning several years later, although this does nothing to lessen British influence over the Chilean economy. Now three-quarters of all exports go via England – and they are almost exclusively saltpetre.

Working conditions at the saltpetre mines in the Atacama Desert were terrible, with sixteen-hour days and wages that were barely enough to survive on. In December 1907 the miners rebelled and marched into Iquique, singing and shouting slogans. This culminated in what became known as the Santa María de Iquique massacre, in which 2,000 men, women and children were mown down by Chilean machine guns.[82]

By then, European researchers had already found a low-cost method for extracting nitrogen from the air. The process went into full production in the 1920s, but demand for Chilean saltpetre persisted until the bottom suddenly fell out of the market halfway through the century.

The Danish author Carsten Jensen went on a visit to the mining area in Iquique at the end of the 1990s and came across industrial ruins that were more dinosaur-like than dinosaur skeletons: 'An archaeological Pompeii of industrialism, buried and abandoned under the rain of ash from falling share prices and plunging stock exchange listings.'[83]

BOOK

William Edmundson (2011)
The Nitrate King:
A Biography of 'Colonel' John Thomas North

The 'Nitrate King' invariably uses a gold toothpick after dinner; but he is not in the habit of shaving with a diamond razor and he doesn't encourage Miss North to curl her fringe with brand-new Bank of England notes

HAMPSHIRE TELEGRAPH

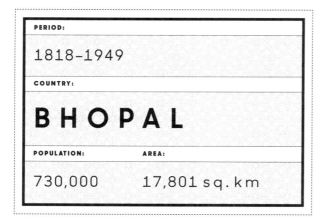

PERIOD:	
1818–1949	

COUNTRY:	
BHOPAL	

POPULATION:	AREA:
730,000	17,801 sq. km

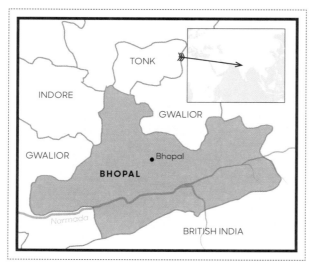

Burka-clad princesses

'We were choking and our eyes were burning. We could barely see the road through the fog, and sirens were blaring. We didn't know where to run.'[84] This account is from an eyewitness to the catastrophe that struck on the night of 2 to 3 December 1984, in the central Indian city of Bhopal.

A pesticide plant belonging to an American company, Union Carbide, had sprung a leak, releasing a gigantic cloud of methyl isocyanate, a corrosive, blinding poison gas. The plant was in the middle of a residential district and more than 15,000 people died in what would later be judged the world's worst industrial disaster.

Since then, the name of Bhopal has almost become synonymous with an earthly incarnation of hell. Before that fateful night, though, the name evoked quite different associations. Because it was here that Kipling's *Jungle Book* had played out a hundred years earlier, following Baloo the bear, Bagheera the panther and Mowgli the jungle boy through hot, dry summers and rainy autumn monsoons. Here and there small sandstone hills pierce the canopy of the forest. The otherwise flat landscape is intersected by rift valleys and canyons, with rushing rivers. Small villages of mud huts lie in clearings and at the centre of it all is the beautiful thousand-year-old city of Bhopal, between its two artificial lakes.

Following the withdrawal of the Persian Moghul empire, Bhopal had been an autonomous monarchy for more than a hundred years by the time it signed a cooperation agreement with the British East India Company in 1818. The country was assigned the status of a princely state. Put briefly, this meant that the British would take care of all foreign policy and trade, while the country would retain a small army, its own flag and its own prince, designated according to local laws of inheritance.

Unlike in most of the other princely states, the population of Bhopal was Muslim. This made it even more remarkable that the first four rulers in the Begum dynasty were all women.

First up was Qudsia, the pioneer princess. At eighteen years old, she insisted on taking over when her husband was assassinated just a few days after the establishment of the princely state. She ruled the country with a steady hand until 1837. She was followed by her daughter Sikander, the warrior princess: a virtuoso when it came to riding and the martial arts, and commander-in-chief of the army. Many of the local imams were angered, because they viewed female monarchs as un-Islamic. And it didn't improve matters that both Qudsia and Sikander refused to submit to purdah, the code of practice that, among other things, required women to cover their bodies and faces. But the princesses were as honourable as they were British-friendly, so the British opted to keep them.

Shah Jahan Begum took the throne in 1860. With minor reservations, we could call her the cultural princess, because she was undoubtedly interested in poetry, art and architecture. How deep this interest actually went is another matter. At any rate, intensive opium farming enabled her to finance the construction of some splendid buildings in and around the city.

After the death of her first husband, she remarried. Her new husband, Siddiq Hasan Khan, of Persian descent, appeared orthodox on matters of religion. And the princess allowed herself to be swept away. She submitted to purdah and Siddiq seized the opportunity to take over all public communication, including with the British. This greatly increased his power and influence.

The first stamps were introduced under Shah Jahan in 1876. The motif is an octagon representing the diamond in the princess's ring, with her name inscribed around it. In the twenty years that follow, the only thing that changes in the different issues is the spelling. On the first stamps, the letters are out of order and almost illegible. This is because, according to Islamic orthodoxy, all perfection leads to jealousy and the distortion of reality. Only Allah is perfect. On my copy, from 1890, most of the letters are in the right order. And it is probably not by chance that this reorganization of letters happens the year after the British have removed Siddiq Hasan Khan following accusations of anti-colonial activities.[85]

The stamps also have more to offer: in the white field inside the octagon an embossed figure is just about visible. Again, it is the princess's name, but this time in Urdu. The embossing process takes place at the castle, under the supervision of the princess, as a personal seal of validity.[86] Note also the rough perforations. They have been pierced by hand using a single needle, hole after hole in bundles of ten sheets at a time. They emanate an intense feeling of presence, influenced by whether the person who made them was on form that day; whether they were diligent or distracted.

In between her many tasks at the castle, Shah Jahan travelled around the princely state. She was well liked, or at least that's the impression given in the autobiography she later wrote:

> As soon as the people of a village become aware of my approach, the women come out in crowds to meet me, with their little ones in their arms, and carrying tiny bowls of water, the sprinkling of which, as they firmly believe, is to bring good fortune to their Chief and protector. As my carriage draws near, they all join together in a song of welcome.[87]

And then comes a passage that may, perhaps, lead us to take the declaration of love with just the smallest pinch of salt. 'I acknowledge by dropping bakshish into their little water vessels.'[88]

The daughter of Shah Jahan, Kaikhusrau Jahan, took the throne in 1901. She was the social princess, known for a series of reforms that strengthened the position of women. She also established a legislative assembly that was elected

1890: Barely visible embossed relief of Shah Jahan's name, framed by the octagonal diamond in her ring.

by something close to a popular vote, and she opened up important administrative posts to Hindus.

At the same time, Kaikhusrau appeared to be even more orthodox than her mother had been. All her decisions were communicated through a screen or through the crocheted lattice of a burka. But there is no doubt that this wasn't just a matter of religion: it also limited the extent to which her many male adversaries, from local aristocrats to delegates of the British colonial administration, could attempt to influence or dominate her.

When Kaikhusrau abdicated in 1926, allowing her son Hamidullah Khan to take the throne, she was breaking with a hundred-year tradition of queenly rulers. The odd thing is that we have no idea what any of them looked like. The first two ruled before the age of the camera, and the last two wore the veil. We know a great deal more about their husbands, all of whom were chosen after painstaking scrutiny by mother or daughter. And all of them without exception were extremely handsome princes with glittering almond eyes: fitting providers of divine bedtime delight or first-class decoration for the royal couch, clad in velvet and silk. The princesses' efforts certainly paid off.

After the British withdrew from the Indian continent in 1947, Hamidullah Khan demanded full independence for Bhopal, but had to give in after massive local protests. Bhopal was then incorporated into the Indian Union from 1949, and was subsequently merged with the even larger state of Madhya Pradesh to the south.

The Bhopal disaster, which struck less than twenty years later, would change almost everything.

BOOKS

Shaharyar M. Khan (2000)
The Begums of Bhopal:
A History of the Princely State of Bhopal

Nawab Sultan Jahan Begum (1912)
An Account of My Life

//

As soon as the people of a village become aware of my approach, the women come out in crowds to meet me, with their little ones in their arms, and carrying tiny bowls of water, the sprinkling of which, as they firmly believe, is to bring good fortune to their Chief and protector

SHAH JAHAN BEGUM

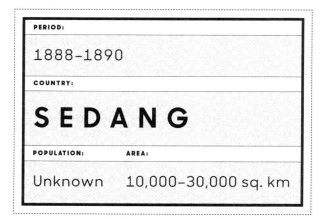

PERIOD:

1888–1890

COUNTRY:

SEDANG

POPULATION: AREA:

Unknown   10,000–30,000 sq. km

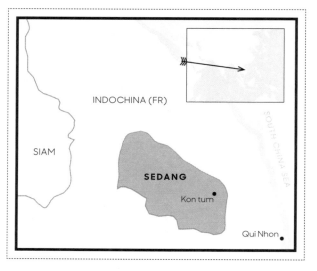

INDOCHINA (FR)

SIAM

SEDANG

Kon tum

Qui Nhon

SOUTH CHINA SEA

From the Champs Elysées to Kon Tum

'I'll get myself a kingdom.' The indications are that this is what Charles-Marie David de Mayréna has in mind as he struggles across the green-clad mountains from the coastal town of Qui Nhon in Indochina. He is accompanied by his business partner, Alphonse Mercurol, four Chinese merchants, two Vietnamese concubines and eighty bearers, with eighteen local soldiers to keep guard. The expedition is aiming for the highland plateau that surrounds the town of Kon Tum. Where possible, they follow small paths between the region's villages; elsewhere they have to hack their way through the wilderness of liana and bamboo. It is humid and muddy, hot and sultry – as far as one could possibly get from the Parisian boulevards where Mayréna has spent many years as a notorious dandy. He has fled after being charged with embezzlement. Now he is mulling his revenge, a splendid revenge.

The ragtag caravan eventually arrived on the plain inhabited by the local tribes: the Bahnar, the Rongao and the Sedang. They were actually the region's original inhabitants, but had been ousted from the coastal areas by the Chinese and the Malays. Here, they inhabited small villages, living off slash-and-burn agriculture and simple livestock farming. At the centre of every village were distinctive buildings called *rongs*. They stood on stilts, rising to heights of up to 20 m (65 ft), and looked like giant sailing ships, with their steep and slightly curved straw roofs. This was where the village council resolved its conflicts and made offerings to the gods. And they didn't use surnames, only a letter to indicate sex – A for men and Y for women – followed by a first name, so that the full name would be, for example, A Nhong or Y Hen. Another peculiarity was the language. It sounded like a gentle song and had over fifty different vowel sounds, more than any other language in the world.

It is 1888 and, a year earlier, France has established Indochina as a French colony. Mayréna has persuaded the French colonial administration that a demonstration of might is required in the western areas, which have not yet been visited by the French government. Moreover, rumour has it that massive gold deposits await discovery.

But as we know, Mayréna also has personal plans. On arrival, he immediately commandeers a *rong* and summons all the local chiefs to a meeting. Here he declares that they owe nothing to anybody, neither the French nor anyone else, and that the time has come to respond. He suggests establishing Keh Sedang, the Kingdom of Sedang, with himself as king. And they agree.

On 3 June, aged forty-six, he is crowned Marie the First. His partner Mercurol acquires the title of the Marquis of Hanoi. Mayréna moves into a huge straw hut in the capital of Kon Tum. The national flag soon flutters there: a white cross on a blue background, with a red star in the middle.

The huge royal elephant is equipped with similarly embellished harnesses.

Over the course of a few days, he gathers an army of 1,400 warriors to subdue the Jarai to the north. They have long been troubling the French missionaries in the area. The punitive expedition proves successful and wins Mayréna some sympathy from the French bishop in Indochina. When he goes on to declare Catholicism the state religion, he is honoured with a private prayer-desk, equipped with red draperies and a special cushion. He doesn't get a great deal of use out of this, though, because he converts to Islam, in part so that he can marry a few of the daughters of the local chiefs.

After a few weeks, Mayréna travels to Hong Kong with the bishop's letters of recommendation in his pocket. He is seeking international recognition for his country and money to run it. Mayréna is tall, charming and good-looking, with coal-black hair and a full bushy beard. He makes a strong impression on those who meet him:

> There was power in every line of that face, in the hard, determined, cruel mouth, the dark and heavy eyebrows which nearly joined one another across the bridge of the nose, in the broad smooth forehead, in the eyes themselves, keen, fierce, piercing and cynical.[89]

This impression is hardly lessened by the fact that he is also dressed like a king, in a scarlet jacket with enormous epaulettes, trousers with a gold stripe, and with copious decorations on his chest. Some Chinese businessmen quickly rise to the bait, ready to pay for the exclusive right to trade with the new country. He uses some of the resulting funds to print stamps in no fewer than seven colours, their values expressed in local currency. The designs are identical: a coat of arms beneath a crown. Later, a new issue is printed in Paris.

My stamp has an 1889 postmark, but there is some question about its authenticity. The local population was illiterate and it is doubtful that there was even any postal system to speak of.

After his success in Hong Kong, everything went rapidly downhill. Mayréna visited Europe, starting in Paris, but met with a lacklustre response. He certainly lived as befitted his rank, staying at the best hotels, and handing out his 'Order of Marie the First' to all and sundry, along with honorific titles and all kinds of rights to mineral exploitation and trading monopolies. But people were unimpressed and the return was meagre.

The French newspaper *Le Temps* described the whole business as 'rather obscure' and eventually there was talk of a Mayréna Scandal. The French state, which had initially assumed it would all fizzle out of its own accord, issued an unambiguous condemnation. It rejected all overtures seeking recognition for the Kingdom of Sedang and launched legal proceedings against Mayréna.

Fearing the very real possibility of a death sentence, Mayréna leapt on a steamer bound for home, but didn't

1888 or 1889: Standard issue bearing a coat of arms with a crown and lion.

dare complete the last leg of the journey through French Indochina into Sedang. Instead, he barricaded himself into a hut on the small, lush but almost uninhabited island of Tioman off the eastern coast of the Malacca Peninsula. The hut had loopholes in the window shutters and was known as the *maison du roi* or 'house of the king'. In addition to two or three women, he was accompanied by his flesh-coloured French poodle, Auguste, from whom he always sought counsel.

The island of Tioman was under British jurisdiction, and by the time a young British officer paid a visit to clarify the situation, Mayréna had only a handful of half-franc coins left to live on. Nonetheless, he greeted the Briton with enthusiasm: 'You are a brave man, and courage we admire, we love. Figure to yourself, we expect an army, and see 'tis only a child that comes to us. Enter, enter!'[90]

Just a few days later, on 11 November 1890, Mayréna was bitten by a cobra and died. In accordance with his own wishes, he was given an Islamic funeral. France quickly ensured that all that remained of the kingdom was wound up, and also took the opportunity to settle accounts with the Catholic mission in the area.

Today, the Sedang district has been renamed Xedang, and is part of Vietnam, close to the borders with Laos and Cambodia. The area was hard hit by the Vietnam War. It is still fairly isolated and, according to guide books, only around five per cent of the villages have been visited by tourists.[91] Here and there lie the ruins of French mission stations. All that remains of the Kingdom of Sedang are its stamps.

BOOKS

Gerald Cannon Hickey (1988)
Kingdom in the Morning Mist.
Mayréna in the Highlands of Vietnam.

André Malraux (1930)
La Voie Royale ('The Royal Way')

Wolfgang Baldus (1970)
The Postage Stamps of the Kingdom of Sedang

//

There was power in every line of that face, in the hard, determined, cruel mouth, the dark and heavy eyebrows which nearly joined one another across the bridge of the nose, in the broad smooth forehead, in the eyes themselves, keen, fierce, piercing and cynical

HUGH CLIFFORD, DESCRIBING MAYRENA

PERIOD:	
1874–1895	
COUNTRY:	
PERAK	
POPULATION:	AREA:
101,000	21,035 sq. km

Tin on the brain

Sampans are lying on the heated slime. Cocoa-nut trees fringe the river bank for some distance, and there are some large, spreading trees loaded with the largest and showiest crimson blossoms I ever saw, throwing even the gaudy *Poinciana regia* into the shade; but nothing can look very attractive here, with the swamp in front and the jungle behind, where the rhinoceros is said to roam undisturbed. There is a general smell of vegetable decomposition, and miasma fever[92] (one would suppose) is exhaling from every bubble of the teeming slime and swamp.[93]

It is the late 1870s and the British adventurer Isabella Lucy Bird and her friend Mrs Daly are travelling across the Malacca Peninsula.[94] They are standing by the mouth of the Bernama River, looking across at the state of Perak on the opposite bank. Bird was bitten by the travel bug after her doctor recommended sea voyages as a general remedy for poor health. In photographs, she looks small and fragile, and has a slightly world-weary air. But this must be a misinterpretation, because in a few short years, she has travelled around the whole world.

Beyond the mangrove swamps, the interior of Perak is covered in huge forests, from which white limestone peaks protrude here and there, eventually merging into a mountain chain to the east. The area is uniquely fertile. But still, the only thing anybody talks about is tin.

As early as the 1500s, large tin deposits had financed Perak's liberation from the Malacca Sultanate, and by the middle of the 1800s it was clear that the jungle regions concealed the world's largest alluvial deposits of this valuable metal. The ore lay piled up in river gravel to a thickness of up to 30 m (100 ft) and was extremely simple to mine. Stones and other impurities were easily flushed away before the tin itself was smelted into a shining, creamy mass in huge furnaces. It was then cooled into bars that were transported out to the coast by rail and elephant.

Tin has always been sought after, and for thousands of years it has been used in an alloy with copper to produce the harder metal, bronze. During the Industrial Revolution the areas of application multiplied, in the rapidly expanding canned goods industry among others. And boys' games with tin soldiers had become extremely popular by the 1800s, although it is unlikely that this, in itself, accounted for a particularly large volume of the metal.

When Isabella Lucy Bird arrived in Perak, the British were already installed, with their own governor. By then he had had full control over the administration of the British-friendly sultans for five or six years.

But the Chinese had been quicker off the mark. As early as 1860, the Hai San and Ghee Hin clans had embarked on intensive tin mining, employing up to 30,000 workers to this end. The two clans had always clashed over the best ore deposits, but apparently irrelevant situations could also flare up into conflicts. It all came to a head after the leader of the Ghee Hin clan was found to be conducting an adulterous affair with the wife of a nephew of the Hai San leader. After catching the adulterous pair in flagrante, the Hai San clan had them tortured, placed in a basket and drowned in a disused mine. When the Ghee Hin clan responded by bringing in 4,000 mercenaries from China, the feud was on. It all escalated into a civil war, in which many local Malayan chiefs also became embroiled, resulting in thousands of murders and the complete annihilation of the mining town of Larut.[95]

An otherwise insignificant chief, Raja Abdullah, exploited the situation. With the aid of a powerful Chinese merchant he drafted a letter to the British in the Straits Settlements colony, a group of strategically placed possessions in other parts of the Malacca Peninsula. In the letter, he begged the British to deal with the chaos and, in addition, to ensure that the reigning – and apparently useless – sultan be deposed and replaced with Raja Abdullah himself.

The British were more than happy to help, especially since the tin deposits had proven much larger than previously thought. After exerting the requisite diplomatic pressure needed to calm both Chinese and local chiefs, Raja Abdullah was installed as the new sultan of Perak in 1874. And a British emissary, later the governor, was sent in to protect and develop British interests in the region.

It soon became clear that Abdullah had no local supporters. He had negotiated entirely on his own behalf and was otherwise quite uninterested in anything that smacked of management. He used his position primarily to get women, smoke opium and arrange cockfights. The British had him removed and sent into exile in the Seychelles. In his place, they appointed a much less troublesome chief, Raja Muda, as regent of Perak.

It is in this period that Isabella Lucy Bird arrives. She travels the length and breadth of the country and makes observations, particularly about flora and fauna, with a special interest in insect life:

> There are 'trumpeter beetles' here, with bright green bodies and membranous-looking transparent wings, four inches across, which make noise enough for a creature the size of a horse. Two were in the house to-night, and you could scarcely hear anyone speak.[96]

But she is also interested in people. She observes the ever-growing crowds of frustrated chiefs who gather outside the governor's house, and complains that the people back home are not informed about what is happening:

> Public opinion never reaches these equatorial jungles; we are grossly ignorant of their inhabitants and their rights, of the manner in which our interference originated, and how it has been exercised.[97]

To strengthen their position, the British provided Perak with stamps, initially Straits Settlements issues overprinted with the word Perak. Only in 1892 did Perak get its very

1892: Perak's first stamps feature a hunting Malayan tiger.

own stamps, bearing the image of a Malayan tiger on the hunt. My crimson specimen is postmarked Taipeng. This name, meaning 'eternal peace' in Chinese, is given to the city built on the spot where Larut was razed to the ground some years before.

In principle, there was still no question of Perak being a British colony, and this remained the case in 1895, too, when Perak was merged with the neighbouring states of Selangor, Negri Sembilan and Pahang to form the Federated Malay

States. But all this happened under the strict direction of the British, with a view to further developing the export-orientated economy through the construction of railways, plantations and dockyards. Everything still revolved almost entirely around tin, although the land had eventually proved to be well suited to the cultivation of rubber trees too.

The British kept tight control over the region up until 1948, when the Malaysian Union was created, but it was only in 1957 that the country finally gained its independence. The global tin industry collapsed in the 1980s. Perak, which is now one of Malaysia's thirteen states, has still not fully recovered.

BOOKS

Isabella Lucy Bird (1883)
The Golden Chersonese

H. Conway Belfield (1902)
Handbook of the Federated Malay States

//

There are 'trumpeter beetles' here, with bright green bodies and membranous-looking transparent wings, four inches across, which make noise enough for a creature the size of a horse

ISABELLA LUCY BIRD

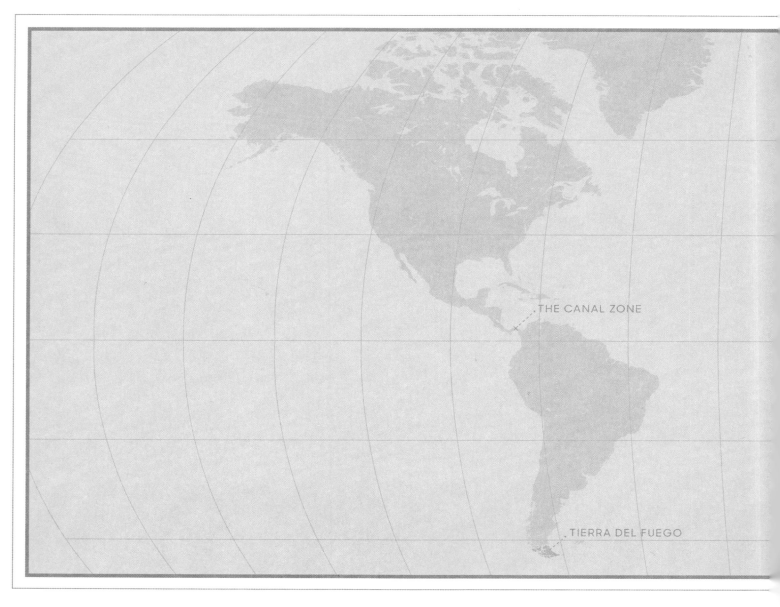

THE CANAL ZONE

TIERRA DEL FUEGO

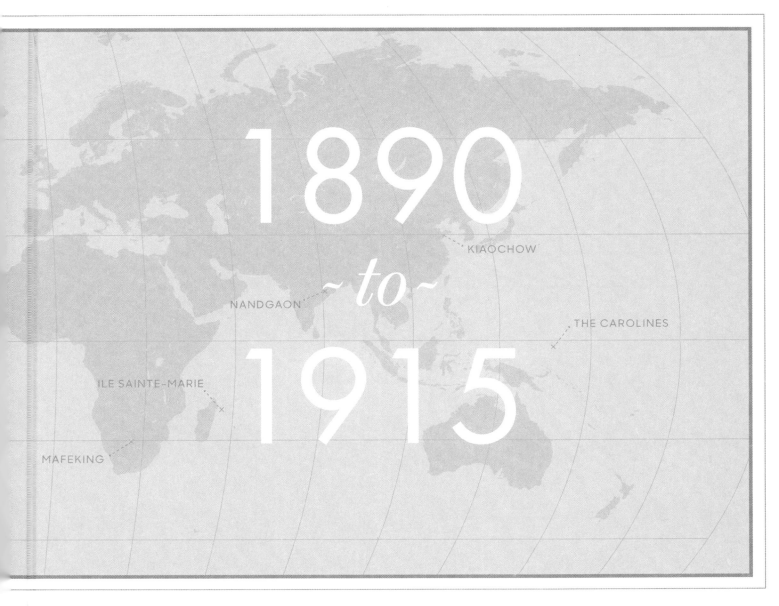

1890 ~to~ 1915

KIAOCHOW

THE CAROLINES

NANDGAON

ILE SAINTE-MARIE

MAFEKING

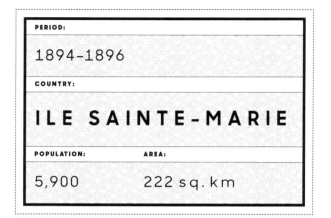

PERIOD:

1894–1896

COUNTRY:

ILE SAINTE-MARIE

POPULATION:

5,900

AREA:

222 sq. km

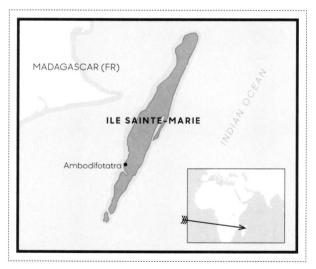

MADAGASCAR (FR)

ILE SAINTE-MARIE

INDIAN OCEAN

Ambodifotatra

Civilized panic in a tropical Utopia

Some time in the early 2000s, the Norwegian author Bjarte Breiteig travelled with his family to Ile Sainte-Marie off the eastern coast of Madagascar in search of a peaceful place to write. The island is 10 km (6 miles) from the mainland. Narrow and just 50 km (30 miles) long, it had been a French colony since the end of the 1800s.

Although Ile Sainte-Marie meets all expectations of South Sea harmony – with high sun, swaying coconut palms and white beaches – the young family's stay there proved anything but romantic. Their encounters with the locals were far from reassuring and the local wildlife was repulsive. A short way from the beach, black ants, cockroaches and rats ruled the roost. And hordes of land crabs made evening walks a revolting experience.

One evening, Breiteig's wife Tonje vanished without a trace. Darkness fell abruptly. Breiteig had only the flame of a lighter to guide him in his search, and his son Askil was on his back in a baby-carrier. Suddenly, there was a violent rainstorm.

> I panicked. I ran in the darkness and the rain, legs sinking into the mud, calling out for Tonje like a madman. Around me I could see small lights gleaming

in the huts, dark faces that were barely distinguishable from the night and the rain. I had the feeling that this was the end, a cyclone – and then I would lose Tonje.[98]

Even though his fears were unfounded, perhaps Ile Sainte-Marie is no place for sensitive authors in search of peace and quiet. But we can assume that the island seemed more than good enough for the European pirates who lived there for nearly two centuries. It ticked all the boxes: close to the trading routes from Asia; sheltered harbours and unlimited access to water, as well as fruit, meat and seabird eggs; and palm sap that can easily be fermented to make wine and then distilled into the rum-like spirit, arak. What's more, the island was full of beautiful women.

Many of the pirates married into the local Betsimisaraka tribe. The wedding ceremonies, which started after the parents and shamans had given their consent, were lively blends of local and European rituals. One account tells of a bridegroom wearing a new white shirt with lace on the breast, a back-combed wig and red knee-length socks from a Dutch prize. He had already showered the bride's parents with gifts, such as dragon-patterned damask, leaf-thin teacups, and a painting of a chalk-white lady in a golden, baroque frame. The bride herself, shrouded in white silk, was promised a secret present that night, and a bridal bed sprinkled with cinnamon.

By the end of the 1600s, more than 1,500 pirates were living on Ile Sainte-Marie, and its economy was good or even sustainable, as we'd put it today. This is the situation that prevails when some French pirates take the initiative to establish the anarchist colony Libertatia under the motto 'For God and Freedom'.[99]

They seem like anti-capitalists, with their declared aim of plundering the rich and sharing out the booty. They are also resolutely opposed to church, monarchy and anything else that smacks of authority. They themselves practice direct democracy, which is organized through a council formed of representatives from the different pirate groups. Anybody who tries to accumulate personal power or thwart the will of his own voters may be recalled with immediate effect. The island is also a cashless economy, and all agricultural activity is carried out collectively. The booty from the pirate expeditions is shared out equally, and the local population is also taken care of.

Unlike other pirate ships, the ones from Libertatia sail under a white flag. When they capture one of the many slave ships crossing the oceans in those days, they immediately set free the prisoners, who are also offered the opportunity to live on Ile Sainte-Marie and to share in the piracy. The resulting ethnic mix eventually gives rise to a unique dialect that steadily becomes more incomprehensible to anybody but the island's own inhabitants. This helps strengthen the sense of fellowship.

So it seems there must have been other reasons why the community of Libertatia nonetheless ground to a halt after just twenty-five years. Perhaps the loot from piracy dried up after England and other European countries sent warships to the area – or perhaps the whole thing was just one great fib. Because in all honesty, nobody can say for a fact that Libertatia ever existed. Written sources, so abundant in the wake of more authoritarian societies, are nowhere to be found.

From the mid-1700s, Ile Sainte-Marie became more or less French, although the story behind this is also poorly documented. It is said that it all started with a French officer, Jean-Onésime Filét. Fleeing punishment for an adulterous relationship on the island of Réunion, a little further out in the Indian Ocean, he was washed ashore on Ile Sainte-Marie.[100] Here he was rescued by none other than Princess Betia, the daughter of King Ratsimilaho, who was the son of a former British pirate. They got married and when the king died in 1750, the island was at once presented as a gift to Louis XV of France.

The local population was angry and a couple of years later a rebellion ensued. Some of the French settlers were massacred and the locals regained control. We do not know what became of Jean-Onésime, but Princess Betia was exiled to Mauritius forever.

Eventually the French returned in 1818 with a large naval force. After a smooth reconquest, the island was used as a penal colony. Beyond that, it would appear that the management of the territory was a half-hearted venture. There simply wasn't much to gained.

Later in the same century, the island served as a poorly prioritized subsidiary of more important French possessions, in particular Réunion, Mayotte and Diego Suarez. Then, in 1894, for reasons unclear, it was assigned the status of a separate colony.

1894: Navigation and trade – a standard French colonial issue.

In the couple of years this lasted, Ile Sainte-Marie issued its own stamps. Needless to say, they were of the prevailing French colonial type, with an allegorical depiction of navigation and trade, in which the woman holding the flag represents navigation. My stamp is postmarked 11 August 1896 and was probably stuck on one of the last letters to be posted before the colony was dissolved and made subordinate to Madagascar. Madagascar, in its turn, remained a French colony until 1946, then became a French protectorate. It gained full independence in 1960.

Today, Ile Sainte-Marie goes by its original Malagasy name of Nosy Boraha again. The island seems like a peaceful, remote corner of the world, with the occasional slightly eccentric tourist sitting in his deckchair by day or panting through the bush by night.

On Ile aux Forbans, an islet just off the coast by the little harbour town of Ambodifotatra, are the remains of the pirates' graveyard, its crumbling gravestones set on a green plain beneath the palms. And in the bay beyond lie dozens of sunken pirate schooners, all in a row, clearly visible below the surface of the crystal-clear water.

BOOKS

Bjarte Breiteig (2013)
Ile Sainte-Marie

Charles Johnson (1724)
A General History of the Pyrates

FILM

Against All Flags (1952)
Directed by George Sherman

//

For God and freedom

SLOGAN OF THE PIRATES OF LIBERTATIA

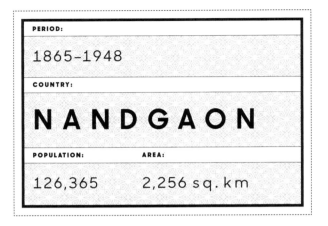

PERIOD:	
1865–1948	
COUNTRY:	
NANDGAON	
POPULATION:	AREA:
126,365	2,256 sq. km

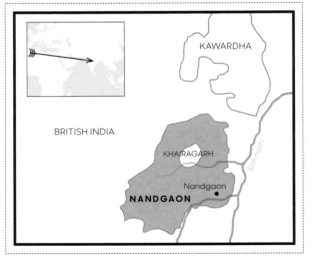

KAWARDHA

BRITISH INDIA

KHAIRAGARH

Nandgaon

NANDGAON

Shivnath

Peaceful fanaticism

Every year during the Holi Festival, a pitcher of buttermilk is suspended on a string high above the main street in Nandgaon. As the boys eagerly try to form a human pyramid to reach up and break it, hordes of girls bombard them incessantly with coloured dyes – pink, yellow, blue and green. In this way, they re-enact the story of the Hindu god Krishna and his friends as impudent butter thieves.

This is probably the wildest thing that happens in Nandgaon, which was said by British officials in colonial times to be the most peaceable of the Indian princely states. There was never any trouble here. There is much to suggest that the reason for this was the princes themselves – every one of whom was a fervently religious Hindu of the Bairagi sect.

The term Bairagi comes from a Sanskrit word meaning freedom from passion. The very purpose of life was the spiritual quest and spiritual development. The Bairagis therefore had little interest in material goods. Not even food should be given much importance. The most dedicated of them would prepare and consume their food in isolation. The noblest life was a celibate one, and failure could carry a severe penalty. Sexual intercourse with a woman was punishable by between 200 and 300 meals' worth of food.[101]

Nandgaon lies in the northwest of the Deccan Plateau: the only city in a lush forest landscape, 300 m (1,000 ft) above sea level. Elsewhere in the area there are a few hundred small villages, where people live simply and self-sufficiently. The little kingdom was originally ruled by the Marathas, a clan that had populated large parts of Central India over the centuries.

At the beginning of the 1700s, Prahlad Das arrived from the Punjab region. As well as being a successful shawl merchant, he was also a Bairagi and rapidly caught the attention of the local monarchs, who employed him as a spiritual advisor. And after him came several Bairagi disciples, whose influence gradually increased until at last the British appointed one of them, Ghasi Das, ruler of the newly established princely state of Nandgaon in 1865.

The prince was given the title of Mahant and, in principle, he also practised celibacy. But Mahant Ghasi Das quickly changed all that. He got married and had a son, Balram Das, who inherited his title. It was Balram Das who first started printing stamps. They met with a fairly lacklustre response: 'The stamps are of the most primitive and smudgiest order of lithography.'[102] It's a bad business. The paper quality is poor and the lines tend to run into each other. And as we saw earlier with the stamps from Obock, a pointless perforation is drawn in (but here it is so wonky that it doesn't even serve as a useful guide for cutting out the stamps). It is difficult to imagine anything further removed from aesthetic vanity and materialism. The whole thing was in line with Bairagi teaching, so Mahant Balram Das was on safe ground.

But one may wonder whether the Mahant went a little too far in 1893, when he allowed the unsold stock to be overprinted with the Latin characters M. B. D. – his own initials. Was this an acute case of vanity or was it all done simply to butter up the British?

The stamps are printed at the Mahant's own newly established printing press. A certain Narayan Vaman Tilak gets a job there. He comes from the west and belongs to the highest caste, the Brahmins, who account for four per cent of all Hindus. It is the priestly caste, in which the priests serve as messengers between man and the gods. Tilak is aware of this. He knows the Veda inside out. He's also in the process of becoming a renowned poet, with a large portfolio of religious poems of praise.

We may assume that it is the pious Mahant who has brought him to the region. Tilak has just decided to embark on *Sannyasa*, the fourth life stage within the Hindu tradition of *Vaishnavism*. This implies that he must offer up his property to Prajapati, the lord of creation, and live his life as a mendicant, meditating and praising Krishna all the while. He doesn't appear to be held back by the fact that he is already married. His wife is called Laxmibai and is also from the Brahmin caste. They entered into an arranged marriage when she was eleven.

In Nandgaon, religious ambition is primarily a man's business. Laxmibai is not especially committed, but all the same she has to put up with her husband's constant sacrifices. Time and time again, she gives away everything she owns to the needy, including food and clothing.

She writes in a journal, using the tip of a used matchstick: 'I'm very like a rubber ball, bouncing back, again and again.'[103] She tells us about her husband, who might suddenly leave her in the middle of the night, setting off without money or food, apparently without any aim: 'All he knew was to walk as far as his feet would carry him.'[104]

Even so, Tilak would sometimes end up on a train; and on one occasion, late at night, he met the American missionary Ernest Ward, who belonged to the Methodist mission that ran several leprosy hospitals in the area. Along with a couple of dozen colleagues, he worked night and day to save as many souls as possible on the brink of death, and his task was made more demanding by his conviction that the sickness was caused by inbred sin.

Ernest Ward gave Tilak a bible and whispered in his ear that he would be converted within two years.[105] Tilak denied it, but since he had promised to read the bible, he did so. And in 1895 he converted, sending a warning home to Laxmibai's sister at the same time: 'I've become a Christian. Take care of your sister. There is a river at Nasik as well as Jalalpur. See that she doesn't take her own life.'[106]

Laxmibai took his conversion very badly and the couple separated. We do not know whether it was love or the lack of rights for divorced women that prompted her to resign herself at last, but after five years she agrees to be baptized and moves back in with her husband. There she faces the same stress as before, accompanied by the same mortification of the flesh and renunciation of material goods. In between his constant journeys, he writes more than a hundred edifying songs before dying in 1919.

1893: Stamp overprinted with M. B. D., standing for Mahant Balram Das, Prince of Nandgaon.

Laxmibai also continues to write, but in her case it all takes a more political direction. Her message is women's liberation and the eradication of illiteracy, and she rejects the caste system. Laxmibai was brought up to believe that some people are clean and others unclean – among others by her father, who suffered from a compulsive disorder linked to hand washing. He was unable to accept clothes or food from lower-caste people without making them undergo an excessive cleansing process. To demonstrate her scorn for this, Laxmibai seeks out the poorest people in the non-caste or untouchable groups, eating from their hands in public.

By the time she dies in 1936, the last Mahant of Nandgaon – Digvijai Das – has already been born. In 1948, without a hint of protest, he signs an agreement that incorporates Nandgaon into the Indian Union.

BOOK

Laxmibai Tilak (2007)
Sketches from Memory

//

I've become a Christian.
Take care of your sister.
There is a river at Nasik
as well as Jalalpur. See that
she doesn't take her own life

NARAYAN VAMAN TILAK

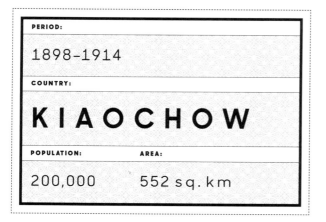

PERIOD:	1898–1914
COUNTRY:	**KIAOCHOW**
POPULATION:	**AREA:**
200,000	552 sq. km

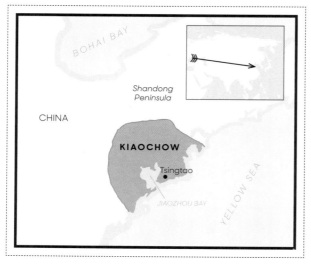

A capricious emperor in a rotten game

It was December 1897 and the century was on the wane when the German Foreign Minister Bernhard von Bülow spoke the words that would later become so famous: 'We do not wish to throw anyone into the shade, but we also demand our own place in the sun.'[107] Today, the phrase is mostly used in arguments about access to sunlight and views in villa neighbourhoods. The original occasion was quite different. Germany had been late joining the race to acquire colonies. On most continents, they were already lagging well behind the other great European powers. Now came the battle for China.

Germany longed to establish a naval base in the region. At the same time, it wanted to have a bridgehead for exporting goods to China, which had become one of the most dynamic markets outside Europe in a few short years.

The occasion presented itself when two German missionaries were murdered in the village of Juye, in the south of Shandong Province, by the shores of the Yellow Sea. The crime was probably committed by members of the nationalistic organization, The Long Knife. Although the Qing Dynasty promised that the culprits would be found and punished, German naval forces soon came sailing into Jiaozhou Bay and took possession of the surrounding coastal area.

The bay was sheltered and offered an ideal base for a fleet. The landscape in the interior was also inviting, with fertile, forested slopes that climbed towards mountain formations. Evenly scattered across it all lay small, peaceful villages, whose inhabitants were farmers and fishermen.

When the Germans arrive, it is still winter, with sub-zero temperatures at night, and the annual growth of algae, with its distinctive smell of rotten eggs, has not yet made an appearance. Nor are there any warning signs of the black syphilis that will later make the area so notorious among sailors on shore leave. It is said that there is no cure for this illness, which causes the penis first to swell up dramatically, and then, over the course of a few weeks, to rot and fall off – testicles and all.

The local population is also scared to death, even though they haven't learnt anything at all about the effect the illness has on women. Not even the local barefoot doctors can offer more information. And perhaps this isn't so strange since the whole business is, in fact, no more than a myth invented by the German authorities to keep the ships' crews out of the whorehouses. Later, it will be used with equal success by the Americans in Okinawa, South Korea and Vietnam.[108]

Officially, Jiaozhou Bay was not occupied. Germany's ambitions of increased trade with China called for diplomatic solutions, although it kept a whip at the ready too. The result was a 99-year lease on the bay and the adjacent coastal area. And the whole thing was ringed by a spacious security zone with a radius of 50 km (30 miles). In addition, China would pay for the construction of three Catholic churches, and would grant Germany all conceivable concessions for coal mining and the construction of railways throughout Shandong Province. The area was christened Kiautschou – more commonly known as Kiaochow in English – and became a regular German colony.

For Germany this provided a long-awaited occasion for celebration. At home in Dresden, Kiautschou cakes appeared in the bakeries, followed by Kiautschou schnapps, Kiautschou cigarettes and Kiautschou cigars, until the whole business became clichéd. The colony also got its own stamps, depicting Wilhelm II's elegant pleasure yacht, with its virile, threatening ram bow. It was identical to most other German colonial stamps of the time, although neither the ship nor the Kaiser ever came to the southern seas.

The Kaiser preferred to cruise in the Norwegian fjords. And it was on one of these trips that he drew the sketch for what would later be called *Völker Europas, wahrt eure heiligsten Güter* or 'Peoples of Europe, Guard Your Dearest Goods', but popularly known as 'The Yellow Peril'.[109] The sketch was developed into a monumental painting – now missing, but widely available as a lithograph – by the national romantic artist, Hermann Knackfuss:

It portrays the arts and industries under the protection of the Army. Beneath a Gothic arch stand ideal female forms, representing Art and Industry.

A threatening cloud is coming up towards them. Fearful hostile forms emerge from it. A Teuton warrior advances to meet the fearful forms.[110]

The fact that the Teuton warrior mentioned here comes equipped with blond curls and angels' wings speaks volumes. Wilhelm II was afraid that the Asians would threaten the white race once again, the way Genghis Khan's hordes had done a few hundred years before. He wanted to unite Europe in a crusade against Asia before it was too late. But the painting was savaged by the critics, while its message was rejected and sometimes ridiculed. Slightly offended, the Kaiser shelved the project.

All the same, we can assume it sent an exciting shiver up his spine when the Boxer Rebellion flared up in 1899. This was sparked by the Germans' annexation of Kiaochow, along with a whole series of similar actions by Great Britain, France and Russia. The Boxers formed a secret confederation, which they preferred to call the Society of the Righteous and Harmonious Fists. They fired up the population to attack anything that smacked of colonialism, mostly at the expense of the mission stations and Christianized Chinese people. The colonial powers responded by sending massive forces deep into China, crushing the rebellion.

Once again, Kaiser Wilhelm seizes the opportunity to get his point across:

> Just as a thousand years ago the Huns, under the leadership of Attila, gained a reputation, by which they still live in historical tradition, so may

1901: Standard German colonial issue featuring Hohenzollern II, Kaiser Wilhelm II's pleasure yacht.

the German name be known in such a fashion in China that no Chinaman will ever again dare to look askance at a German.[111]

Now that the power relations had thus been settled once and for all, Kiaochow embarked upon a period of expansion, backed up by German capital. Rail links to Peking were completed and connected up with the Trans-Siberian railway. This allowed German businessmen to make the journey from their homeland in three weeks. Tsingtao, formerly a fishing village, was expanded, with port facilities, broad streets, elegant administrative buildings and banks. Electricity and sewage systems were introduced. The surrounding areas were cleared of forests, and silk factories, sawmills, tile factories and breweries were set up. And along the border in the west, a series of twelve forts was built.

Eventually, many wealthy Chinese also moved in to enjoy all the modern comforts. Even Sun Yat-sen, later a revolutionary leader, was taken by it: 'I am impressed. This city is a true model for China's future.'[112]

In November 1914, it all came to an end when the colony was invaded by Japan, which had entered the First World War on the Allied side a couple of months earlier. After the war, the Chinese took over again. Once more the area was incorporated into Shandong Province, today one of the wealthiest provinces in China. The city of Tsingtao was renamed Qingdao.

The Red Guards laid waste to the churches in the 1950s, but there are still some remains of the more secular colonial buildings. Still, the most notable reminder of that time is Tsingtao Beer, a brand developed by German brewers in 1903 that is now viewed as China's best beer.

BOOKS

Hans Weicker (1908)
Kiautschou

S. C. Hammer (1917)
William the Second as Seen in Contemporary Documents and Judged on Evidence of His Own Speeches

ART

Hermann Knackfuss (1895)
Völker Europas, wahrt eure heiligsten Güter
('Peoples of Europe, Guard Your Dearest Goods')

///

Just as a thousand years ago the Huns, under the leadership of Attila, gained a reputation, by which they still live in historical tradition, so may the German name be known in such a fashion in China that no Chinaman will ever again dare to look askance at a German

KAISER WILHELM II

PERIOD:	
1891	

COUNTRY:	
TIERRA DEL FUEGO	

POPULATION:	AREA:
10,000	74,000 sq. km

ARGENTINA

Punta Arenas

Strait of Magellan

ATLANTIC

TIERRA DEL FUEGO

PACIFIC

Cape Horn

Dictator in gold

Right at the southern end of the South American continent lies the archipelago of Tierra del Fuego, Land of Fire. Actually, it was originally called Land of Smoke, after the Portuguese explorer Ferdinand Magellan, who navigated the area in 1520 and noticed the locals lighting interconnected and unusually smoky bonfires along the shoreline. The expedition ship then travelled further west, into a labyrinth of bays, coves and fjords. Here, it first encountered a series of low, grassy islands, dense with forest. The further west it sailed, the hillier the terrain became, culminating in the high, sharp mountain chains interspersed with glaciers where the land met the Pacific Ocean. Magellan sent home reports of a short, cold and damp summer. To the south, where the Pacific and Atlantic finally meet beneath the cliffs of Cape Horn, the climate was sub-arctic; and over the centuries that followed, the violent storms there made the region notorious as one of the world's largest ship graveyards.

Although Tierra del Fuego was long deemed economically uninteresting, the situation quickly changed when gold was found in the area in the 1800s. This sparked a lengthy conflict between Chile and Argentina, both of which wanted dominion over the archipelago. Tierra del Fuego never became a separate country, although it would soon seem to be once Julius Popper came on the scene in 1886.[113]

Although he was only twenty-nine, Popper's hair was already thinning, but he compensated for it amply with a neatly trimmed moustache and a full beard. This only partially concealed his pronounced underbite, a feature he shared with Austria's royal house of Hapsburg, which contributed for a while to the myth that he was actually Archduke Johann Orth. Johann had vanished without a trace en route from Salzburg to La Plata in Argentina – a tremendously convenient occurrence for him, since he had gradually built up a harem of sixteen lovers and had undertaken to pay annual upkeep for all of them. Julius Popper did little to dispel the myth. In fact, though, he was Romanian, born into a Jewish family in Bucharest, and had trained as an engineer in Paris. He had since travelled the length and breadth of the planet, via Egypt, China and Siberia and as far as the American continent, working as an itinerant expert in expansion and modernization. In Cuba, he helped breathe new life into the seafront at Havana by designing a modern city plan.

Leading a heavily armed expedition, he soon found large quantities of gold and took over the firm *Compañía de Lavaderos de Oro del Sud* (the 'Southern Gold-Washing Company'). Shortly afterwards, Argentina granted him the rights to all gold deposits in Tierra del Fuego. This marked the beginning of an empire based in Punta Arenas, on a sandy headland on the mainland side of the Strait of Magellan in the far north.

Popper quickly made a name for himself as a man about town with a large appetite for champagne and caviar. He always wore a uniform and established a hundred-strong private army whose members all dressed up in brilliantly coloured regalia, and where nobody was ranked below lieutenant. The army was constantly on the move, punishing thieves and unauthorized gold-diggers with great brutality. After a while, they also started hunting down the indigenous people.

Tierra del Fuego was originally inhabited by the Yaghan people, making them the world's most southerly population. According to the 1889 edition of *Encyclopaedia Britannica*, they were around 1.5 m (5 ft) tall with low brows, large lips, flat noses and wrinkled skin. Over the course of several hundred years, other tribes also settled on the archipelago, including the Selk'nam people, who were nomads. Captain James Cook, who travelled through the area in 1769, describes their living conditions:

> Their Hutts are made like a behive and open on one side where they have their fire, they are made of small Sticks and cover'd with branches of trees, long grass etc in such a manner that they are neither proof against Wind, Hail, rain or snow.[114]

When the British settlers put large flocks of sheep out to pasture, the indigenous people assumed they were fair game, and embarked on a massive hunt. That is what sparked the genocide. Yet it is said that Popper and his army were not the keenest participants: the farmers were the main culprits. The bounty offered was one bottle of whisky or one pound sterling per Indian. People could claim this only after delivering a pair of hands or ears, although this was later changed to the head, after it transpired that hands and ears were sometimes being reused. The orgy of killing continued for fifteen years. And those Indians who were not murdered soon died of infectious diseases that were trivial for Europeans but to which they themselves had no resistance. In this way, both indigenous groups were effectively wiped out.[115]

It is in this period that Julius Potter introduces his stamp (because there is only one issue), with a face value of ten centigrams of gold dust: *diez oro*. Intended to bolster Potter's empire, it portrays standard gold-mining equipment, including a wash pan, sledgehammer and pickaxe, around a centrally placed P for Potter. The whole image has a certain sense of depth, in which the individual elements appear three-dimensional.

The stamps are never postmarked. And since there are no traces of gum left on my slightly yellowed stamp, I reckon it has been used, possibly on a letter or a package sent between the widely dispersed gold fields and Punta Arenas. The stamps are never recognized by Argentina, which charges extra postage on all onward dispatches.

Popper's empire is now in its heyday. He starts to plan an expedition to the Antarctic to claim territorial rights, apparently on behalf of Argentina, although he undoubtedly

1891: Standard issue with a face value of ten centigrams of gold dust, with a motif of gold-mining equipment.

has his own agenda, too. His ship, the *Explorador*, is fitted out in Buenos Aires and the Norwegian whaling skipper C. Hansen is hired as captain. It is on a journey to inspect the final arrangements that Popper is poisoned and dies. There are plenty of indications that this was an assassination instigated by a powerful sheep farmer. Another theory suggests that the English wanted to frustrate the

Antarctic expedition. Popper has no heirs, and after his death his empire rapidly crumbles. Even his mother in Romania doesn't inherit a penny.

Argentina and Chile eventually manage to clear up the division of the territory. It reflects the population base, with one-third going to Argentina and two-thirds to Chile. Some fishing and farming takes place and in the 1950s oil extraction starts up in the north of the country. Further south, tourism has long ago taken over as the most important industry.

BOOKS

Arne Falk-Rønne (1975)
Reisen til verdens ende
('Journey to the World's End')

Carlos A. Brebbia (2006)
Patagonia, a Forgotten Land

Martin Gusinde (2015)
The Lost Tribes of Tierra del Fuego

//

**Their Hutts are made like
a behive and open on one side
where they have their fire, they
are made of small Sticks and
cover'd with branches of trees,
long grass etc in such manner
that they are neither proof against
Wind, Hail, rain or snow**

JAMES COOK

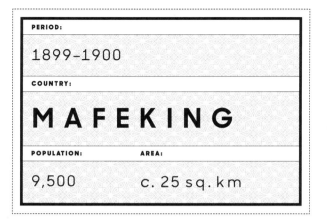

PERIOD:

1899–1900

COUNTRY:

MAFEKING

POPULATION: AREA:

9,500   c. 25 sq. km

BECHUANALAND
(GB)

Molopo

● MAFEKING

TRANSVAAL

STELLALAND

Vaal

ORANGE FREE STATE

Boy Scouts using diversionary tactics

When a horse was killed his mane and tail were cut off and sent to the hospital for stuffing mattresses and pillows. His shoes were sent to the foundry for making shells. His skin, after having the hair scalded off, was boiled with his head and feet for many hours, chopped up small, and with the addition of a little saltpetre was served out as 'brawn'. His flesh was taken from the bones and minced in a great mincing machine and from his inside were made skins into which the meat was crammed and each man received a sausage with his ration.[116]

This is the situation in January 1900 at the little station town of Mafeking in the British Cape Colony, just across the border from the Boer republic of Transvaal to the east. Mafeking was founded in 1860 out on the veldt, the stony steppe-like highland landscape where the great Molopo River has its source. We are halfway through the Boer War, which the British started in order to get their hands on the huge diamond and gold deposits the Boers had been managing for almost fifty years.

Half a year earlier, before the outbreak of war, the British colonel Robert Baden-Powell had decided to place himself under voluntary siege in Mafeking. His aim was to lure Boer troops away from the battlefields further to the southeast where their presence might prove decisive. His preparations took three months. Food and other consumables were stockpiled, and fortifications and trenches were built, all connected with a tangle of telephone lines. Most importantly, the whole town was encircled with a dense network of landmines, which, practically speaking, made it impregnable.

The Boers rose to the bait and advanced with 6,000 men, who besieged the town just a couple of days after the British had issued their declaration of war in October 1899.

Mafeking had a black district and a white one, all within a circumference of 10 km (6 miles). The white district had clearly been designed on a drawing board, with broad streets that met at right angles, and identical houses built of sun-dried mud bricks and with corrugated iron roofs. At the centre was a square with shops, a bank, a printing press, a hotel and a public library. More than 1,700 men were living here, including Baden-Powell's own division. In addition, there were 229 women and 405 children who, for one reason or another, could not be evacuated before the Boers struck.

The black district in the northwest consisted of scattered groups of round, straw-roofed huts, which accommodated around 7,500 members of the Baralong tribe. They were the original inhabitants of the region, and put simply they favoured the British over the Boers. It was easy for them to pass through the front line, and they helped out as spies and couriers, taking messages in and out of the besieged town.[117] But they were kept away from armed duties, because this was supposed to be a 'white man's war'.

The Boers' main plan was to starve the Britons out. At the same time, they launched a heavy bombardment against the town. But their cannons were small and inaccurate. Few of the towns' inhabitants were hit, and any damage to the mud-brick houses was easy to repair with damp clay rolled up in burlap and stuffed back into the holes.

The food situation was worse. It hit the indigenous population hardest, as they got much smaller rations.[118] Even so, everybody was soon reduced to eating donkey and horse. They also soaked the oats from horse-feed to use as gruel. The patients in the field hospital were served rice pudding made out of rice powder requisitioned from the town's hairdressers (where it was used as a sort of dry shampoo).

Beyond that, life in the town continued almost as normal – ostentatiously so to some extent: the hope was that this would discourage the Boers, who monitored every tiniest detail from the scaffolding set up beyond the minefield. For their part, the Boers strictly observed the Sabbath peace, and there was no cannon fire on Sundays. The British seized the opportunity to arrange open-air concerts, theatre productions and sporting events, especially cricket. And everyone attended in their Sunday best, the women in fluttering frocks, hand in hand with their neatly dressed children.

The Boers couldn't believe their eyes. The high point came when the British produced stamps for internal post within the town. There was probably no real need for them, but the British knew what they were up to. Because there's no better way to prove that a society is working properly than to give it its own stamps. In terms of quality and design they were close to perfect, too, with perforations, gum and all. They were printed at Townsend & Son on the town square. A photographic process was used, which involved placing the negatives directly onto paper coated in light-sensitive chemicals produced from *ferro gallate*, an extract of acacia sap. The design was formed from different shades of blue, all impressively precise.

It is almost impossible to get hold of genuine examples of these stamps today, and there are many forgeries. My slightly yellowed specimen has obviously been damaged at some point: a tear in the upper-left corner has been repaired. I assume that this at least increases the chance that it is real. The motif is a boy on a bicycle and is based on a photograph of thirteen-year-old Warner Goodyear. He was the Sergeant Major of the town's cadet corps, for boys aged nine and older. The child soldiers were dressed up in khaki uniforms and broad-brimmed hats with a yellow band, and their mission was to keep watch and deliver post. They went everywhere by bicycle once all the donkeys had been eaten.

The Boers soon realized that Mafeking was impregnable. After a couple of failed attempts to occupy it, more than half of the Boer forces were withdrawn. For the British, the operation had been a success, helping their troops in the east go from strength to strength. And in May 1900,

1900: Sergeant Major Warner Goodyear on a bicycle.

the 217-day long siege was broken by British forces, who saw off the remaining Boers.

All this time, the British newspapers had correspondents on the ground in Mafeking,[119] and people back home followed events with growing enthusiasm. When victory was achieved, the Lord Mayor of London went out onto the balcony of Mansion House on Queen Victoria Street: 'We never doubted what the end would be. British pluck and valour when used in the right cause must triumph.'[120]

Robert Baden-Powell became a great national hero. In 1907, he used this prestige to start the Boy Scout movement, which aimed to combat further degeneration in the British race. Baden-Powell held up the Liberal government as a ghastly example: 'Free feeding and old age pensions, strike pay, cheap beer and indiscriminate charity do not make for the hardening of the nation or the building up of self-reliant, energetic manhood.'[121]

Warner Goodyear died aged just twenty-six after being hit on the head by a hockey ball. For many years, his sisters, Lottie, Maude and Lorna, continued to run the library on the square in Mafeking.

BOOKS

Solomon Plaatje (1990)
The Mafeking Diary

Hope Hay Hewison (1989)
*Hedge of Wild Almonds: South Africa,
the Pro-Boers & the Quaker Conscience, 1890–1910*

//

Free feeding and old age pensions,
strike pay, cheap beer and
indiscriminate charity do not make
for the hardening of the nation
or the building up of self-reliant,
energetic manhood

ROBERT BADEN-POWELL

PERIOD:
1899–1914

COUNTRY:
THE CAROLINES

POPULATION:	AREA:
40,000	1,167 sq. km

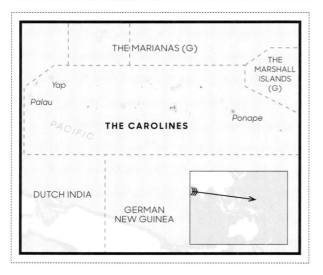

THE MARIANAS (G)

THE MARSHALL ISLANDS (G)

Yap

Palau

PACIFIC

THE CAROLINES

Ponape

DUTCH INDIA

GERMAN NEW GUINEA

Sea cucumbers for stone money

On the island of Yap just north of New Guinea in the western Pacific Ocean, people had been using a very special monetary system for more than a thousand years. The monetary unit itself was a so-called *fei* wheel, a kind of flattened doughnut made of grey-white limestone, which varied from palm-sized to more than head height. Their value was primarily reflected in their size, with the smaller stones corresponding to a small pig and the largest as much as a whole village. But it wasn't always all that simple. If there was a good story attached to the stone, preferably one involving misfortune and death, the value increased dramatically regardless of the size. And this applied to many of the stones.

The big challenge was that the raw material could only be found on the island of Palau, more than 400 km (250 miles) across the open sea to the southwest, and this distance had to be covered in sometimes fragile outrigger canoes and rafts. Things often went wrong. But if the transport met with an accident and the stone sank to the bottom in the breakers off the coral reef, it wasn't the end of the world. The sunken stones would also, in fact, be accepted as valid tender. Everybody on the island knew roughly where they were and this knowledge was passed down from one generation to the next. The stone wheels that did arrive safely were placed around the landscape, apparently at random. And all subsequent trade took place by verbal agreement, without the stones being moved again.

Yap was part of the archipelago called the Carolines, which consisted of around 500 islands scattered in a slightly ragged half-moon shape across an area of ocean twice as large as the North Sea. The combined land mass was surprisingly large, and consisted principally of low coral islands, along with a few scattered volcanic islands, such as Palau and Yap in the west and Ponape in the east.

The Spanish had already colonized the Carolines by 1686, calling them the New Philippines, but they hadn't made much use of them. The local population was aggressive, and the missionaries who tried their luck there were either killed or thrown into the sea.

Yap was deemed the most impossible island. It actually consists of four islands separated by narrow channels, all of it surrounded by a green lake ringed in turn by a broad reef. The largest island, Rul, is fish-shaped, 16 km (10 miles) long and 5 km (3 miles) across at its widest point. To the north lie the Burra Hills, whose red clay slopes rise to a height of 200 m (650 ft) and are overgrown with dense brush. The southern part is a fertile plain, which rises steadily up to the foot of the hills. Rul together with the next-largest island, Tomil, provides a sheltered harbour, and this is where most of the 8,000 inhabitants of the island live. They live off fishing and gardening, and have divided themselves into villages, observing an internal ranking system that is strict yet constantly shifting as a result of small wars, marriages and changes in holdings of the *fei* wheels. It is a patriarchal society in which many of the men have their own harem. And the island's shamans are at the top of the heap.[123]

In 1872, Yap is ruled by Shaman Fatumak. One day while he's out looking for a few extra-fat lizards for the regular sacrificial ceremony, he meets an American captain, David Dean O'Keefe, who has just washed ashore after being shipwrecked. He is of Irish stock, tall and muscular with wiry red hair and a full beard. Fatumak takes him under his wing.

It isn't long before the enterprising Irishman realizes that the use of *fei* wheels offers some commercial opportunities. He gets himself first one, then several more schooners, which he uses to transport the locals and their wheels to and from Palau. The transport is both quicker and safer than before, and the wheels can also be made larger: up to 4 m (13 ft) in diameter, with weights of up to 5 tonnes. Overwhelmed, the locals make him their king.[124]

O'Keefe makes sure he is paid in copra – dried coconut flesh – and sea cucumbers, delicacies that he dispatches to Hong Kong and sells to Chinese merchants who can pay well. Within a few years, he has become extremely wealthy. He sets up a harem for himself and builds a white house in European half-timber style, with a colonnade leading down to the harbour and a roof of gleaming corrugated iron. The shining building is visible from all the islands and looks like jewel, like a message: this is the very centre of the universe.

On one of his trips to Hong Kong, O'Keefe meets a younger fellow-countryman, Johnny O'Brien. When it turns out that both of them were born in Cork on the south coast of Ireland, O'Keefe makes him an offer:

Come to Yap and I will give you a half interest in all that I own, including my harem, and if I should pass on, I will have arrangements made for you to take my place as King of Yap.[125]

They had certainly been drinking heavily, and O'Brien chose to forget the whole business.

An orderly group of barracks was built on Yap for German marines after Germany bought the Carolines from Spain in 1899 for 25 million pesetas. Germany's regional head there quickly got wind of O'Keefe's ingenious business concept and decided to expropriate it, either on Germany's behalf or his own. After one of his trips to Hong Kong, O'Keefe was placed under house arrest, but the local population united behind him and threatened an uprising.

It is spring 1901. The German colonists have already introduced German stamps, with the usual symbol of the eagle, overprinted with *Karolinen*. Letters and packages are picked up by smaller steamers on their way from New Guinea to Hong Kong, where the mail sacks are transferred to ships bound for Europe.

My stamp is postmarked 29 March and was almost certainly stuck on a letter describing the menacing situation, sent either from the island's administration or by one of

1899: German stamp with a coat of arms bearing an eagle, overprinted with 'Karolinen'.

the marines stationed there. Some days later, O'Keefe is released but he feels unsafe and decides to flee the island. He takes a couple of his sons with him and sets out in one of his schooners in early May. But a severe typhoon catches him by surprise, and he is shipwrecked and drowns.

The relationship between the Germans and the locals on Yap remained chilly in the years that followed. In 1914, the Japanese occupied the entire archipelago. They held out until the end of the Second World War, when the Americans took over, and divided the Carolines up into Micronesia and Palau.

Yap became part of Palau, which gained its independence in 1994. In the meantime, after the German regime had prohibited the system that ensured constant shifts in the ranking between the villages, the island had developed a society with rigid class divisions. Some of the *fei* wheels disappeared along with the Japanese, who used them as building blocks and anchors. Those that remain are still in use, although mostly for social transactions such as weddings, or to ratify different types of agreements.

All that remains of O'Keefe's villa, it seems, is the foundation wall. Many of the island's inhabitants still firmly believe that he did not die in the hurricane in 1901 but travelled onwards to a distant island elsewhere in the Pacific. There, he established a new dynasty, which flourishes to this day.[126]

BOOKS

William Furness (1910)
The Island of Stone Money

Lawrence Klingman & Gerald Green (1952)
His Majesty O'Keefe

FILM

His Majesty O'Keefe (1954)
Directed by Byron Haskin

//

Come to Yap and I will give
you a half interest in all that
I own, including my harem,
and if I should pass on, I will
have arrangements made for you
to take my place as King of Yap

DAVID DEAN O'KEEFE

PERIOD:

1903–1973

COUNTRY:

THE CANAL ZONE

POPULATION:	AREA:
51,000	1,432 sq. km

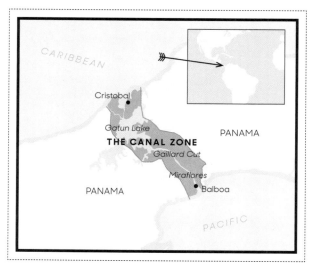

A Siberia in the Caribbean

As early as the 1500s, the Spanish were already fantasizing about a canal connecting the Atlantic and Pacific Oceans. This wouldn't just provide the ultimate short cut to expansion and trading links further west, but would also make the perilous journey around Cape Horn unnecessary.

The French were the first to start digging, in 1880, but the project collapsed nine years later. By then more than 20,000 workers had lost their lives, most of them victims of yellow fever and malaria. Every single engineer had fled back to France.

It's difficult to see how things could have gone otherwise. With its waterlogged rainforests and endless swamps, the place was a veritable paradise for malaria-carrying mosquitoes. When, in addition, the insects were offered unlimited access to thinly clad, sweaty male bodies, they took it as an invitation to out-and-out gluttony. The victims didn't even know what had hit them. The mosquitoes' ability to spread deadly illnesses was still quite unknown.

Just after the turn of the century, the Americans decided to try their luck. Meanwhile a Cuban doctor, Carlos Finlay, had discovered the mosquitoes' particular talent. This made it possible to take countermeasures, such as draping mosquito nets over hammocks, and putting oil in the water in the hatching areas. At that time, Panama was a province of Colombia, and the Colombian government refused to grant the USA the rights it wanted. The USA then changed tactics, offering its active support to groups that had long been working for Panamanian independence. At the same time, the American navy was sent south.

Only a few days after the resulting uprising broke out, the Colombian government army was forced to beat a retreat. In 1903, the newly formed state of Panama signed an agreement giving the USA a long-term lease on the Canal Zone, with a 20-km- (12-mile-) wide corridor from coast to coast. When Colombia started sabre-rattling again, President Roosevelt was careful to pacify it with cash, in one of the first cases of the dollar diplomacy that the USA has used with great success so many times since.

The USA was going to both build and administer the canal between the two oceans. The works were launched in 1904, and were completed ten years later. The canal is 80 km (50 miles) long, with a height difference from end to end of 26 m (85 ft), which is dealt with via a series of locks.

Gatun Lake was the largest man-made lake of its day, and when the water level was established in 1913, it covered an area of around 425 sq. km (164 sq. miles). The old twists and turns of the Chagres River remained upon the bed of the canal. The river had previously been the quickest route over the Panama Isthmus and became especially popular after gold fever took hold in California in the mid-1800s. Along its banks, there had been a row of villages built of bamboo and planks, with roofs of banana leaves or corrugated iron, 'where bongo-loads of California travellers used to stop for refreshments on their way up the river, and eggs were sold four for a dollar and the rent for a hammock was $2 a night'.[127]

In those days, the rainforest pressed in densely on all sides, and it still does. The flooded mahogany trees simply do not rot. The Canal Zone issued its own stamps as early as 1904. Mine is from 1931 and shows the passage through the Gaillard Cut,[128] named after Major David Du Bose Gaillard, who led the works in this area. The Gaillard Cut, the greatest bottleneck in the excavation work, ultimately formed an artificial valley more than 14 km (9 miles) long, which crossed the watershed between east and west.

The Americans put tens of thousands of men to work on the project. Between the two large daily dynamite blasts, one trainload of excavated material left every minute. But constant mudslides almost forced them to give up. Gaillard described the soil as: 'a tropical glacier – of mud instead of ice'.[129] It was too soft to be moved with diggers and had to be flushed away laboriously instead.

The work was tough and demanding, with constant accidents. Still, the mortality figures were lower than for the French. By the time the canal was ready in 1914, 5,609 people had died in all, most of them West Indian workers.

Cristobal on the Atlantic side was the main port of the Canal Zone, while the administrative functions were assigned to Balboa on the Pacific side. By 1940, the population had climbed to 51,000 and was ethnically diverse. All had attended an induction course that gave them guidance on acceptable behaviour in the colony. If they still proved unable to hold themselves in check, Panama had its own police, justice system and judges on hand to deal with them.

Maintenance and stevedoring work were carried out by hired hands from other countries in the West Indies. Americans filled the posts higher up in the system. Positions such as governor went straight to retired senior officers in the American Engineer Corps, without any democratic fuss and nonsense. The governor also automatically became the president of the state-owned Panama Canal Company.

And the company ran everything, including the shops, where food could be bought at cost price. There was a prohibition on taking lodgings in private homes. Bachelors were placed in motel-like complexes, with shared domestic help, while families were assigned to standard-issue four-family buildings painted grey and with corrugated iron roofs. The size of the apartment varied according to income: one extra dollar per month gave you an extra square foot of living space.[130]

All in all, the Canal Zone bore a remarkable resemblance to the many industrial cities Soviet Russia was building in Siberia around this time. This was how it was planned, and probably executed too, in the early years. But it had all become slightly more laid back by the time I passed through it as a first-time crewman on the slightly ageing cargo ship MS *Theben* in 1973. This was before the days of containers: the cargo was packed on open pallets with nets lashed around them, and there were piles of bright blue plastic owls between the bulkheads from a pallet that

1931: Canal Zone issue showing the Gaillard Cut.

had tipped over during bad weather a few days earlier. We were heading for Venezuela and entered the canal from the Pacific side. The passage took around ten hours.

As a greaser, I spend my days down in the machine room, doing maintenance work on the pistons and washing the cast-iron floor. It had been boiling hot for several days. We did all our work in shorts. I was knocking back salt tablets to keep myself going and my belly was already bloated from all the iced water I'd been drinking. My downy cheeks were brown and lumpy with eczema from the oil and I'd tied a dirty bandanna around my head.

First-timers in the machine room are allowed to come up on deck when the boat enters the Miraflores Locks. It's towed in by small locomotives, and the rainforest closes in tightly along the banks. The second engineer from Østfold tells us about an island in there so full of snakes that when an ox was lowered down from a helicopter, it was stripped clean to the bone before it even hit the ground. 'Ah, damn it, lads. Back to work. There'll be time enough to rest in the grave.'

The same year, Panama and the USA agreed on a transition to shared administration of the canal. The division of Panama had long been a source of diplomatic conflict. This escalated into disturbances in 1964, in which twenty-one Panamanian civilians and four American soldiers lost their lives. Even so, Panama was not granted full control of the region until 1999, and there is still a significant American presence there.

The hot topic of the day is future competition with the Northwest Passage, which is highly likely to become free of ice in a few years. The route will not only be free but also much quicker.

BOOKS

Georg Brochmann (1948)
Panamakanalen ('The Panama Canal')

Noel Maurer & Carlos Yu (2010)
The Big Ditch: How America Took, Built, Ran, and Ultimately Gave Away the Panama Canal

//

A tropical glacier – of mud instead of ice

DAVID DU BOSE GAILLARD, ON THE CONDITIONS DURING CANAL CONSTRUCTION

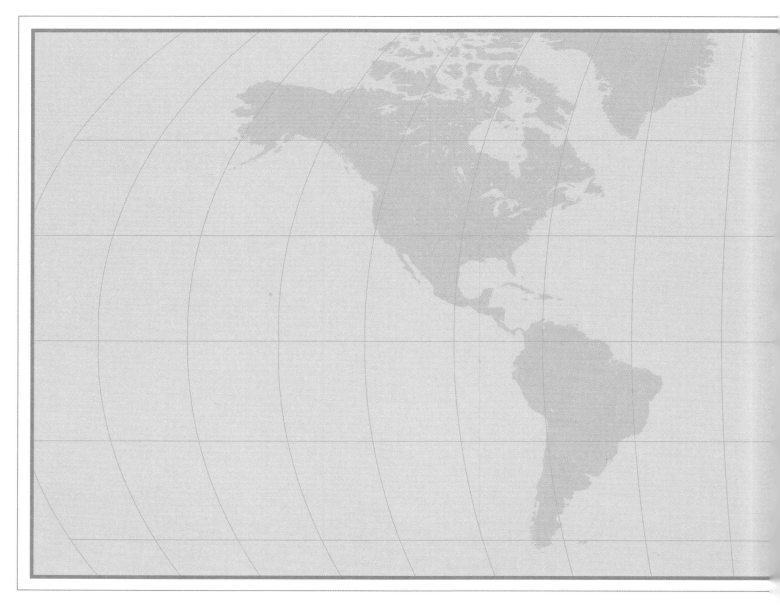

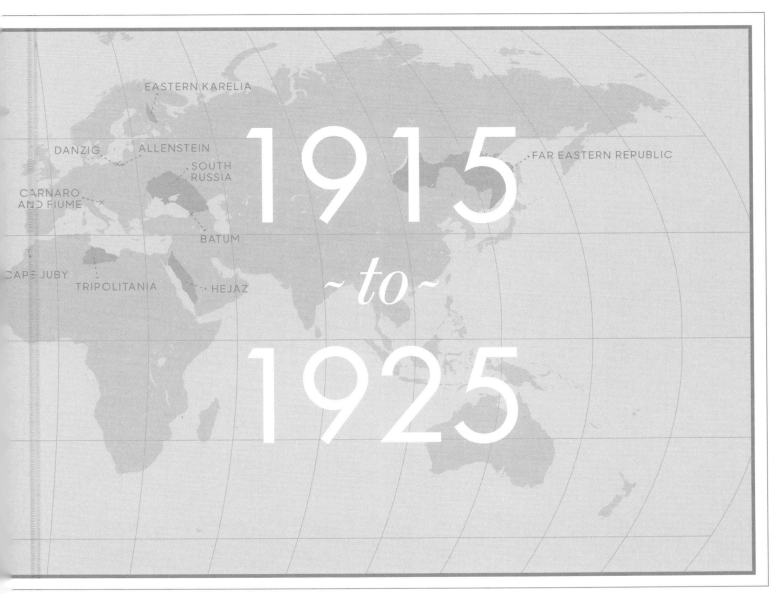

EASTERN KARELIA

DANZIG   ALLENSTEIN

SOUTH
RUSSIA

CARNARO
AND FIUME

BATUM

CAPE JUBY

TRIPOLITANIA   HEJAZ

FAR EASTERN REPUBLIC

1915
~ to ~
1925

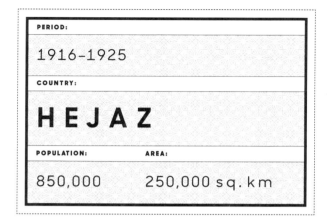

PERIOD:

1916–1925

COUNTRY:

HEJAZ

POPULATION: AREA:

850,000   250,000 sq. km

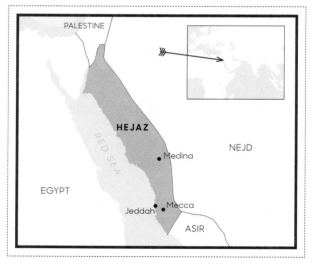

Stamps with a bitter strawberry taste

It is summer 1916 in Cairo. The First World War has already been raging across Europe for two years. Egypt has also been touched by these events. The year before, Ottoman forces on the German side made an attempt to capture Suez, but gave up after an effective British pushback.

Two British officers, Thomas Edward Lawrence and Ronald Storrs, are on their way up the steps of the red building that houses Egypt's history museum. They're looking for motifs for the stamps of the new kingdom of Hejaz. Just a couple of months earlier, it had declared its liberation from Ottoman rule, taking Sayyid Hussein bin Ali, the Sharif of Mecca, as its king. But, as so often elsewhere, the British have been pulling the strings. The people of Hejaz aren't even allowed to choose their own stamps. Still, the British do accept the ground rule that no portraits must be used: Islam forbids the depiction of people.

Hejaz lay on the western side of the Arabian Peninsula, stretching along the shores of the Red Sea from the Gulf of Aqaba in the north all the way towards Yemen in the south. On the seaward side of the kingdom, the coastal plain of Tihama quickly rose up into ridges and plateaux, then into a chain of mountains more than 2,000 m (6,500 ft) high that served as a barrier against the Arabian Desert to the east. Through the hills wound a caravan trail linking the spice growers in Yemen to Syria and the Mediterranean. It was also used by pilgrims on their way to Mecca and Medina, two of the most important holy sites in the Muslim world. Including the harbour town of Jeddah, Hejaz was a populous country of more than 850,000 inhabitants.

The area is hot, sometimes baking hot in the summer half of the year. The townhouses, built of carved coral stone from the Red Sea, are four to five storeys high in order to cast as much shade as possible onto the narrow streets. They are generally placed at a slight distance to one another to allow a little air to circulate freely around the outer walls. And the exteriors are covered in rows of wooden balconies, to reduce direct sunlight. Even the streets are twisted into angles designed to capture the most possible shade:

> Its winding, even streets were floored with damp sand solidified by time and as silent to the tread as any carpet. The lattices and wall-returns deadened all reverberation of voice. There were no carts, no shod animals, no bustle anywhere. Everything was hushed, strained, even furtive. The doors of houses shut softly as we passed. There were no loud dogs, no crying children.[131]

The Ottoman Empire had been present in the area since the early 1500s. But the Ottomans only took direct control in 1845, and retained power until the First World War. Towards the end of the period, a railway was built between Damascus and Medina. It was called the Hejaz Railway and was used to transport troops and strengthen positions in the south. The occasional well-heeled pilgrim could hitch a ride too.

The Arabs in the Ottoman areas were on the German side when the First World War broke out. The British dealt with this by starting secret talks with selected Arab leaders, including Sayyid Hussein bin Ali. This is where the so-called Arab Revolt was planned. The aim was to drive the Ottomans out of the Arabian Peninsula. For their part, the British also wanted to tie up the Ottoman army to prevent it from increasing its presence on the European battlefields. The strategy was guerrilla attacks, particularly on the Hejaz Railway.

Britain's leading representative in these secret talks was Thomas Edward Lawrence, better known as T. E. Lawrence. He was both an officer and an archaeologist, spoke fluent Arabic, and also had great sympathy for the Arabs and Arabic culture in general. He was somewhat androgynous in appearance, with thinning hair, a large, hooked nose and dove-like eyes – quite unlike Peter O'Toole, who later played him in the film *Lawrence of Arabia*. On the other hand, his upper lip was not quite as stiff as that of many other British emissaries. He was good at collaborating. During the early years, Lawrence played an active role in the guerrilla warfare, and made such an impact that the Turks put a price on his head. By then, though, the king of Hejaz had already given him the status of a son and nobody dared touch him.

Together with his mandate from England, it is also with this trust invested in him that Lawrence travels to Cairo to find motifs for the stamps. He is convinced that the stamps must go into circulation as quickly as possible to create the necessary stir about the new country. He is also aware that the design must have Arabic associations. But there's nothing suitable the Egyptian museum. Lawrence and Storrs continue through the town. Their first find is the carved pattern on the main door of the Al Salih Tayi mosque; the next, the stucco relief above the entrance to the train station; and the third, the ornamented final page of the copy of the Koran in the El Sultan Barquq mosque. In the end, they have a complete set of motifs, which they hand over to the typographer, Agami Effendi Ali, who will be responsible for the fine work. Lawrence issues one last instruction: no European script must be used. The whole thing must be archetypically Arabic.

Lawrence also oversees the final printing work. The story goes, although this is not fully documented, that he mixed strawberry flavouring into the gum. One slightly unexpected effect of this is that many people buy the stamps just to lick them, especially the cheapest ones with a face value of half a piastre.

I've checked my own stamp, but the aroma probably vanished after the first lick; still, the motif is the one Lawrence found at the railway station in Cairo. The text enclosed in the circle reads *makkah al mukarrama*: 'Venerable Mecca'.[132]

When the war ended, the Arabs expected autonomy in their own areas, an expectation that had also been held out to

1916: Motif from stucco work above the entrance to Cairo Railway Station.

them in their talks with the British.[133] Instead, France and Great Britain nonchalantly carved the region up between them into spheres of interest. Lawrence was in despair, as he made quite clear in his autobiography *The Seven Pillars of Wisdom*. And he felt he had been badly treated. The promises he himself gave to the Arabs were not kept.

Hejaz remained a separate kingdom under British influence, still with Sayyid Hussein bin Ali as ruler. But the past would soon catch up with him, because when he declared himself King of Hejaz, he couldn't resist the temptation of throwing in the title King of all the Arabs, *Malik bilad-al-Arab*. His rivals in the Sultanate of Nejd to the east pondered this for several years and their frustration gradually built up into rage. In 1925, they invaded Hejaz and formed the Kingdom of Nejd and Hejaz, which stretched right across the Arabian Peninsula from the Red Sea to the Arabian Gulf. The British, who had few objections, recognized the country and were soon on good terms with it. In 1932, it was renamed the Kingdom of Saudi Arabia.

BOOKS

T.E. Lawrence (1922)
The Seven Pillars of Wisdom

E.M. Dowson (1918)
A Short Note on the Design and Issue of Postage Stamps Prepared by the Survey of Egypt for His Highness Husein Emir & Sherif of Macca & King of the Hejaz

Mohammad Arif Kamal (2014)
The Morphology of Traditional Architecture of Jeddah: Climate Design and Environmental Sustainability

FILM

Lawrence of Arabia (1962)
Directed by David Lean

//

Its winding, even streets were floored with damp sand solidified by time and as silent to the tread as any carpet

T. E. LAWRENCE

1915-1925

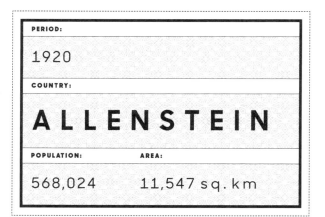

PERIOD:

1920

COUNTRY:

ALLENSTEIN

POPULATION: | **AREA:**

568,024 | 11,547 sq. km

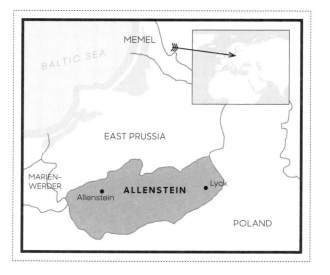

MEMEL

BALTIC SEA

EAST PRUSSIA

MARIEN-
WERDER

ALLENSTEIN

Allenstein

Lyck

POLAND

A summer of independence

The heat of the day is alleviated by a cooling breeze through the maple trees that line the fields of ripening crops on the way into the town. Church bells chime in the distance. It is 11 July and less than two years since the end of the First World War. On the narrow gravel roads, people are on their way to the polling stations. They are walking in family groups, and some of them are singing to keep time. Their brown lunch sacks contain pretzels, smoked cheese and honey cakes, because today is a holiday.

Allenstein was never a country in the strictest sense of the word. In the summer of 1920, though, many people probably feel almost independent. They are going to choose whether they belong to East Prussia in Weimar Germany or Poland, and everybody over fifteen gets to vote.

The Allenstein region was generally referred to as Thousand Lakes, although, in fact, there were only 200 of them. The area outside the densely populated towns consisted of forest and farmland, and this is where the majority of the population of half a million lived in 1920, mostly in enclosed smallholdings, with steep roofs of straw or wood shingles. The main farmhouses were single-storey timber buildings facing outwards onto the country roads, with brightly coloured window frames and intricate carvings.

At regular intervals, the towns rose like fortresses from the gently rolling agricultural landscape. The buildings within the walls strutted in familiar North European style, with churches and brick houses several storeys high lining the broad streets and spacious squares. And wherever you turned there were traces of disused military installations. Throughout its history Allenstein had rarely been left in peace, constantly ravaged by everybody from the Swedes to Teutonic knights – and Napoleon, of course. Throughout the First World War, the area had been a battlefield almost continuously, following Russia's fatal defeat in the Battle of Tannenberg during the heatwave of August 1914.[134]

The borders that were drawn up for the electoral area of Allenstein in 1920 largely followed the region that the Masurs had inhabited since the Middle Ages. And the descendants of this ethnic group were now on their way to the polls along with a large cohort of Poles and ethnic Germans, who could also lay claim to centuries-long traditions in the area. Their coexistence had been anything but harmonious, often teetering on the edge of conflict. These were the problems the victors of the First World War wanted to clear up through the Treaty of Versailles, signed the year before.

The treaty had ended the four-year state of war between Germany and the Allies, and required Germany to take responsibility for the war. It must also pay out substantial war reparations and unconditionally relinquish all its colonies and disputed territories to neighbouring countries. But in a few places, like Allenstein, the final choice was left to the inhabitants themselves.

> Versailles Treaty Article 94: In the area between the southern frontier of East Prussia... and the line described below, the inhabitants will be called upon to indicate by a vote the State to which they wish to belong: The western and northern boundary of Regierungsbezirk Allenstein to its junction with the boundary between the Kreise of Oletsko and Angerburg; thence, the northern boundary of the Kreis of Oletsko to its junction with the old frontier of East Prussia.[135]

In order to increase awareness of the plebiscite, a special stamp had been issued, admittedly in the form of an overprint on a German stamp. The stamps were valid from 3 April and would lose their face value once the result of the plebiscite was clear.

The motif on the stamp was 'Mother Germania', for which the actress and silent movie star Anna Führing had modelled. She is presented as a romantic personification of the German nation, a crowned, blonde woman in armour with a striking breastplate. We can also just about see an olive branch, a symbol of peace, and a sword, unambiguously representing the opposite. The overprint bears the text *Traité de Versailles*.

My stamp is postmarked Lyck (now Ełk), a town in the far east of Allenstein with 13,000 inhabitants. Often referred to as 'the Pearl of Masuria', it stood on the shore of the Ełk Lake entirely surrounded by forest.

The Englishman Ernest Rennie is appointed president of the plebiscite commission and he aims for a quick and efficient conclusion. In order to ensure a peaceful process, he has posted troops from an Irish and an Italian regiment at the polling stations.

But this soon proves to have little effect. Observers report large-scale fraud, especially on the German side. Among other issues, Polish polling cards have been removed, while the electoral rolls have been falsified and filled with dead people. And transport between the polling stations is arranged so that people can vote several times.

The legitimacy of the vote is further weakened by the fact that many Poles opt to stay at home after being threatened by the *Heimatsdienst*, a patriotic German organization that has been making its presence felt throughout the electoral region for some months. Another factor is the ongoing conflict between Poland and Soviet Russia, and Lenin's clear ambitions of pushing Communism further west. It is feared that Poland will fall, and many Masurs vote for Germany out of sheer fear.

All this meant that the outcome of the plebiscite was essentially a foregone conclusion, although the German victory was more decisive than anybody had thought, at 97.8 per cent. The electoral commission nonetheless concluded that the plebiscite must be recognized as valid, and Allenstein must be incorporated into East Prussia from 16 August. Four days later, the provisional stamps were declared invalid.

1920: Overprint on a 1916 German stamp featuring Mother Germania, for the occasion of the plebiscite.

There were many Jewish people in Allenstein, and they had probably voted for Germany, too. Reha Sokolow, who later emigrated to the USA, tells of her childhood memories of arriving with her family as an eight-year-old in the middle the 1920 plebiscite. They had travelled from Löbau[136] in Poland, where they were increasingly subject to harassment. 'Everything was left behind – our house, our property, and my father's businesses.'[137] In Allenstein they feel safe. The family is as German as anybody else. Reha has grown up singing 'Deutschland, Deutschland über alles', and felt it in the very depths of her heart. And her mother loves the Kaiser. She knows he will look after the Jews. Reha quickly makes a lot of non-Jewish friends, and goes on cycling adventures with them in the forest and along the lake.

But it doesn't last long. Gradually, the friends disappear. And after 1933 come laws restricting the activities permissible to Jews. The family flees again, to Berlin, not realizing that this will bring them even closer to the fire.

In January 1945, Allenstein is occupied by Soviet forces and is eventually incorporated into Poland as part of Olsztyn Province,[138] this time without a plebiscite.

BOOKS

David A. Andelman (2014)
A Shattered Peace: Versailles 1919 and the Price We Pay Today

Reha Sokolow, Al Sokolow & Debra Galant (2003)
Defying the Tide: An Account of Authentic Compassion During the Holocaust

//

In the area between the southern frontier of East Prussia... and the line described below, the inhabitants will be called upon to indicate by a vote the State to which they wish to belong

TREATY OF VERSAILLES, ARTICLE 94

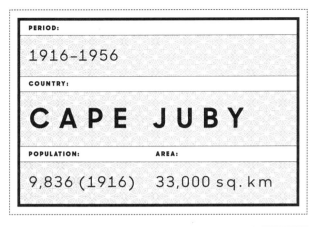

PERIOD:

1916–1956

COUNTRY:

CAPE JUBY

POPULATION: 9,836 (1916) **AREA:** 33,000 sq. km

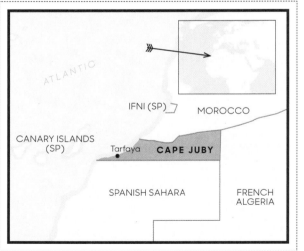

ATLANTIC

IFNI (SP)

MOROCCO

CANARY ISLANDS (SP)

Tarfaya **CAPE JUBY**

SPANISH SAHARA

FRENCH ALGERIA

Mail planes in the desert

Originally, Cape Juby is just the name of a headland in the far south of modern-day Morocco. It lies on the border of the Western Sahara and has been sporadically inhabited by nomads throughout its history. The adventurer Thor Heyerdahl was almost shipwrecked there during his first *Ra* expedition in 1969: 'a treacherous low sandbank like a licking tongue that sticks out into the dangerous ocean current just where the coast of Africa curves off to the south'.[139] He manages to save himself by the skin of his teeth.

The Romans also spoke of Cape Juby as a fearful place. Anyone who rounded the headland faced the risk of violent confrontations with all sorts of sea monsters, and they also thought a white sailor's skin would turn black. This was why, according to Pliny the Elder (AD 13–79), Cape Juby marked the absolute limit of all responsible navigation.

In spite of that, the Spanish, British and French all showed a certain interest in this desolate collection of sandstone cliffs around 100 km (60 miles) east of the Canary Islands. As early as the 1400s, the Spanish conquistador Don Diego de Herrera had built the fort of Santa Cruz de la Mar Pequeña on a little island 100 m (330 ft) offshore, to protect Spanish sardine fishermen from hostile nomadic tribes.

These nomads belonged to the Sahrawi people, descended from a mixture of Berbers in the north and Tuaregs from the desert areas of the interior in the east. In summer, they lived by the coast, where they fished while their herds of camels, sheep and goats grazed on the sparse tufts of grass. Here, the families camped in pale-brown tents made of wool and goat-hair, which were tethered to the ground with hemp rope or dried dromedary gut. The Sahrawis had nothing but scorn for settled populations, and no respect for either land ownership or borders. And they were absolutely unaccustomed to acknowledging superiority or monarchs of any kind. They themselves had a long tradition of making decisions through representative councils, in a form of anarchism where even the chief had to behave properly if he wanted to remain in power.

At the end of the 1800s, a fearless Scot named Donald Mackenzie investigated the Cape Juby area. 'I carefully examined a coast-line of about 200 miles in extent, and came to the conclusion that Cape Juby was the only safe harbour that could be found on the whole coast.'[140]

In 1876, he established the Port Victoria trading post on behalf of the London-based North West Africa Company. It was secured with high fences, and was there to establish trade with the interior of the Sahara.

During his travels in the desert to the east, Mackenzie discovered a depression that seemed to continue as far as Timbuktu. This prompted him to launch the 'Flooding the Sahara' project, which aimed to open up the way for shipping right into the heart of the Sahara. But the idea failed to spark any interest back home in England. At the same time, conflicts were becoming increasingly frequent with the Sahrawis, and eventually with the sultan of Morocco, too, who sent an army of 20,000 men to wipe out the trading station in 1888. And he won, although almost one-third of his forces died of hunger and thirst.

You really have to ask whether it was worth it. There was absolutely nothing of value here: no raw materials, no women, no glory. Spain must also have realized this when it, in turn, occupied Cape Juby in 1916. It nevertheless marked the occasion by issuing the first local stamps: overprints from the Spanish colony of Rio Oro to the south. My stamp, from 1919, is a simple overprint on long out-dated unsold stock of Spanish stamps from 1872, bearing a royal crown. But it still incorporates the important feature of the stamp's history: the printing ink. The red overprint was almost certainly done using synthetic aniline dye, which came onto the market around the turn of the century. It was first made from coal, then oil, and was soon used in all printing ink. The original stamp used mineral pigment thinned out with linseed oil. It appears to be green earth, a cheap pigment that was extracted in large quantities in Italy. But it's a mystery why it was used on the stamps, since it was known to be especially hard on printing plates.

Later, Cape Juby used stamps from Morocco, which was a Spanish protectorate until 1956. The protectorate was divided in two: the northern section encompassed a little strip heading up towards the Strait of Gibraltar, while the southern section, including Cape Juby, was generally referred to as the Spanish Sahara.

With Spanish permission, the French established a landing strip just north of the headland in the 1920s. It served as a staging post for mail planes on their way to South America and Dakar. Their usual cargo was 30,000 letters and the occasional passenger. The author Antoine de Saint-Exupéry was station manager at the base from 1927 to 1928:

In Cape Juby, day lifted the curtain on what seemed to me an empty stage. A set without shadow, without a backdrop[141] ...my sole fortune consisted of a shack built against the Spanish fort, and in this shack, a basin, a pitcher of saltwater and a bed that was too short.[142]

Aviation is in its infancy and he tells of a risky venture involving long distances, poor materials and constant breakdowns. What's more, trouble with the nomads persists, and vigilance is required:

The nights in Cape Juby were divided up into quarter hours like clockwork: the sentries called out the alert to one another, one man to the next, with a loud, regulation call...and we, the passengers on this blind vessel, we heard the call grow louder as it came closer and closer, circling above our heads like seabirds.[143]

There is less to fear by day:

When they [the chiefs] met us outside the forts, they wouldn't even insult us. They turned aside and

1919: Overprint on a Spanish stamp from 1872 featuring a royal crown.

spat. And they drew this pride from the illusion of their own power. How often have I heard them say, after placing an army of three hundred rifles on war footing: 'It's lucky for France that it's more than a hundred days' march away from here.'[144]

To pacify the chiefs, they are taken on plane trips, sometimes all the way to France. Some of them burst into tears at the sight of the lakes, trees and green fields. In Cape Juby, water is worth its weight in gold. It takes hours to dig down through the sand to 'some mud mixed with camel urine? Water! In Cape Juby...the little Moorish children don't beg for money, but hold out a tin can for water: "Give me a little water, give me..."'[145]

The Cape Juby era ended in 1956 when Morocco finally gained its independence. The name for the area was changed to Tarfaya Strip, named for some hardy tamarind bushes that grow wild there, and it was downgraded to a Moroccan province. The population has held steady at around 5,000 to this day. The inhabitants live off fishing and some trade with the Sahrawi, who still travel in the area.

The buildings inland from the headland consist of a cluster of modest two- or three-storey houses lining a main street of brown gravel. They are typical of the first half of the 1900s, with flat roofs and walls of only partly dressed concrete blocks. Most of them are very dilapidated and at constant risk of being buried by sand.

BOOKS

Antoine de Saint-Exupéry (1954)
Night Flight

Antoine de Saint-Exupéry (1952)
Wind, Sand and Stars

Arthur Cotton (1894/1912)
The Story of Cape Juby

//

In Cape Juby, day lifted the curtain on what seemed to me an empty stage. A set without shadow, without a backdrop

ANTOINE DE SAINT-EXUPERY

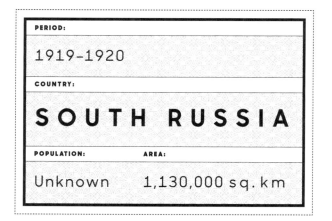

PERIOD:

1919–1920

COUNTRY:

SOUTH RUSSIA

POPULATION: AREA:

Unknown 1,130,000 sq. km

LATVIA

Moscow

SOVIET REPUBLIC

POLAND

Kiev

SOUTH RUSSIA

ROMANIA

Crimea

BULGARIA

BLACK SEA

Novorossiysk

TURKEY

PERSIA

A white knight loses his grip

There were at least five 'times' in use in Novorossiysk: (1) local time; (2) ships' time; (3) Petrograd time – standard throughout Russia for railways and officially used by the Volunteer Army; (4) Cements Works' time, announced by hooters every hour; (5) British Mission time, according to the Mission clocks, which were unreliable. There was about 1½ hours' difference between the fastest and slowest of the times, the others coming in the middle. It was, therefore, difficult to keep appointments, though one could always excuse oneself for being late![146]

The British journalist Carl Eric Bechhofer was confused. He had arrived in the port of Novorossiysk on the northeast coast of the Black Sea late in November 1919. It was a month since he'd travelled there by boat from London. At that time, the Volunteer White Army had been on the offensive, ready to attack Moscow. Now, the fortunes of war had turned and the White Army forces were fleeing south at breakneck pace, towards the town where Bechhofer had just landed.

It had all started a couple of years earlier in the wake of the Russian Revolution. After the coup against Tsar Nicholas II in 1917, a group of generals loyal to the Tsar had fled to the Caucasus to consolidate resistance against the red Bolsheviks. Among them was General Anton Ivanovich Denikin. His generous waistline, Hindenburg moustache and goatee beard gave him a solid appearance, but he may have been lacking on the intellectual front, according to the British agent, Sidney Reilly.[147] Even so, he managed to scrape together a considerable force that would serve as the southern flank of the Volunteer White Army. An equivalent group under the leadership of General Kolchak would cover the area to the east and further into Siberia. It was an exaggeration to describe this as a volunteer army: forced conscription was widespread.

The Whites were supported with weapons and money from France, the USA, Poland and England, all hoping that a victory would help return the market for European goods to pre-war levels. They also expected the Whites to recognize the substantial loans Nicholas II had contracted with American and European banks during his reign.

In spring 1919, Denikin informally established what was known as the South Russian Government. It stretched all the way from the Caucasus Mountains in the southeast to Kiev, with fertile plains on either side of the Dnieper River, and an extensive coastline, which Crimea in the south. He established a number of local administrative posts, with awe-inspiring military courts. Treason and assisting the enemy resulted in summary execution, without any fuss. On the whole, Denikin ruled with a firm hand.

In autumn of the same year, the Whites embark on a major offensive against Moscow. It is a failure, largely because of bickering among the generals. In addition, the soldiers are poorly trained and there are no logistics in place for securing provisions. The soldiers have to find their own food along the way. This leads to extensive looting and conflicts with the local population, and ends in the massacre of whole villages, particularly those with Jewish inhabitants, who are assumed to be supporters of the Bolsheviks. The Bolshevik leader, Leon Trotsky, describes the behaviour of the Whites as 'a comet with a filthy tail of robbery and rape'.[148] Many who have been fairly uninvolved in the conflict up until now join the Reds.

It is also a cold autumn. A porter at the railway station in Novorossiysk answers without hesitation when Carl Eric Bechhofer asks him who he thinks will win: 'The Bolshevists, for sure. You see, they have warm clothes.'[149]

On the train north, Bechhofer meets a beautiful young woman with a big basket of butter. She is thinking of selling it closer to the front line, where the profits are higher. He shakes a finger at her jokingly: 'So you're a speculator.' She laughs. 'Well what about it? Who isn't a speculator nowadays?'[150] For Bechhofer, the next question is where it is safe to get off the train, because the front line is constantly shifting backwards and forwards. In the recent past, Kiev has been captured and recaptured a grand total of sixteen times. The city's great cathedral has been alternately refurbished as a place of worship by the Whites and a corn store by the Reds.[151]

Denikin had also seen to it that the South Russian Government got its own stamps. My block of four is from the first batch produced in May 1919. There is plenty of residual gum, which is golden brown and probably produced from slaughterhouse waste, unlike later issues. I can confirm that it still tastes of boiled down horse-carcasses.

The main motif is tiny, set in an inner oval and surrounded by floral ornaments. Nonetheless, there is little doubt that it portrays a knight wielding a lance. It is, of course, Don Quixote's antithesis: Saint George. He had already earned a place on the Tsar's coat of arms for saving towns and beautiful maidens from Muslims and greedy dragons, if only in the world of myths. It is clear that Denikin identifies with this. Much of his motivation comes from religion – he is strictly Russian Orthodox and is taking an increasingly indignant view of the blasphemous behaviour of the Reds.

In the wartime winter of 1920, South Russia experiences a period of severe inflation. My block of four stamps, which is postmarked 20 January, consists of thirty-five-kopeck issues, the individual value of which was insufficient to cover the postage of even the smallest letter. A couple of months later, all the unused stamps are collected up, and much higher prices are overprinted on them. The price of just one of my stamps is raised to five roubles, equivalent to 500 kopecks.

By that time, South Russia is very much heading into the sunset. At the end of March, only Crimea remains, with a little strip of coast right in the north. The South Russian Government under General Denikin is dissolved on 30 March, and he hands over leadership of the White Army to Baron Pyotr Nikolayevich Wrangel, a fanatical aristocrat who looks as decrepit as a superannuated high

1919: Miniature motif of St George on the Denikin army issue.

The brown sticky side of the same stamp, which indicates a production date in May 1919.

court judge. As Denikin is being evacuated on a British man-of-war, Wrangel sets up the Government of South Russia – in other words, he just reshuffles the original name.

Wrangel's forces keep a firm grip on Crimea through the summer and autumn. Many are killed in constant skirmishes with the Reds. The following winter looks set to be even harsher than the year before, and soldiers freeze to death, even after stuffing their shirts with moss. In November, the Whites give up and the remainder of the army (almost 150,000 people, including the soldiers' families) is evacuated with what's left of the Russian Black Sea fleet. In the years that follow, most of them are settled in the Balkan region.

The generals flee further. Denikin settles in the USA, where he dies of a heart attack in 1947 after writing five fat volumes of memoirs.[152] Wrangel starts an association for what remains of the White officer corps, the object of which is revenge. He is probably poisoned by a Soviet agent after settling in Belgium.

BOOKS

Carl Eric Bechhofer (1923)
In Denikin's Russia and the Caucasus 1919–1920

Anton Ivanovich Denikin (1975)
The Career of a Tsarist Officer: Memoirs 1872–1916

//

A comet with a filthy tail of robbery and rape

LEON TROTSKY, OF THE WHITE ARMY

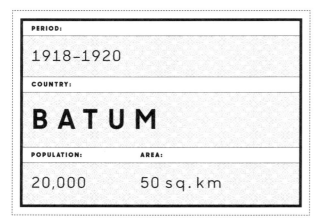

PERIOD:
1918–1920

COUNTRY:
BATUM

POPULATION:	AREA:
20,000	50 sq. km

SOVIET REPUBLIC/
SOUTH RUSSIA

CASPIAN SEA

BLACK SEA

GEORGIA

BATUM

Baku

ARMENIA

AZERBAIJAN

TURKEY/
OTTOMAN EMPIRE

PERSIA

Oil fever and bluebottles

The history of Batum is almost exclusively about the interests of the great powers and the lust for oil, and follows a pattern that has persisted ad nauseam right up to the twenty-first century. And as so often elsewhere, Great Britain is right at the centre of events. It ruled Batum from December 1918 to July 1920.

Batum started out as little more than an average seaside town on the Caucasian Black Sea coast. Nonetheless, as the terminus of the Trans-Caucasian Railway, it had gained a certain international lustre by the time Norwegian writer Knut Hamsun came on a visit in 1899:

> The city lies in a fertile region, surrounded by forests, cornfields, vineyards. High up, the mountains are burnt here and there, and on these bare patches, Kurds walk about herding their sheep. The ruins of castles protrude from the velvety forests.... There is something South American about life in Batum. People come into the hotel dining room dressed in modern clothing and silk dresses and jewelry.... Its streets are broad but not cobbled: you drive and walk on sand. The harbour is teeming with ships, with small sailing vessels from southerly towns all

the way down to Turkey, and big European coastal steamers on their way to Alexandria and Marseille.[153]

Hamsun is fascinated, but even so is struck by the large 'unhealthy' swamp areas close to the city, an impression shared half a century later by the travel writer, Erik Linklater, who mentions the tremendous numbers of bluebottles. 'Our bedrooms were noisy hives, and the restaurant by day a buzzing cloud.'[154] Rainfall is the cause, and there is a lot of it, more than anywhere else in the entire region.

A couple of years after Hamsun's visit, the young Joseph Stalin cut his revolutionary teeth in the town, organizing strikes and repeatedly being jailed for agitation. Stalin was so proud of these feats that he asked the author Mikhail Bulgakov – best known for his surreal novel, *The Master and Margarita* – to write the biographical play, *Batum*. But Stalin felt that the play depicted him as too naive and romantic, and ordered the destruction of the entire edition, much to the dismay of Bulgakov, who died a few weeks later, albeit from a kidney disease that had tormented him for a long time.

Norway's Fridtjof Nansen came to Batum in 1925 in his role as the High Commissioner in the League of Nations. The aim was to help survivors of the Armenian genocide to find a better life, deeper in the Caucasus region. Nansen was travelling with his secretary, Vidkun Quisling.

The city made a positive impression on them. Nansen was not a man to be bothered by flies, but the ill-kempt avenues of fan palms along the main boulevards irritated him greatly: 'Like worn-out tassels on top of long poles, they look like tattered besoms on long handles.'[155] And he had some plain advice on the matter for the city administration: 'Leafy maple and linden trees would have done much better.'[156]

Nansen and Quisling also went to inspect the pipeline that had been transporting oil overland from Baku by the Caspian Sea since the turn of the century. This was the site of the world's largest oilfield.

Production had started in the 1870s and it was soon delivering more than fifty per cent of the world's oil. At the centre of it all was the Swedish company Branobel, run by Ludwig Nobel, Alfred's brother. He had been quick to declare that petroleum, previously deemed a non-resource, had 'a bright future',[157] then went on to design the world's first oil tanker, and to develop technology for transporting oil through pipelines.

The pipeline between Baku and Batum had an internal diameter of 20 cm (8 in.), was 900 km (560 miles) long and was carried over a ridge almost 1,000 m (3,300 ft) high with the help of an intricate system of pumping stations. Nansen was impressed.

And so were the English, some years earlier, when they decided to occupy the port in Batum. Since the English fleet had switched from coal to oil in 1913, the motivation was greater than ever. Oil fever was absolutely raging throughout post-war Europe. The British foreign minister, Lord Curzon, had already declared: 'The Allies floated to victory on a wave of oil.'[158]

Batum was captured by 20,000 British soldiers at Christmas in 1918 after the withdrawal of the Turkish Ottomans. Engineers immediately set to work upgrading and repairing the pumping stations along the pipeline.

The occupation was unpopular with the local inhabitants. At the same time, regional ethnic groups were constantly coming into conflict with one another as they fought for their own sovereignty, and from the north, the Bolsheviks were steadily pressing forward, driving great streams of refugees before them.

When the British saw the game wasn't worth the candle, the project was abandoned, and the navy shipped out the last soldiers in summer 1920. Batum was handed over to the Turks led by Kemal Atatürk, who quickly presented the region to the Bolsheviks, after securing guarantees for the safety of the local Muslims.

During the occupation, the British had initially left the management of the postal system to Batum's city council. So when it came to producing stamps, there was no question of using beautified portraits of British monarchs. Instead, the city council designed a stamp with local associations: a beautiful aloe tree beneath the text *Batumskaya Pochta* ('Batum Post'), in Cyrillic script. It was printed at a local press, came in several different colours, had no perforations and the first issue came out on 4 April 1919. But when the city council later supported a general strike against the British occupation, the entire stock was confiscated and overprinted with 'British Occupation' before being released again.

1919: Local 'aloe tree' issue, overprinted by the British.

My seven-rouble stamp belongs to this group. It is probably genuine, even though stamps from Batum have been extensively forged over the years. Its authenticity is indicated by the fact that the third and fourth branches from the left form a clear V, whereas they are usually parallel in forgeries.

Those of us who are less concerned with time than place will probably always be intrigued by a thought experiment involving a chance meeting between Hamsun, Stalin, Nansen and Quisling – over a meal of boiled sturgeon and vodka at the station restaurant, for example. From a purely political standpoint, they would have had little to fight about, but it is easy to imagine some heavily in-depth discussions about the management of whiskers and moustaches, with Quisling as an impartial moderator.

BOOKS

Knut Hamsun (1903)
I Æventyrland ('In Wonderland')

Fridtjof Nansen (1927)
Gjennom Armenia ('Through Armenia')

Erik Linklater (1941)
The Man on My Back

//

There is something South American about life in Batum. People come into the hotel dining room dressed in modern clothing and silk dresses and jewellery

KNUT HAMSUN

| PERIOD: |
| 1920–1939 |

| COUNTRY: |
| # DANZIG |

| POPULATION: | AREA: |
| 366,730 | 1,966 sq. km |

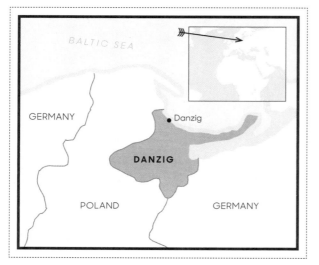

BALTIC SEA

GERMANY

• Danzig

DANZIG

POLAND

GERMANY

Sponge cake with Hitler

To celebrate the National Socialists' victory in the Free State of Danzig's parliamentary elections in 1933, Hitler issues an invitation to an afternoon of coffee and cakes at his Reich Chancellery in Berlin: 'They were literally coffee and cakes, "just like mother", *Streuselkuchen* and *Napfkuchen* (German teacake specialities). And Hitler was the *Hausfrau*. He was in a gay mood, and almost amiable.'[159]

Hermann Rauschning was contented. He was a landowner in Danzig and had just been elected president of the Free State's senate. Now at last they would bring some order to the situation in the little country, which he felt had long been neglected.

The Free State of Danzig lay in the fertile delta either side of the Vistula River (later the Wisła). Apart from smaller hilly areas in the west, it consisted entirely of first-class agricultural land, flat and easy to cultivate. This, combined with its strategic location right in the far southeast of the Baltic Sea, had made it coveted and disputed territory over the centuries. And its bustling harbour town – christened Giotheschants, Gidanie, Gdancyk, Danczik, Dantzig, Gdańsk or Danzig depending on who was in charge – was the jewel in the crown. The Prussians had ruled since the Middle Ages, except for a brief interlude under Napoleon from 1809 to 1814. In 1871, the area was incorporated into the newly formed German Empire.

After the Germans lost the First World War, the Treaty of Versailles stipulated that Danzig should be established as a free state under the protection of the League of Nations. Poland was behind this move. After winning back its independence in 1918, it was keen to have its own trade corridor out to the Baltic Sea, free of German influence. And it wanted to have full control over the railway links and harbours.

Ninety-five per cent of the 350,000 inhabitants were German and, naturally enough, they opposed the idea, but they failed to gain support for a plebiscite of the kind conducted in Allenstein a little further southeast. When the Free State was established in 1920, all those who would not accept their new nationality had to abandon the area and their properties within two years. Most of them stayed, but they protested vociferously when it became clear that the Poles would also have a military transport depot on Westerplatte, a little peninsula outside the city.

The Poles would also be allowed to run their own post office, where all post was franked with Polish stamps overprinted with the text 'Gdańsk', the Polish rendering of Danzig. My specimen is from 1926, and shows a Spanish galleon in full sail; it is an overprint on Polish stamps from the previous year. This can be seen as a slightly infantile dig at a fairly similar stamp issued by the national postal system in Danzig in 1921. Admittedly, it doesn't portray a galleon, but a more modest vessel – a Hansa cog. Here, too, we can sense a political game. The League of Nations had firmly opposed the term 'The Free Hansa City of Danzig'. It didn't want to stir up associations with Danzig's golden age of extensive industrialization, shipbuilding and trade links deep within Eastern Europe. The Hansa cog was an unambiguous symbol of those times.

The stamp with the Hansa cog is postmarked Langfuhr, a small suburb of Danzig. It lies just west of the city and is an upper-middle class district. This is where the author Günter Grass grows up, in a spacious apartment in a four-storey dressed stone building. His parents run a grocery shop on the ground floor. Several of his books begin with childhood experiences in the nearby arable land, which is criss-crossed by canals and drenched in marshy soil. In *The Tin Drum*, the narrator Oskar is taken by his mother on trips to the mudbanks by the sea. He struts along, light-footed, in his sailor coat with golden anchor buttons – hand in his mother's, too inquisitive and boisterous for his mother to dare loosen her grip. On one of these trips, they meet an elderly fellow in a longshoreman's cap and quilted jacket who is fishing for eels with a horse's head. The eels come squirming out of every orifice beneath the shining black mane:

'Take a little look!' he grunted now and then. "Let's just see!" He wrenched open the horse's mouth with the help of his rubber boot and forced a stick between the jaws, so that the great yellow horse teeth seemed to be laughing. And when the docker – you could see now that his head was bald and egg-shaped – reached into the horse's gullet with both hands and pulled out two at once, at least as thick as his arm and just as long, my mama's jaw dropped – she spewed her whole breakfast, clumps of egg white with yolk trailing threads among lumps of bread in a gush off coffee and milk.[160]

It was the early 1930s and the Nazis had been making their presence felt in German politics for several years now. In January 1933, Hitler was elected Chancellor of the Reich and immediately launched a campaign to strengthen the anti-Polish forces in Danzig. This enabled Hermann Rauschning and the Nazis to win the local parliamentary elections later the same year. Under the slogan 'Back to the Reich', they followed up with systematic harassment of all Poles, who now accounted for more than twenty per cent of the Free State's population. The Jews, who numbered more than 10,000, were persecuted, too. And Danzig was also involved in *Kristallnacht* on the night of 9 to 10 November 1938. Many people fled in fear.

In 1938, the German foreign minister Joachim von Ribbentrop demanded that Danzig be returned to Germany. The USA, France and England rejected this in no uncertain terms. They sided with Poland, which was threatening an armed invasion if Germany tried its luck.

On 1 September 1939 the Second World War starts when German troops cross the border into Danzig. They meet no resistance from the local population, but the small

1926: Polish post office overprint on a 1925 Polish stamp featuring a Spanish galleon.

1921: Stamp featuring a Hansa cog, issued by Danzig's national postal system.

Polish force on Westerplatte puts up a fight. The Polish post office further inside the town also resists during a fifteen-hour siege. The entire building is reduced to ashes, stamps and all.

The Germans immediately set about arresting more than 4,500 Poles, beheading the main leaders. Later, the Jewish inhabitants are also arrested, and campaigns are launched to sterilize Polish women.

The former president of the senate, Hermann Rauschning, has long since repudiated Hitler and fled to the USA. He despairs as he sees his worst nightmare come true: 'Here, one man is leading a whole age ad absurdum.... The "beast from the abyss" has been let loose.'[161]

Günter Grass joins the Hitler youth: 'Christened, vaccinated, confirmed, schooled./ I played with bomb fragments./ And I grew up between the Holy Spirit and the portrait of Hitler.'[162] Later, he fought as an SS soldier on the Eastern Front.

During the war, Danzig is bombed to bits and occupied by Russian forces on 30 March 1945. Under the Potsdam Treaty signed a couple of months later, the area is incorporated into Poland and the city of Danzig is renamed Gdańsk for good. All remaining Germans are deported and replaced with Poles who move in from the southeast.

BOOKS

Hermann Rauschning (1939)
Hitler Speaks

Günter Grass (2009)
The Tin Drum

FILM

Die Blechtrommel / The Tin Drum (1979)
Directed by Volker Schlöndorff

//

> The docker – you could see now that his head was bald and egg-shaped – reached into the horse's gullet with both hands and pulled out two [eels] at once, at least as thick as his arm and just as long
>
> GÜNTER GRASS

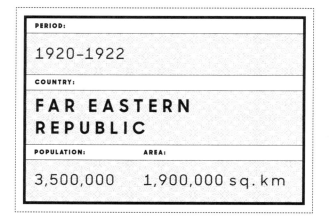

PERIOD:
1920–1922

COUNTRY:
FAR EASTERN REPUBLIC

POPULATION:	AREA:
3,500,000	1,900,000 sq. km

Utopians on the tundra

It is late at night in 1921 in the city of Perm in the Urals. Many of the sledges outside the station building are already white with heavy sleet. Two people hurry across the slippery platform, both in brown fur hats, thick fur coats and galoshes. First comes a stocky man, gesticulating a little. A slender woman follows, somewhat reluctantly. The locomotive has already worked up a full head of steam – it's the Trans-Siberian Railway's extra train to the newly established Far Eastern Republic, in transit from Moscow. Expected arrival in the capital of Chita: one week later.

The above is a rough summary of a scene change in Boris Pasternak's semi-documentary novel *Doctor Zhivago*.[163] Larissa Feodorovna, Lara, has moved to the Urals to escape the chaos of the revolution in Moscow without obtaining the necessary permits. She is caught out but saved at the last minute by the lawyer, Komarovsky, who smuggles her further east. Despite the apparent heroism of this feat, the lawyer is actually an unscrupulous rogue acting in his own interests. In part, he wants Lara for himself and in part he is, in fact, working for the Bolshevik regime, which has sneaked him in as justice minister in the newly established republic there in the east. Komarovsky was modelled on

Mstislav Petrovich Golovachev, who served in real life as assistant foreign minister of the Far Eastern Republic.[164]

The Far Eastern Republic first saw the light of day in April 1920. It was initially limited to an area just east of Lake Baikal, and stretched across a sub-arctic climate zone, from tundra and steppes in the north to the mountainous areas towards Mongolia in the south. For several hundred years, the region had been dominated by Mongolian nomads and different tribes of Turkish extraction, along with the occasional Chinese trader.

Russian Cossacks founded what would later become the capital of Chita at the end of the 1600s. But it remained an insignificant garrison town until the beginning of the 19th century, when the Tsar used it as a place of exile for political opponents and criminals from Europe. Even though the buildings were laid out over a tight grid of streets and squares, the town gave an impression of chaos matched in few other places. In style and format, it went off in all directions – from imposing public buildings in classical Greek style to Russian wedding-cake romanticism and tremendous numbers of small timber huts – all piled up randomly against each other without any overarching plan.

The Far Eastern Republic was apparently the work of a group of socialists who were much more democratically inclined than the communist Bolsheviks. They claimed to be adherents of libertarian socialism, and Prince Pyotr Kropotkin was among their sources of inspiration. His political programme was formulated in his 1892 book, *The Conquest of Bread*, in which he sketched out a social model that involved neither central state nor private profiteers. In the Far Eastern Republic, free elections and universal suffrage were soon declared. All indications were that these ideals would be pursued and that this was an independent country ruled by its own people. But, in fact, the whole thing was an elaborate fraud staged by the Bolshevik government in Moscow.

Since the revolution in 1917, the Bolsheviks had been marching steadily eastwards, driving throngs of increasingly demotivated Tsarist White Guards before them. But by the Pacific Coast, a well-equipped Japanese army of 70,000 men was waiting. They supported the Whites, albeit with rapidly waning enthusiasm. Nevertheless, the Bolsheviks weren't going to risk an open confrontation with the Japanese and therefore opted to set up a buffer state, the Far Eastern Republic, as an interim solution.

It was also hoped that the democratic veneer of the new country might pacify the rest of the world. But not one country was taken in, and no recognition was forthcoming. The British activist, pacifist and philosopher Bertrand Russell had a great deal of sympathy for the new republic. And it was mutual. When he was lying on his sickbed in Peking in 1921, he received constant dispatches of champagne from the leaders in Chita – in one case, personally delivered by the official emissary and future foreign minister, Ignatius Yourin. 'One of the kindest men I ever met,' wrote Russell in a letter in June 1921,[165] which likely establishes that the leaders of the Far Eastern Republic didn't know they were the victims of a plot either. If they did have any suspicions, these were overshadowed by the fact that they were fundamentally a bunch of naive and well-meaning idealists.

Japan withdrew its forces the autumn after the Far Eastern Republic was formed. The borders went with them, so that the country soon stretched as far as the Pacific Ocean and the port of Vladivostok, taking in more than 3.5 million inhabitants. And stamps were issued, initially using unsold stocks from the times of the Tsar, which were collected up and stamped with overprints. Gradually, these were supplemented with four stamps that were newly designed but offered no aesthetic improvements. My stamp belongs to this group and, at first glance, it has a fairly old-fashioned appearance, remarkably like the stamps the Whites used in South Russia a couple of years earlier. On closer examination, though, the central coat of arms turns out to be formed of an anchor crossed over a pickaxe, against a background of a ripe wheat sheaf: quite different from the symbolism of the lance-bearing knight in South Russia. We can sense a message of peace and brotherhood. On the surrounding wreath appear the Cyrillic letters Д, в and Р, short for Дальневосто́чная Респу́блика, the Russian rendering of Far Eastern Republic.

In what might be described as a death throe, the remaining Whites tried their luck once again in Vladivostok in May 1921. With a bit of half-hearted support from the Japanese, they managed to hold the city until October of the following year, but that was the end of it. The Whites were wiped out once and for all, and the Japanese lost interest. With

1921: Miniature coat of arms bearing an anchor crossed over a pickaxe, against a backdrop of a ripe wheat sheaf.

that, the point of the buffer state also vanished. On the suggestion of the Bolshevik leader, Lenin, the Far Eastern Republic was dissolved on 15 November 1922. This marked the end of the Russian civil war.

M. P. Golovachev, alias the villain from *Doctor Zhivago*, travelled onwards to Peking, where he eventually became one of the Bolsheviks' most talented spies.[166] Boris Pasternak won the Nobel Prize for Literature in 1958. Rumour had it that this was the result of pressure from the USA, which wanted to exploit the win for propaganda purposes. Many felt the book itself was bad. The Russian author Vladimir Nabokov, normally critical of the Soviets, described it as 'a sorry thing, clumsy, trite and melodramatic, with stock situations, voluptuous lawyers, unbelievable girls, romantic robbers and trite coincidences'.[167]

BOOKS

Richard K. Debo (1992)
Survival and Consolidation:
The Foreign Policy of Soviet Russia 1918–1921

Boris Pasternak (1958)
Doctor Zhivago

FILM

Doctor Zhivago (1965)
Directed by David Lean

//

One of the kindest men
I ever met

BERTRAND RUSSELL,
OF FOREIGN MINISTER IGNATIUS YOURIN

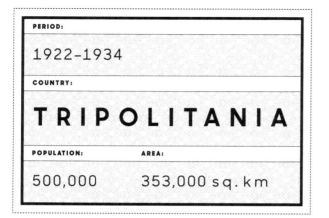

PERIOD:	
1922–1934	
COUNTRY:	
TRIPOLITANIA	
POPULATION:	AREA:
500,000	353,000 sq. km

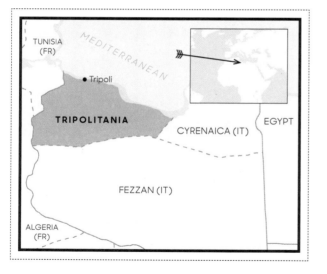

Fascist air race
in the cradle of Islamism

The air quivered. It was hot, improbably hot in fact. The young man was on his way to check the wind, rainfall, pressure and temperature readings at the little weather station rigged up on a hilltop beside the caravan station of El Azizia on the Sahel Jeffare plateau. Far to the north he could see a glimpse of the blue strip of the Mediterranean, interrupted only by the minarets in the capital of Tripoli. And a little nearer lay the almost unnaturally sharp divide between the bright green agricultural areas out there and the bone-dry, yellow-brown desert in which he stood. Off to the west, it rose in abrupt drifts, before gradually evening out into an endless rocky grey plain that led towards the mountain chain in the south. This was where the Ghibli came from, an incessant föhn or southerly wind that just made everything even hotter.

He couldn't even sweat as he clambered up the last few steps to the wooden box containing the instruments and struggled to note the temperature: 57.8 °C (136 °F). That was a lot. But he hadn't the faintest idea that he had just measured the highest temperature ever recorded on the earth's surface. It was 13 September 1922 in the Republic of Tripoli.

The Republic of Tripoli, or Al-Jumhuriya al-Trabulsiya, had declared its independence from Italy in November 1918 and was the first ever Arab republic.

The initiative came from the city-dwellers of Tripoli, who had been promised independence after Italy captured the area from the Ottomans in 1911. Instead, the whole region had ended up as an Italian colony. While Italy was licking its wounds after the First World War, they seized their opportunity. The aim was a secular state that would unite the population of Arabs, Berbers and Tuaregs, with their differing social systems and denominations of Islam.[168]

A deputation was sent to the 1919 peace conference at the Palace of Versailles near Paris to seek international recognition. The delegates from Tripoli were not allowed into the negotiations themselves, but stood waiting in the gilt colonnades for whenever the other attendees took a break. However, they were given the cold shoulder. The thirty-two participating countries had more important things on their mind. What's more, no oil had been found in the area, unlike other Arab countries in the east. The deputation returned home, disappointed.

In the meantime, Italy had adopted a tougher tone. It flooded the area with leaflets dropped by plane, threatening a massive invasion if the independence efforts were not shelved. Nothing comes of the invasion, but the leaders of the Republic of Tripoli agree that Italy will be consulted when the final constitution is written in June 1919. So there is never really any question of full independence. The newly established republic does manage to gain some concessions: that the Arabic language will be on an equal footing with Italian, as well as some points related to civil rights and freedom of the press. And they get a parliament elected by a popular vote of sorts.

Everything proceeds fairly peacefully until September 1922, when the record temperature is measured in El Azizia. In October, Mussolini and the fascists take power in Italy and the very next month, Italian troops are sent in – and they don't stop at Tripoli, crossing also into Cyrenaica to the east. On paper, Cyrenaica is still Italian, but local rebels have long been making life difficult for Italy's representatives in the area. The Italian troops don't give up until they have crossed Fezzan, an extensive desert territory to the south of Tripoli. Mussolini's vision is for the whole region to be incorporated into a Greater Italy spanning both sides of the Strait of Sicily. He wants to turn the Mediterranean into an inland sea, a *Mare Nostrum*.

The Republic of Tripoli is ill equipped in military terms. And once the Italians have successfully used divide-and-rule tactics on the various tribes, it abandons all resistance.[169] The new colony is rechristened Tripolitania and Italian settlers quickly take possession of the fertile coastal areas while the local population is driven further inland. The few who take the risk of staying must commit themselves to working free of charge on whatever roads and other infrastructure projects the Italians might come up with.

The Italian troops face bigger problems in Cyrenaica, particularly with a large group of combative, well-armed Muslim militias. They see Islam, nationalism and anti-colonialism as three sides of the same issue.[170] The Italians intern more than 100,000 prisoners in concentration camps. There are constant massacres, which even involve the use of chemical weapons.

General Pietro Badoglio is appointed governor of the whole region in January 1929. He promises amnesty to those who abandon the resistance movement, hand over their weapons and show respect for the law:

> We have also brought under our government a population that we must care for and steer towards a more civilized way of life. It is obvious that we shall never achieve our goal if this population does not feel the moral and material benefit of siding with us, submitting to our customs, to our laws.[171]

The atmosphere in the area never becomes wholly positive, but by 1931 the back of the resistance has been broken. The population slowly starts to return to the city and coastal areas, only to discover that the Italians have taken most of it over. The best they can hope for is tolerable conditions as farmhands or factory workers.

The Republic of Tripoli never got its act together enough to issue its own stamps, but the Italians needed to have a functioning postal service, and got started on it as soon as the colony of Tripolitania was established.

In letters to the old country, people talk about life as a master race with the locals taking care of all the dirty work. They complain about the heat, but boast about the

1934: Special issue in connection with the Oasis Circuit air race and a trade fair in Tripoli.

newly built racetrack, with its annual international motor-racing competition. And if the letter is from a man in the expanding upper class, it may well talk about the flying club, *L'Aereo Club della Tripolitania*. It is extremely active and in summer 1934, two stamps are issued to mark the *Circuito delle Oasi*, the Oasis Circuit, an international air race along the outer borders of Tripolitania. The race starts at the seaplane base in Tripoli harbour. We can imagine the atmosphere: redolent of perfume, newly tanned leather and oil fumes, with learned discussions about engine performance. Some of the first planes are forced to return after trouble with the Ghibli wind over the mountains. After three intermediate landings, the others return to a champagne reception on the jetty outside the Uadden hotel. My stamp comes equipped with its own special postmark celebrating the air race. It is placed with flawless precision. The postal worker must have leaned back in his chair with a self-satisfied air afterwards. We can guess that he loved flying machines, a love bordering on the ideological that he shared with most fascists.

Tripolitania was merged with Cyrenaica and Fezzan on 3 December 1934, to become Italian Libya. During the Second World War, the Italians lost the entire colony to the Allies. The part that included Tripolitania remained under British administration until Libya was declared an independent kingdom in 1951. Tripolitania operated as a separate province until 1963, when a system of smaller administrative regions was imposed.

During the civil war in 2011, Muammar Gaddafi was bombed out of power by the same countries that refused to recognize the Republic of Tripoli in 1918 – with the addition of Norway. The following year, the heat record from El Azizia was overturned by leading meteorological researchers. They said that it could not possibly be right,[172] and claimed that the boy who read the record temperature must have been badly trained. Possibly, the usually precise Bellani Six Thermometer was also poorly calibrated. As a result, the USA took the lead, with a temperature of 56.7 °C (134.1 °F) in Death Valley in California.

BOOKS

Lisa Anderson (1982)
The Tripoli Republic

Ali Abdullatif Ahmida (2011)
Making of Modern Libya: State Formation, Colonization and Resistance

//

We have also brought under our government a population that we must care for and steer towards a more civilized way of life

PIETRO BODOGLIO, ITALIAN GOVERNOR

PERIOD:

1922

COUNTRY:

EASTERN KARELIA

POPULATION: AREA:

c. 100,000   50,000 sq. km

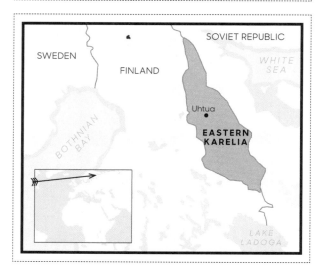

SWEDEN

FINLAND

SOVIET REPUBLIC

WHITE SEA

BOTHNIAN BAY

Uhtua

EASTERN KARELIA

LAKE LADOGA

National romanticism and brooding woodland pathos

My stamp from Eastern Karelia shows a raging bear beneath a sky sparkling with Northern Lights. It has cast off its chains and is ready to fight. The motif was produced by artist Akseli Gallen-Kallela, otherwise known for his illustrations of Finland's national epic poem *Kalevala* – more or less the equivalent of Norway's *Poetic Edda*. *Kalevala* is based on material collected in Eastern Karelia; the first part is a creation story in which a teal comes flying across the taiga: 'The beautiful bird came gliding over the water and caught sight of the maiden's kneecap in the bluish billows; it thought it was a hillock, took it for lush turf.'[173]

Akseli Gallen-Kallela was a cosmopolitan who had been educated in Paris, where he was greatly inspired by symbolism and art nouveau. He had a joint exhibition with Edvard Munch in Berlin and later took long study trips to Kenya and Mexico. At the same time, he was a sworn nationalist, with strongly romantic inclinations.

Along with fellow Finns such as the architect Eliel Saarinen and the composer Jean Sibelius, he founded the Karelianism movement. They believed they had found the cradle of Finnish culture in Eastern Karelia, an archaic region of lakes and acidic turf bog densely interwoven with

Norway spruce, fir and birch trees; on scattered clearings, small silver-grey farmsteads were inhabited by desiccated men and wiry-haired women.

A slash-and-burn farming technique called *huuhta* (meaning 'spruce tree') was developed to perfection here over several thousand years, and farmers continued to use it well into the twentieth century. The principle was simple: spruce trees were cut down and dried out over the winter before being burnt on the same spot. Rye or turnips were then planted in the ashes, usually in two rotations, after which the soil was exhausted but still rich enough in nutrients to use as sheep pasture or meadow until new woodland had grown.

But slash-and-burn farming required large areas of land, so it goes without saying that the farms had to be widely dispersed. This not only cultivated eccentric personalities but also meant that everybody needed to have their own drying kiln for the rye. Along with the chimneyless main house and the sauna, this resulted in the farm buildings being organized in a somewhat less orderly fashion than on farmsteads elsewhere in Scandinavia. And because of the unlimited access to wood, people kept the fires going intensively, everywhere, all the time. In the resulting scenery, shrouded in turn by smoke and frost, the Karelianists found an ancestral atmosphere that appeared, at least from the outside, to be authentic and unsullied by any other culture.

Finland is a relatively young country. For 700 years, the Finnish peninsula was ruled by Sweden, until it was conquered by Tsar Alexander I of Russia in 1808 and became a Russian dependency with the slightly misleading name of the Grand Duchy of Finland.

Once the Bolsheviks had overthrown the old rulers in the Russian Revolution of 1917, the Finns came to believe the conditions for their previously close relationship with Russia no longer applied. They declared Finnish independence on 6 December of the same year, a move that was accepted by the newly formed Soviet regime. New borders were agreed in Tartu in 1920.

But as part of that agreement, large Finnish-speaking areas in Eastern Karelia were left on the Soviet side of the border. The population felt betrayed and rebelled. Some 500 Finnish volunteers joined their fight, many of whom dreamt of a Greater Finland that would also include parts of northern Sweden and Finnmark – like a miniature version of the Nazis' vision of a Greater Germany some years later.

The rebels quickly set to work, systematically purging everybody who could be suspected of Soviet sympathies. At the same time, they worked intensively to secure official support from Finland. Their overtures were rejected by the Finnish government. In despair, one of the leaders, the 21-year-old philosophy student Bobi Sivén, committed suicide. He wrote a suicide letter dripping with pathos to the Finnish foreign minister Rudolf Holsti, which was later described as 'the most overblown letter ever sent'.[174]

Sivén shoots himself in the heart rather than the head, a symbolic act that places him in the same class as many other Finnish heroes, for whom aesthetic concerns remain crucial even in death.

The war follows its course, initially with considerable success for the separatists under Gustaf Svinhofud, who gains control of much of Eastern Karelia during the autumn of 1921. The winter is cold, the conflict brutal, and they fight it out in the forest. 'The shrapnel sounds like taut steel cables suddenly splitting asunder, and the treetops shake as if a storm were blowing up.... The trunks splinter, so that the pale wood shines out beneath the bark.'[175]

But a major Soviet offensive early in January quickly changes things. The Karelian rebels are suffering from lack of food and frostbite, and at the beginning of February the resistance falls apart. The rebels panic and quickly retreat towards the Finnish border.

And it is only now that the stamps with the raging bear come into circulation. In practice, they are only valid for a couple of snowy winter weeks: from 31 January to 16 February 1922. My stamp is postmarked Uhtua, a village on the shore of Lake Kuittijärvet,[176] which was already lost by 6 February.

The postmaster going through the letters must certainly have been made nervous by the distant but identifiable crackle of machine-gun fire, the sharp cries of command in the street outside, the echo of hobnailed boots on icy roads. Yet the postmark is steady and neat, which doesn't seem to make sense, so I'm inclined to believe it is one of many forgeries, even if the stamp itself is genuine enough.

The conflict ended with a treaty between the Soviet Union and Finland later in the spring, whereby Karelia was even granted a degree of autonomy, as the Karelian Autonomous

1922: Coat of arms with a raging bear.

Soviet Socialist Republic. For a period, those who wished were offered safe conduct to Finland, an opportunity some 30,000 Karelians seized. In the early years, instruction in Finnish was permitted in the schools. But the reins were quickly tightened and by the mid-1930s the region was effectively a regular Soviet republic.

Eastern Karelia was recaptured in the Second World War, once again driven by ambitions of a Greater Finland. But now the Finnish state was behind the plan itself, with strong support from Germany. The invasion was part of Operation Barbarossa, in which Hitler's primary aim was to conquer the Soviet Union across the whole of the line stretching from Kola in the far north to Crimea, and Finland held a substantial part of Eastern Karelia from 1941 until the evacuation in 1944.

Today the territory is a part of Karelia, one of Russia's twenty-one federal republics. It stretches from the White Sea in the north to lakes Ladoga and Onega in the south-east, and its most important industries are forestry and wood processing.

After *perestroika* at the end of the 1980s, a certain cultural softening becomes evident, including a suggestion that Finnish could be permitted as a second language in the schools. But the megalomaniac Greater Finns are gone, and Karelianism is dead forever. That said, perhaps there is a hint of Bobi Sivén's spirit to be found in the nationalist True Finns party formed in Helsinki in 1995.

BOOKS

Eino Friberg (1989)
The Kalevala (English translation)

Hagar Olsson (1965)
The Woodcarver and Death: A Tale from Karelia

MUSIC

Jean Sibelius (1892/94)
Karelia Suite Opus 11

///

The most overblown letter ever sent

RUDOLF HOLSTI, OF THE SUICIDE LETTER
FROM SEPARATIST LEADER BOBI SIVÉN

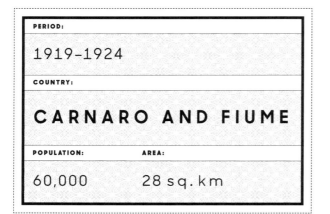

PERIOD:

1919-1924

COUNTRY:

CARNARO AND FIUME

POPULATION: **AREA:**

60,000 28 sq. km

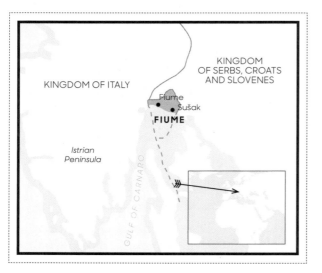

KINGDOM OF ITALY

KINGDOM OF SERBS, CROATS AND SLOVENES

Fiume
Sušak
FIUME

Istrian Peninsula

GULF OF CARNARO

Poetry and fascism

Few places offer such stark contrasts in climate as the barren, south-facing slopes in the heart of the Adriatic. Even in late spring when the bathing temperatures along the coast are more than acceptable, there's still plenty of snow on the mountains a short distance inland. And throughout the winter half of the year, the unpredictable Bora wind can strike, arriving without warning from the northeast, and gusting at speeds of more than 30 m (100 ft) per second.

For the Romans, this was crucial to their planning of the coastal town of Rijeka 2,000 years ago: they consistently placed the main roads at right angles to the main wind direction. The buildings were also constructed in robust natural stone masonry, a building style that was maintained in all subsequent modernizations right up until the 1900s. The same principles were applied in the villages to the north along the cliffy coasts and further inland in the narrow wooded valleys.

In the 1920s, Rijeka was the centre of a small autonomous state that had adopted the Italian name of Fiume, with a three-month interlude in autumn 1920 as Carnaro. The population in the area was predominantly Italian, with a minority of Croatians and Hungarians. Everyday conversations took place in Italian, interspersed with a few Croatian words.

Fiume had already been a free state for a period in the 1700s. Later, it switched to a more limited autonomous status, known as *corpus separatum*, within the kingdom of Hungary. This was maintained until Hungary and Austria merged in 1867.

Serious argument over the small area's future only started during the settlements that followed the First World War. Austria-Hungary had suffered a resounding loss, and the victorious great powers envisaged a buffer state at the innermost end of the Adriatic. This was in direct opposition to the wishes of both the Kingdom of Italy and the Kingdom of Serbs, Croats and Slovenes (later the Kingdom of Yugoslavia), both of which had territorial rights in the area. But the victors stood their ground: Fiume would be established and organized as a free state. The American president, Woodrow Wilson, went even further, seeing the free state as a future base for the League of Nations, alongside supranational institutions for the promotion of disarmament and peace.

But the disagreements continued, and internal conflicts between the different ethnic groups became ever more frequent. British, American and French troops were sent in to cool tempers and take control.

This is how the situation stands when the ageing Italian poet, the Prince of Montenevoso, better known as Gabriele D'Annunzio, steps in.

Born in 1863, he grows up in the secure environment of a landowning family in Pescara, a little coastal town further along the Adriatic coast. He writes his first poetry collection, *Primo Vere*, when he is only sixteen. He soon joins the decadents in Paris and over the years, he produces an abundant stream of poems, novels and plays the common feature of which is that they are passionate to the point of being overheated. When not writing, D'Annunzio indulges wholeheartedly in the pleasures of life, leading a notoriously debauched existence that involves experiments with drugs and eroticism, all of it neatly logged in his diary. He also develops some sympathy with the Futurist movement that emerges in Italy at the beginning of the 1900s. The Futurist manifesto takes a forward-looking stance, adopting speed and technology as its central themes. D'Annunzio loves planes, torpedoes, machine guns and fast cars.

Most of his literary work is already on the shelves by 1910, when he enters political life; here, he is similarly temperamental, as evidenced by his continual swings between right- and left-wing ideology. However, things settle down during the First World War when he is quick to advocate Italy's involvement in support of the French, in a 'Latin war against the Germanic barbarians'. And he signs up immediately when Italy eventually goes to war on the side of the Allies.

It is said that D'Annunzio was named Gabriele because he looked so angelic as a child. Something of that impression remains intact in photographs taken after the end of the war, although he also has a severely receding hairline and something about his eyes betrays a passion beyond any normal emotional life. In addition, he is fairly short, although not quite as short as his hero Napoleon. The war has convinced him of the superiority of nationalism. He joins the Irredentists, who want to unite all the areas with Italian-speaking inhabitants into one huge Italian state. This is where Fiume belongs, its population of 60,000 dominated by a majority of 40,000 Italians. He declares that Fiume will become part of Italy, whatever the cost: *O fiume o la morte* – 'Fiume or death'.[177]

On 12 September 1919, D'Annunzio enters Fiume at the head of an irregular army of 2,600 enraged and single-minded Italian nationalists, many with combat experience from the First World War. They force the Allied occupation forces to beat a retreat, and are given a hero's welcome by the local Italian population.

The occupation lasts fifteen months. D'Annunzio repeatedly attempts to get Italy to officially recognize and support his project, but to no avail. Instead the authorities in Rome ask him to surrender, and threaten him with a blockade. The president Francesco Nitti declares that after losing half a million citizens in the war, Italy cannot be lost through the folly of romantic and literary fops.[178]

Unsurprisingly, D'Annunzio responds in September 1920 by declaring the establishment of the *Reggenza Italiana del Carnaro*, the Italian Government of Carnaro, named after the nearby Gulf of Carnaro (now known as the Kvarner Gulf). With his feeling for form and ornamentation, he sets to work at once designing a flag, which bears a snake biting its own tail above the inscription *quis contra nos* – 'who can oppose us'.

1920: Issue to mark the anniversary of D'Annunzio's march into Fiume. The stamp was overprinted following the occupation of the islands of Arbe and Veglia.

The fledgling state organizes itself using a model that will later be taken up by Italian fascists, with D'Annunzio as *Il Duce*, the leader. It has several surprising features, including full suffrage for women and music as a cornerstone for both the exercise of power and cultural education.

In every district, a choir and orchestra is to be established with public funds, and D'Annunzio sets to work planning a concert hall to seat 10,000, with free entry.

The well-designed stamps being printed in large quantities are intended to be a significant source of income for the new state. The motifs include a portrait of D'Annunzio himself, and they are distributed to collectors worldwide.[179] After the official establishment of Carnaro in September 1920, they have *Reggenza Italiana del Carnaro* overprinted on them. My stamp, with a dagger and rope, belongs to this group, and it leaves one in little doubt about its message.

At this time, D'Annunzio launches the idea of the March on Rome, which will contribute to an eventual revolution. Many Italians sympathize with him and whole ships' crews in the Italian navy sign up as volunteers. Soon, Carnaro has an army of 4,000 well-trained soldiers. But although impressive this is still not enough to repel a surprise attack by superior Italian troops at Christmas in 1920. D'Annunzio himself flees north by motorcycle on 29 December after an Italian cruiser, *Andrea Doria*, has subjected the city to heavy bombardment.

And so the Free State of Fiume, *Stato Libero di Fiume*, at last becomes a reality. It had already been agreed on paper under the Treaty of Rapallo a couple of months earlier. The agreement implied that all disagreements between the Kingdom of Italy and the Kingdom of Serbs, Croats and Slovenes would be set aside. The land area, a modest 28 sq. km (11 sq. miles), would include a corridor along the coast in the west, linking the new state to Italy.

In line with the wishes of the USA and the great powers of Europe, the state acquired full sovereignty. And in return it quickly gained international recognition.

In the spring of 1921, parliamentary elections were held in the free state, ending in a clear victory for the Autonomists, who favoured independence, although the Italian nationalists had tried their luck again. Old stamps were destroyed and new ones were printed, generally a little less melodramatic than their predecessors. My second stamp, from 1922, shows a Venetian galley overprinted with *Costituente Fiumana*, to demonstrate that this was now a serious country with its own constitution.

But the stability was only illusory: there were constant disturbances and repeated coup attempts, put down each time by Italian troops.

Back in Italy, D'Annunzio had been wounded in an assassination attempt. As a result, he had to withdraw from the March on Rome in summer 1922, which was now relaunched and taken over entirely by an up-and-coming politician, Benito Mussolini.

It ends in a coup, with Mussolini seizing the role of *Il Duce*. He immediately adopts many of the rituals and expressions used during D'Annunzio's time in Fiume, such as the use of black shirts, the well-choreographed parades and the emotive balcony speeches, complete with almost excessive gesticulation.

D'Annunzio is angry. He feels passed over. What's more, he has a lot of reservations about the fascist politics Mussolini is introducing. This irritates Mussolini. 'When your tooth is rotten you have two possibilities: pull it out or fill it with gold. I've chosen the latter for D'Annunzio.'[180]

D'Annunzio has medals and honours heaped upon him until he dies of a stroke in 1938. He is interred at the state's expense and is buried standing up in a niche at his home by Lake Garda, in accordance with his own wishes.

After the fascists took over in Italy, the Fiume question gained traction. Under heavy pressure from the Italians, the Kingdom of Serbs, Croats and Slovenes signed the Treaty of Rome at the end of January 1924, in which the free state was dissolved and divided up. Italy got most of it, while the Kingdom of Serbs, Croats and Slovenes was left with the unappealing urban district of Sušak in the east. The whole thing was done without recourse to the elected government in Fiume, which went into exile.

The British writer Rebecca West, travelling through the area just before the Second World War, describes a dismal encounter:

> There we found a town that has the quality of a dream, a bad headachy dream. Its original character is round and sunburnt and solid, like any pompous southern port, but it has been hacked by treaties into a surrealist form.[181]

When the war ended in 1945, the rest of the old government in exile returned home after more than twenty years abroad. Their desire to take matters in hand again was brutally rebuffed by the Yugoslavian authorities, which

1922: Overprint on a stamp from 1919, showing a Venetian galley. It marks the constitution of a new parliament.

had now captured the city. Many of the aged Autonomists were killed, without attracting much attention. And after the peace treaty in Paris in 1947, Fiume was officially incorporated into Yugoslavia under the new name of Rijeka.

After the break-up of Yugoslavia, Rijeka became Croatia's most important port, and still is to this day. And D'Annunzio has been rehabilitated as one of Italy's greatest poets.

B O O K S

Lucy Hughes-Hallett (2013)
The Pike: Gabriele D'Annunzio,
Poet, Seducer and Preacher of War

Alceste de Ambris & Gabriele D'Annunzio (1920)
La Carta di Libertà del Carnaro
('The Charter of the Freedom of Carnaro')

F I L M

Cabiria (1914)
Directed by Giovanni Pastrone

//

There we found a town that has the
quality of a dream, a bad headachy
dream. Its original character is
round and sunburnt and solid,
like any pompous southern port,
but it has been hacked by treaties
into a surrealist form

REBECCA WEST

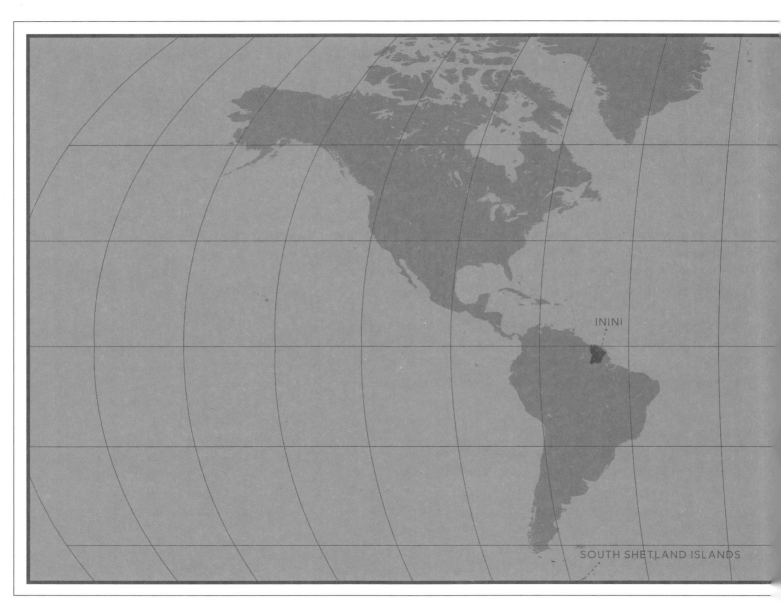

ININI

SOUTH SHETLAND ISLANDS

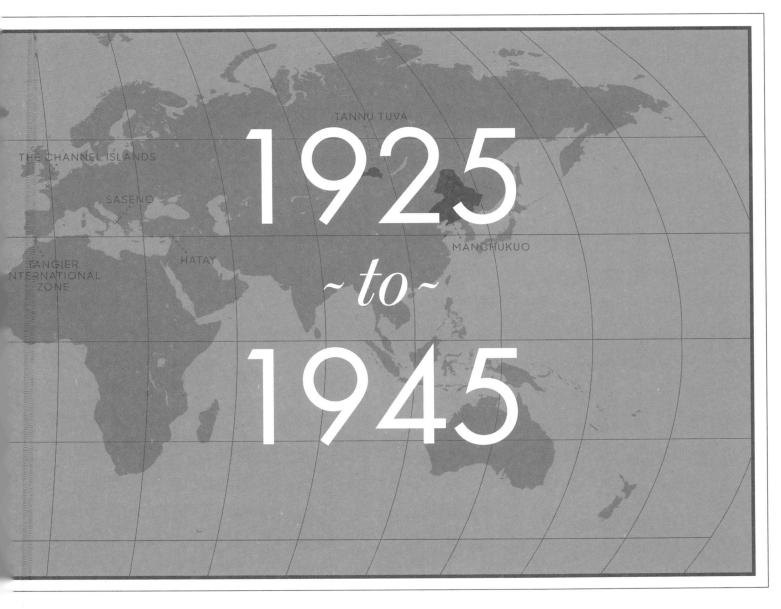

1925
~ *to* ~
1945

TANNU TUVA

THE CHANNEL ISLANDS

SASENO

MANCHUKUO

TANGIER
INTERNATIONAL
ZONE

HATAY

PERIOD:

1932–1945

COUNTRY:

MANCHUKUO

POPULATION: | AREA:

30,880,000 | 1,554,000 sq. km

SOVIET UNION

MONGOLIA

● Harbin

MANCHUKUO

BOHAI GULF

SEA OF JAPAN

CHINA

KOREA (JP)

JAPAN

At the epicentre of evil

The macabre experiments Nazi doctor Joseph Mengele performed on prisoners at Auschwitz in the Second World War have made his name a byword for humanity at its most evil. Even so, his activities pale in comparison with the scenes that played out in the East Asian country of Manchukuo some years earlier.

Few were aware of what lay ahead when the new state was created in early spring 1932, the year after the Japanese invasion of Chinese Manchuria. Chinese historians later insisted on referring to Manchukuo as 'the *false* Manchurian state', because it was clearly nothing but a Japanese puppet state right from the start. Nonetheless, it gained recognition from El Salvador and the Dominican Republic, soon followed by the future axis powers, Germany and Italy, as well as Vatican City, which had lots of missionaries in the area.

Manchukuo stretched from the sub-Arctic areas along the river Amur in the north to the fertile plains of the Bohai Gulf in the south. Here, the border with China coincided with the end of the Great Wall that had been built between the thirteenth and sixteenth centuries to keep out the Mongolian hordes.

Until the 1900s, the area had been a purely agricultural district, divided up into prefectures controlled by the

Chinese emperor. The inhabitants lived in villages that had grown up without any overarching plan. The straw roofs had generous cornices to protect the outer walls against the periodic downpours. And the light walls were filled with thin panels and sliding doors, making it easy to open up large areas to the outside on hot summer days. Still, any modern European would be surprised by the total lack of insulation, given the often-harsh winters. But the people of Manchukuo had their own strategy. When the cold set in, they retreated instead to smaller rooms in the centre of the house. The sitting places on the floor here were warmed with wood-fired heating and they kept their outer clothing on.

With the construction of the Manchurian railway at the end of the 1800s, many of the villages along the route were expanded into towns, and sometimes big cities. Polish and Russian engineers contributed to the planning, adding a European touch to things.

The urbanization that had already taken place gave Japan a flying start. The population of the new state quickly grew from 30 to 50 million, mainly as a result of Japanese immigration. And the propaganda claimed that collaboration across the Sea of Japan would contribute to peace between the brother nations. In line with this, my stamp depicts a peaceful crane gliding airily across the water. But at the lower edge – right above the text in Hanzi script – we can see a glimpse of the flagstaff of a naval vessel.

There is little doubt that the region's mineral resources were the first thing to stir Japan's interest, especially the large iron ore deposits. To give the project an air of greater legitimacy, the former Chinese emperor, Pu Yi, was brought in as head of state. He was frail and hollow-chested. His round horn-rimmed glasses dominated his face and had to be balanced out by a grand uniform, laden with epaulettes, silk ribbons and medals. Pu Yi didn't exactly thrive in the role, which mostly involved signing Japanese decrees and cutting ribbons at steelworks, road bridges and railway platforms. Nonetheless, he remained in power until the Russians took over after Operation August Storm, a major offensive in the final phase of the Second World War.

Pu Yi tried to flee to Japan, to hand himself over to the Americans, but was captured by the Red Army and sent to Siberia. Later he was returned to China, and ended his days as a sworn Maoist, if we are to believe Bernardo Bertolucci's 1987 film, *The Last Emperor*. By then, he had also written his autobiography, *From Emperor to Citizen*, in which he frankly acknowledges his guilt: 'I shamelessly became a leading traitor and the cover for a sanguinary regime which turned a large part of my country into a colony.'[182]

Pu Yi probably wasn't aware of the very darkest side of Japan's activities in Manchukuo. Under the pretence of running a water purification business, Unit 731 had already started to use the country as a laboratory for the development of chemical and biological weapons for Japan's expanding war machine by 1935.

At six foot, the project director, General Shiro Ishii, towered above most of his countrymen. Like Pu Yi, he wore round horn-rimmed glasses but his body and soul appeared much more in harmony. He was always well dressed, his hair neatly pomaded, and although he may have been slightly self-centred he was still well liked by his colleagues. Admittedly, there was the odd slip with heavy drinking and his nightly raids on the local geisha house, but he was still respected and even more beloved as a result.[183]

The facility was set up in Pingfang, a treeless plain just south of the provincial town of Harbin. Here, 150 rectangular concrete buildings, large and small, were built over an area of 6 sq. km (2½ sq. miles). The buildings included a Shinto temple to ensure the spiritual well-being of the employees, as well as schools for their children. Every morning Shiro Ishii commuted in his armoured limousine from Harbin, where he lived with his wife, seven children and servants in a mansion that dated back to an earlier Russian era – an idyll his eldest daughter later described as being straight out of *Gone with the Wind*.[184]

The core of the experiments was testing on living people. This included the removal and modification of brains and intestines, injections with horse's blood, testing in gas chambers, pressure chambers and centrifuges, but most importantly of all, systematic testing of contagious biological substances. Experiments were carried out with anthrax, typhus, dysentery and cholera, as well as a selection of lesser-known but similarly horrific plague bacteria. The chosen carriers of infection were flies, which were bred in several thousand specially made containers.

The subjects of the experiments, mainly Chinese and Russian civilians, were referred to as 'logs' and included children, women and old people. In all, more than 10,000 of

1940: Manchurian cranes above a ship's mast.

them died in Pingfang. Nobody survived. In addition, more than a million people died elsewhere, for instance when infection-bearing flies were released over Chinese cities. On one occasion, soldiers planted hundreds of paratyphoid-infected cakes around Nanking,[185] then suffering a famine.

Unlike Pu Yi, most of the staff of Unit 731 managed to flee to Japan in 1945. Here they handed themselves over to the American forces and after a short time, they were given general immunity on the orders of the Supreme Commander in the Pacific, General Douglas MacArthur. At the same time, the war crimes evidence files were destroyed. Many of the former workers, including Shiro Ishii himself, quickly became affiliated to the newly launched United States Biological Development Program. Shiro Ishii died peacefully in 1959 and therefore did not live to see the USA applying its newfound knowledge with great success during the Vietnam War.

In 1945, Manchukuo was reincorporated into the Chinese state, and today constitutes the provinces of Liaoning, Jilin, Heilongjiang and parts of Inner Mongolia. Few visible traces of Unit 731 remain, but beneath the hill broods one of the world's most horrific chemical dumps. For now, it seems to be stable. But a combination of severe temperature increases and more intense rainfall in the Harbin area over time may waken the sleeping vampire.

BOOKS

Hal Gold (2004)
Unit 731: Testimony

Simon Winchester & Aisin-Gioro Pu Yi (1987)
From Emperor to Citizen:
The Autobiography of Aisin-Gioro Pu Yi

Haruki Murakami (1999)
The Wind-up Bird Chronicle

FILM

The Last Emperor (1987)
Directed by Bernardo Bertolucci

///

I shamelessly became a leading traitor and the cover for a sanguinary regime which turned a large part of my country into a colony

PU YI

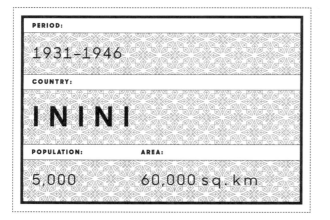

PERIOD:

1931–1946

COUNTRY:

ININI

POPULATION: | AREA:
5,000 | 60,000 sq. km

ATLANTIC

St Laurent

FRENCH GUIANA

• Cayenne

St Elie

SURINAM (NL)

ININI (FR)

BRITISH
GUIANA

BRAZIL

Mortal sins in an impenetrable rainforest

From 1932 onwards, Inini issued its own stamps in the form of French Guianan issues with an overprint. Mail delivery in the area was minimal, and nobody wanted to put more effort into it. When Inini ceases to exist as a separate colony in 1946, crate-loads of unused stamps are left. These are eventually distributed to collectors all over the world. My stamp is probably one of these, nicely steeped in fungal spores and jungle damp, I hope, after lying in an attic in St Elie, St Laurent or Cayenne for several years; not as good as a postmarked stamp, but nearly. I lick the back of the stamp carefully and my mouth fills with a cloying, bittersweet taste. Promising.

French Guiana lies in an area of heavy rainfall just north of the Equator. A little way inland from the coast, the whole place is overgrown with impenetrable rainforest, and goods and people must be transported in small boats along a network of rivers. The first colonists were drawn there by gold. Countless expeditions set out to find the golden city of El Dorado, which, according to legend, was towards the west of this area. And gold was found, albeit in relatively modest quantities – although still enough to ensure that gold-mining would remain the principal industry up until the present day.

The American travel writer Hassoldt Davis visited the area and told of his meeting with a Creole gold-digger, Fanfan. One night the prospector dreamt that a headless woman pointed out a place by the bank of the Petit Inini River. She was holding out a gold nugget the size of a water-melon. After the dream was repeated the following night – and this time the woman was furious – Fanfan persuaded his friends to go with him. He found the tree the woman had pointed out and after just a couple of minutes' digging, it was as if he'd struck a head down there. It turned out to be the legendary 'La Grand Pépite' nugget.[186]

Most of the gold-digging was illegal activity, some of it involving high levels of violence. The fact that the area was simultaneously being used as a penal colony imbued the whole thing with an almost apocalyptic atmosphere of mortal sin, temptation and repentance.

As early as the French Revolution, troublemakers were being exiled to Guiana, and from the middle of the 1800s, a good many prisons were built there. They were placed along the coast and were to be used for both French convicts and agitators from the colonies. One well-known example is Devil's Island, where prominent nuisances such as Alfred Dreyfus and, later, Henri Charrière were held – although admittedly the latter managed to escape in a sack of coco-nuts in 1941 and went on to write a book about it.[187]

At the very beginning of the 1900s, the colonial administration started looking for other means of support. And the decision was taken to use the inland areas of French Guiana primarily for agriculture, forestry and controlled gold mining. To make these efforts more efficient, the interior was made into a separate colony in 1930. It was assigned a governor, in St Elie, and named Inini after a tributary of the much larger Maroni River, which forms the border with Surinam in the west.

Inini was twice the size of Belgium by surface area, but still had only 3,000 inhabitants, not including some indigenous people, whom nobody had bothered trying to count. They lived in small, scattered villages deep in the rainforest, belonged to the Arawak, Kalina, Emerillon, Palikur, Wayampi and Wayana tribes, and lived off the natural resources in various ways. While the Wayampi tribe were slash-and-burn farmers, the Emerillon people were primarily hunters and bowfishers. The villages housed between ten and a hundred individuals. They were built in clearings by the riverbanks and generally consisted of large shared houses, oval and cool, built from arm-thick branches and thatched with palm leaves.

The local people knew the natural environment, but it was seen as a hopeless project to use them to clear roads and build railways in Inini. Prisoners were thus brought in to form the workforce.

On 3 June 1931, the steamer *La Martinière* arrives with 523 Annamites[188] from Indochina after thirty-five days at sea. All of them have been jailed for rebellious activity against the French colonial bosses. One of them is Nguyen Dac Bang, who came from a village in the Son Duong district in the far north of Vietnam, close to the border with China. As he recalled it, 'We arrived at our penitentiary home upstream from St Laurent within a few weeks of our departure from Cayenne. The river was beautiful with hundreds of islets along the stream.'[189]

Nguyen and his fellow prisoners are set to work at once, building prison camps and clearing the land to grow their own food. After that, they are sent out to various road and railway projects. It rains every day and the temperature rarely falls below 30 °C (85 °F). Many die of malaria, but the situation could have been worse. Nobody starves. The camps are not enclosed because the jungle is seen as good enough insurance against escape, and in between their shifts the prisoners can hunt and fish as much as they like.

But there's no question of their returning home once they've served their sentence. Under the Doublage Act they must remain in the country for a period equivalent to the length of their sentence if it is shorter than eight years, and for the rest of their lives if it is longer than that. Admittedly, they are given both land and domestic animals by the French authorities, and even get help bringing their wives and children over from Indochina. But they are not allowed to leave. Eventually war breaks out in Europe; Inini drifts into a new status, as a colony of the German-friendly Vichy regime in France.

One night, Nguyen manages to escape and over the course of several weeks he makes his way to British Guiana in the north. There, he seeks asylum by promising loyalty to General de Gaulle's Free France. Eventually he opens a Franco-Oriental restaurant in the port of Georgetown and marries a local woman.

1931: Overprint on a 1929 stamp from French Guiana featuring an archer from the Kalina tribe.

The Inini project was a fiasco from beginning to end. Little land was ever cleared and the few railway lines and roads that were built quickly disintegrated. And today we can count ourselves lucky that it was so, because the jungle here is extremely biodiverse, with more than 1,200 types of trees as well as myriad other plant species and animals such as howler monkeys, pumas and tapirs. It is said that the biodiversity on a single hectare of land here is greater than in the whole of Europe.[190]

French Guiana ceases to be a penal colony in 1946 after growing protests in the homeland. By then, more than 80,000 prisoners have served their sentence here. The country is still French, although the fairly undiplomatic term 'colony' has been abandoned in favour of *départment d'outre-mer* or 'overseas department', and it is divided into arondissements, as if we were in central Paris.

BOOKS

Hy V. Luong (1992)
Revolution in the Village.
Tradition and Transformation in North Vietnam 1925–1988

Henri Charrière (1970)
Papillon

FILM

Papillon (1973)
Directed by Franklin J. Schaffner

//

We arrived at our penitentiary home upstream from St Laurent within a few weeks of our departure from Cayenne. The river was beautiful with hundreds of islets along the stream

NGUYEN DAC BANG

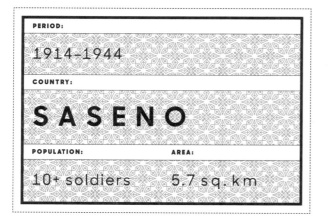

PERIOD:	
1914–1944	
COUNTRY:	
SASENO	
POPULATION:	AREA:
10+ soldiers	5.7 sq. km

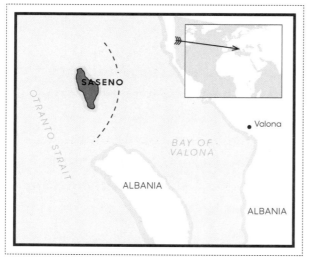

Childhood paradise in the world's most dismal place

Homer's epic poem *The Odyssey*, from 700 BC, describes Odysseus's journey home from the Trojan War. Along the way, he sails past the island of Ogygia, home to a nymph called Calypso, who is the daughter of the Titan Atlas. She captures the ship and puts the warriors on a diet of bread and water for seven years.

Historians are unanimous in the view that much of the Odyssey is based on actual events, and Ogygia is said to be identical to the little island of Saseno by the mouth of the Adriatic Sea.[191] One objection to this must be that Saseno has absolutely no water sources. How even a nymph could survive there, let alone in the company of Odysseus and his thirsty crew, is a mystery.

But although the island is dry as a bone and correspondingly barren, it has always been coveted. Long before modern times, it was already occupied by pirates – perhaps a more sober term for a nymph – then later by great powers such as Turkey, Greece and England, and repeatedly by Italy. Its location just outside the Bay of Valona (the Bay of Vlorë in modern-day Albania) gave it full oversight of shipping through the Otranto Strait, like a kind of Adriatic Gibraltar.

In 1914, the island was being guarded by a dozen poorly equipped Greek soldiers. They surrendered without a struggle when blue-clad, plume-hatted Italian Bersaglieri troops landed one evening late in October. The lack of water was an important reason why the invading force quickly continued to the mainland, where it also occupied the port of Valona (now Vlorë). Valona was recaptured by the Albanians in 1920, and in the years that followed, the Italians on Saseno had to content themselves with the slightly stale water brought over in barrels from Italy to the west.

Saseno measures less than 6 sq. km (2½ sq. miles) and emerges from the sea like the back of a mangy brown camel, its two humps rising to a height of just over 300 m (1,000 ft). On the western side, the Otranto Strait is met by steep cliffs, while the coast facing Albania in the east is calmer, with a narrow, stony shore between two sheltered bays. St Nicholas Bay in the north was viewed as the best, and was equipped with a mole and a quay.

And a naval base was soon built here, initially for small motor torpedo boats. The base was reinforced with a flotilla of submarines after Mussolini took power in Italy in 1922 and declared, in good, old-fashioned Latin, that the Mediterranean was *Mare Nostrum* – 'Our Sea'.[192] U-boats were viewed as a crucial component of this strategy.

My stamp bears a portrait of King Victor Emmanuel III of Italy, with a well-groomed moustache and a courageous gaze. But the image is misleading, because he is generally known to have been a shy and reserved person. He disliked politics and kept his distance from it. One of the few exceptions to this was the cautious support he offered Mussolini, who spent the following years wreaking havoc at will. The plain, simple overprint of 'Saseno' was only used in 1922. After that, they switched to regular Italian stamps.

My specimen was most likely used on a letter from a marine to his family back home. The censor made sure it didn't include any descriptions of exhausting patrols in rough seas north along the Balkan coast. The sender, for his part, probably also avoided mentioning his ill-fated trysts with a soldier in the neighbouring barracks. But perhaps he told them about the swordfish they caught just off Corfu. They'd used a rotten mozzarella as bait and the fish had bitten right away. In the end, it's all about missing people, homesickness and unbearable boredom. For many conscripts, Saseno was the most dismal place in the world.

One person who took a quite different view was Rina Durante. She moved to the island as a three-year-old with her mother, father and three sisters – the only civilians among 1,500 soldiers. Her father was the commanding officer and they lived in a little house on the top of the southern hump, far away from the barracks – she said it was like those towers you only read about in romantic novels.

Rina Durante went on to become a notable journalist and author. She was a socialist and feminist who sympathized with the student radicals of 1968. She constantly harked back to her childhood experiences on the island, monochrome yellow in the summer when the broom was in flower, 'like a gold nugget in the azure sea.'[193]

She recalled the rich, if specialized, fauna: the brown European copper skink, the Dalmatian wall lizard and the green Balkan lizard, rarely more than 20 cm (8 in.) long. She remembered the wire-haired cat she got from a sailor and was allowed to keep despite her father's objections. She remembered the sisterly love and bathing trips with plenty of diving. Rina loved Saseno, which the family had to leave in the end when the Second World War began in 1939.

For a period from 1943, the Germans took over the island, which was then captured by Albanian forces a year later and renamed Sazan.

During the early years of the Cold War, the Soviet navy established a major U-boat base here. This was later enlarged with the addition of a factory producing biological and chemical weapons. After a rapid cooling in relations between the Soviet Union and Albania, the base was closed in 1961. After that, the Albanians ran the facility themselves for several years, with support from China.

Nowadays, the quay in St Nicholas Bay has a little coastguard base, managed jointly by Albania and Italy. Up on the nearest hump lie the remains of a group of faded yellow military buildings in functional style, and here and there some much more intact specimens of the specially constructed Albanian bunkers for civilians, thousands of which can be found elsewhere on the mainland. And everywhere, scattered about at regular intervals, are piles of rusting scrap metal, interspersed with mounds of gas masks from Soviet weapon experiments.

1922: Overprint on an Italian stamp from 1906 bearing a portrait of King Victor Emmanuel III.

The island looks more dingy than ever, and things can only get worse. Forecasts indicate that the southern Adriatic will see a severe reduction in rainfall. At the same time, the temperature is set to rise considerably over the course of this century. Soon, there'll be nothing left but a cloud of dust. This wouldn't be a problem for Greek gods, and would almost certainly be good enough for Rina Durante, who wanted, above all else, to see her island again. She made repeated attempts, even after the Iron Curtain had descended, but was always rebuffed because of the island's military significance.

Even so, some years after Rina's death, the author and filmmaker Caterina Gerardi – a close friend of Rina's – managed to get permission to land there. She took a film crew with her and used the material in a documentary about Rina's childhood.

BOOKS

David Abulafia (2011)
The Great Sea: A Human History of the Mediterranean

Caterina Gerardi (2013)
L'Isola di Rina. Ritorno a Saseno
('Rina's Island. Return to Saseno'; with DVD)

///

Like a gold nugget in the azure sea

RINA DURANTE

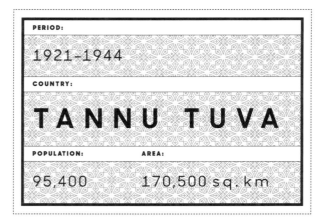

PERIOD:

1921–1944

COUNTRY:

TANNU TUVA

POPULATION: AREA:

95,400   170,500 sq. km

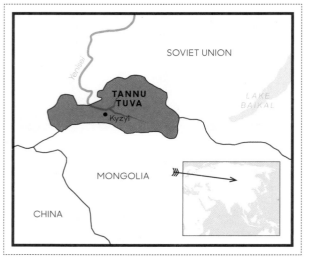

SOVIET UNION

Yenisei

TANNU TUVA

Kyzyl

LAKE BAIKAL

MONGOLIA

CHINA

Closed country with eccentric stamps

In his 1931 book, *Reise ins Asiatische Tuwa* ('Journey to Asian Tuwa'), the Austrian writer Otto Mänchen-Helfen tells of a rich, sporty English adventurer – a bit like a hero from a Jules Verne novel. He travels with a single goal in mind: to place a monument in the geographic centre of all the parts of the world with the inscription 'I was here at the centre of this continent'.[194] It is easy to picture him: clean-shaven, tanned, a mop of fair hair and slightly worn khaki trousers laced up the sides. He peers out across the immense carpet of grass that stretches as far as the Altai Mountains in the south. He stands there, self-satisfied, hands on hips. He has already dealt with Africa and North and South America. Now Asia, too, has been conquered.

The continent's midpoint is said to be a hilltop right beside the village of Saldam in Tannu Tuva. The memorial stone placed there will later be removed and replaced with a concrete Soviet sculpture.

In the chaos that followed the Russian Revolution, Tannu Tuva was proclaimed an autonomous republic in 1921, with the Lamaist monk Donduk Kuular as prime minister and Buddhism as the state religion. Even so, the new country was very Soviet-friendly, having been part of the Tsarist Russian protectorate of Uriankhai since 1911. Before that, the area had been alternately under Turkic, Chinese and Mongolian rule. It was the size of Great Britain and consisted, in addition to the grassy plains, of occasional patches of forest alongside the small rivers that mark the source of the great Yenisei River. The population was largely nomadic, with a strong penchant for shamanism. They travelled round with their herds of camels, sheep and longhaired yaks, and lived in yurts.

A yurt is a spacious tent that is easy to dismantle and transport by pack camel. Its construction has remained unchanged for 3,000 years, and is based on a latticework of criss-crossed laths that form an encircling wall, with a gently sloping conical roof. The whole structure is covered with a layer of thick wool felt, which keeps out both rain and winter cold. The interior is furnished with a circle of benches around a central fireplace, where the Tuvans prepare their meals of meat and dairy products. During the evenings, they enjoy their favourite delicacies of butter tea and Tsampa rolls in the dim light of the wax lamps.

Many families were beginning to give up the nomadic life. There was well-paid work to be had in the mines outside the capital of Kyzyl, and in the grassy hills north of the city, hundreds of yurts popped up. Many of them were decorated in bright colours with geometric patterns, as well as images of lions and tigers, fiery sun eagles and hissing dragons. They presented a great contrast to the unpainted, much more stolid wooden houses within the city, inhabited almost exclusively by Russian immigrants.

In 1944, Tannu Tuva was annexed by the rapidly expanding Soviet Union and lost its autonomy for good. Quite how this happened is a little unclear, but it almost certainly had something to do with newly discovered natural resources – primarily uranium. It is important to remember that the world was then on the brink of the Atomic Age.

Otto Mänchen-Helfen was one of the few West Europeans who got to see the autonomous state of Tannu Tuva with his own eyes. And even in 1929, he'd had great difficulties obtaining a visa: 'I ran to thousands of agencies and offices; obtained certificates, stamps, signatures and attestations; and filled in hundreds of columns of questionnaires ("What did you do in the year 1917 and why?").'[195]

After the Soviets took over, the area was entirely shut off. The Cold War was under way, and the Americans assumed that a large atomic weapons facility had been established in the area, the equivalent to Los Alamos in the USA.

On the other side of the planet, the American physicist and Nobel Prize winner Richard Feynmann confesses that he is obsessed with the idea of visiting Tannu Tuva, almost pathologically at times. After repeated failed attempts, a book detailing the quest, *Tuva or Bust!*, is published in 1991. And if we are to take him at his word – as, perhaps, we must – his interest is not primarily professional in nature: he is simply fascinated by the unique language, the two-tone throat singing and, of course, the stamps.

The stamps of Tannu Tuva developed into something unique. The first issues, in 1926, bore images of the Buddhist wheel of life, as well as numbers and text in the Hudum alphabet. Not especially original, in other words. But then came a series of surprisingly modern stamps, large and generally triangular or diamond-shaped. They bear exuberant depictions of camels, lynxes, bears, yaks, horse racing, hunting and wrestling. The assumption is that the idea came from the Hungarian stamp-collector, Bela Sekula, who was better known as a great forger of valuable Ethiopian stamps.[196]

The stamps bear the inscription 'Postage Tuva' in Roman script, as is usual on European stamps elsewhere. And there is little doubt that most are sold directly to collectors without passing through the country at all. All of them are designed in Moscow, printed in Moscow and also often postmarked Moscow. There are even motifs of airships over the steppe landscape, and camels racing trains, despite the absence of any evidence to indicate that Tannu Tuva was ever visited by an airship, or that so much as a single metre of railway track was ever laid in the country.

The stamps that do have some local colour often prove to be nothing more than mirror images of Otto Mänchen-Helfen's photographs. The stamp with the camel driver is originally taken from his book. Although there was little need for stamps in Tannu Tuva, I reckon my specimen has actually been in the country. It isn't just postmarked but is also simply too worn and ragged to have made its way straight into a stamp album.

Today, Tannu Tuva operates as a satellite republic of the Russian Federation. It has a population of just over 300,000, of whom two-thirds are deemed to be ethnic Tuvans. Many

1936: Motif with camel driver, based on a photograph in Otto Mänchen-Helfen's 1931 book.

still live as nomads, while the Russians pursue mining and more conventional agriculture.

The Norwegian Johnny Haglund travelled through the area in the early 2000s, and maintained that the small villages built up under Stalin had barely seen a spade or hammer since. The buildings, roads, electricity supply and sewage system were either out of order or in a wretched state. But the villages were still inhabited and people drank their butter tea and still kept their shamans. The latter had abandoned their ritual slippers spun from asbestos, known as rockwool, and no longer danced on burning coals, but they hadn't stopped cleansing souls: Haglund, who had been warned in advance not to go outdoors after dark, defied the warnings and quickly met a couple of shamans equipped with drums and whips. They at once insisted that he must be cleansed and gave him a thorough going-over, following the well-known principle of 'casting out evil with evil'.[197]

//

I ran to thousands of agencies and offices; obtained certificates, stamps, signatures and attestations; and filled in hundreds of columns of questionnaires ('What did you do in the year 1917 and why?')

OTTO MÄNCHEN-HELFEN

BOOKS

Otto Mänchen-Helfen (1931)
Reise ins Asiatische Tuwa
('Journey to Asian Tuva')

Ralph Leighton (1991)
Tuva or Bust! (including throat-singing CD)

BUTTER TEA (FIVE PORTIONS)

100 g (4 oz) tea leaves
1 l (35 fl. oz) water
200 g (7 oz) butter (preferably from yaks)
Salt

Mix the tea leaves in the water and boil for twelve hours, skimming off the scum. Top up with water as needed. Pour the mixture into a closed container with the butter and a little salt, then shake. It should have the consistency of thick oil. Serve in a ceramic mug.

TSAMPA

Butter tea
Barley meal

Toast the barley meal in a frying pan on a low heat. Pour a little butter tea into the bottom of a bowl then stir in the meal and shape into rolls. Keep adding tea until the rolls become moist and slightly sticky. Eat with butter tea.

PERIOD:

1923–1956

COUNTRY:

TANGIER INTERNATIONAL ZONE

POPULATION:

150,000

AREA:

373 sq. km

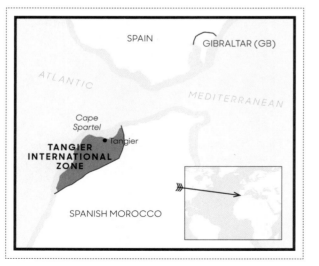

SPAIN

GIBRALTAR (GB)

ATLANTIC

MEDITERRANEAN

Cape Spartel

• Tangier

TANGIER INTERNATIONAL ZONE

SPANISH MOROCCO

A modern-day Sodom

With yellow masonary shining, the lighthouse on Cape Spartel stands on a cliff some 300 m (1,000 ft) above the turbulent Atlantic Ocean. The tower containing the verdigris-coated lantern is square and built in the style of a Moorish fortress, complete with embrasures. The structure was completed in 1864, an international collaboration in which the USA and Europe's major shipping nations – among them Britain, France and Spain – signed a reciprocal agreement for its management and maintenance in perpetuity.

Far to the north you can see the mouth of the Mediterranean, as well as the Spanish mainland and Gibraltar. And if you turn around, you gaze across a landscape that was entirely covered by dense forest 2,000 years ago, and roamed by great herds of elephant. At the beginning of the 1900s, the area looks much more barren, and there are signs that a desert is forming. To the west lies Tangier, its white houses stacked like shoeboxes in the hills around the harbour. From a distance, it is impossible to make out what is going on there, but the farmers and locals in the periphery must have viewed what was then called the Tangier International Zone as something like a new Sodom, a morass of sin – the very manifestation of Allah's wrath.

Many people had wanted to have a piece of this headland, including the British, who already had Gibraltar. After Germany's Kaiser Wilhelm began to cultivate an association with the local Sharif in Tangier, they feared that their free access in and out of the Mediterranean might be under threat.

The British felt safer after their victory in the First World War, but nonetheless took the initiative with the creation of the Tangier International Zone. It was formally established in 1923 through an agreement between the sultan of Morocco and the same countries that had previously taken responsibility for the lighthouse. The zone would encompass the city of Tangier and the immediately surrounding areas. It would be entirely demilitarized and administered by diplomats from the different signatory countries, in collaboration with a small group of local representatives. And the whole thing would follow the principle of the least possible state intervention. All forms of economic regulation were ruled out, as was anything that smacked of taxation or tariffs. That also eliminated the basis for any kind of social security net related to health and poverty. What little remained of the legal system was managed by four international judges and the cases had to be extremely serious to be considered at all.

The zone didn't have its own postal service either but three parallel systems: one British, one Spanish and one French. And it was up to the inhabitants themselves to decide which one they wanted to use. It was said that the Spanish stamps were cheapest and the British the most expensive, but also the most reliable. And the French stamps were unquestionably the most artistic.[198] While the British used stamps from home overprinted with the word Tangier, and followed their tradition of using solemn portraits of monarchs, the French based their stamps on issues from the colony of French Morocco. Mine is designed by Luc-Olivier Merson, and the postmark partially conceals a seated Berber woman on the right. She is staring slightly flirtatiously at the buyer of the stamp. With her strong upper arms and clad in something reminiscent of chain mail, she looks more than ready to deal with the harvest season. The Spanish quickly followed up this use of local colour with issues specific to Tangier, including a portrait of an anonymous Moor. He is looking over his shoulder, evident fear in his gaze. We can never know whether this was intentional on the designer's part, but there is little doubt that this portrait sums up the prevailing atmosphere – at least among the indigenous population. Because at least one in three of Tangier's inhabitants was involved in some shady business or another.[199] Most commonly, this was smuggling, money-laundering or international arms dealing. An array of international banks and several thousand postbox companies stood ready to offer their services and take care of all the cash flows.

The economic liberalism was accompanied by a culture that was also liberally inclined. Camel caravans laden with opium and hashish came in regularly from the Rif Mountains in the south, and the city centre soon had more than thirty brothels for both heterosexuals and homosexuals, generally offering child prostitutes as well.

The Tangier International Zone therefore attracted a motley selection of characters who weren't just after economic profit but also wanted their special requirements met. In addition, there were many who had fled prison sentences in their own countries for murder, bankruptcy, war crimes, conscientious objection or prohibited political activism. It all added up to 'a place where nations, languages and cultures could mix promiscuously'.[200] And the package included a growing group of eccentrics, beatniks and hipsters from the USA. One of them was author Paul Bowles, who bought himself a little house in the upper part of the old town, the Medina – 'A very small and uncomfortable shoe box stood on end'.[201] He loved Tangier from the first instant:

> Its passageways were full of people in bright outlandish costumes.... The back streets of the Medina, crooked, sometimes leading through short tunnels beneath the houses, sometimes up long flights of stairs, lend themselves to solitary speculative walks.... At the end of each street there is almost always a natural view, so that the eye automatically skims over that which is near at hand to dwell on a vignette of harbour with ships, or mountain ranges, or sea with distant coastline.[202]

Bowles was joined by fellow writers Truman Capote, Tennessee Williams, Allen Ginsberg and William Burroughs, who all hurled themselves into an extravagant social life bankrolled by filthy rich patrons such as Barbara Hutton,

1936: Overprint on a stamp of Edward VIII from the same year, issued by the British post office.

1948: Portrait of a Moor on an issue from the Spanish post office.

1918: Overprint on a 1902 stamp from French Morocco, issued by the French post office.

the Woolworth heiress. And when they weren't partying they carried on writing what would later become cult books – with all the concentration that required. Few cities have meant more to American literature than Tangier.[203]

It all came to an abrupt end on 29 October 1956. The rest of Morocco had recently gained its independence from the colonial powers of Spain and France. It was clear that the Tangier International Zone could not continue to exist, even under a fairly liberal Islamic regime. The bordellos were closed overnight, and all trade in narcotics was prohibited. What little remained of western extravagance was handled by the local Coca-Cola bottling plant, which was quick to donate a thousand crates of soft drinks to the popular celebration that followed.[204]

After that, Tangier entered a phase of industrialization and modernization. The city changed its appearance entirely. Paul Bowles, who hadn't yet managed to leave, nonetheless found some consolation:

There must be few places in the world which have altered visually to such an extent in the past quarter of a century.... With everything old being systematically destroyed (and the new European buildings are almost without exception eyesores, while the ones the Moroccans put up are even worse), how is it that Tangier escapes becoming an aesthetic nightmare?[205]

BOOKS

Paul Bowles (1958)
The Worlds of Tangier

Graham Stuart (1931)
The International City of Tangier

FILM

Tangier (1946)
Directed by George Waggner

//

At the end of each street there is almost always a natural view, so that the eye automatically skims over that which is near at hand to dwell on a vignette of harbour with ships, or mountain ranges, or sea with distant coastline

PAUL BOWLES

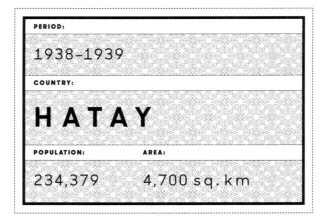

PERIOD:
1938-1939

COUNTRY:
HATAY

POPULATION:	AREA:
234,379	4,700 sq. km

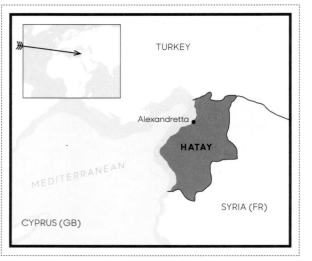

TURKEY

Alexandretta

HATAY

MEDITERRANEAN

SYRIA (FR)

CYPRUS (GB)

Genocide and a rigged referendum

On 15 September 1915, the Ottoman Secretary of the Interior, Talaat Pasha, issued a directive on the deportation of all Armenians living in Turkey:

> Anybody who opposes this order cannot be reckoned a friend of the regime. Regardless of whether they are women, children or sick, no matter how grim the means of destruction can seem, an end must be made to their existence, without heed to feelings or conscience.[206]

After several hundred years of flourishing ethnic diversity, a strongly nationalistic movement had developed in the Turkish part of the Ottoman Empire. It demanded ethnic cleansing.[207] Initially, it was a matter of getting rid of the Armenians, an increasingly numerous Caucasian group. Before the end of 1916, between half a million and a million of them were killed in the massacre that would later be known as the Armenian genocide.

The persecution had extended down as far as the Hatay area in the south. This was the gateway to the Arabian Peninsula, where military leaders such as Alexander the Great and Richard the Lionheart had passed through

186

with their armies. And, every time, they had left the area ravaged – there was a lot worth taking from the extensive and fertile shores of the Orontes River. At the same time, the population had become an ever-more diverse mixture of Syrians, Greeks, Circassians, Jews, Kurds and Armenians – in addition to a large group of Turks.

After the Ottomans were defeated in the First World War, France and England carved up the central parts of the Middle East between them. The basis for division was determined by oil, both deposits and transport routes. The French got the northern sector, including the Hatay area, which they named Alexandretta after the port of the same name. They were quickly challenged by the Turkish Republic, which had grown out of the ruins of the Ottoman Empire. The leaders of the republic were no less nationalistically inclined than their predecessors, and early in the 1930s they declared that the Hatay area had been a Turkish homeland for forty generations, and that it was now time for it to return to Turkish rule.

In order to calm things down, the League of Nations, France and Great Britain drew up a constitution that would be the basis for establishing a neutral and independent country in the area.

The Republic of Hatay, Hatay Devleti in Turkish, was proclaimed on 4 July 1938. To secure democratic elections, the League of Nations sent a delegation to register all men over twenty-one with voting rights. Jonas Lie, then a police official, was Norway's representative. He had also made a name for himself as a talented crime writer under the pseudonym Max Mauser, and had just published his novel *Fetish*, set in the African jungle. The delegation took the Orient Express from Berlin, giving Jonas Lie time to absorb himself in T. E. Lawrence's *The Seven Pillars of Wisdom*, which partly took place in the area he was travelling to.[208] Once there, he was given the task of registering those entitled to vote in the Amanus Mountains:

> The landscape lies exhausted in the oppressive heat, the sun burns from a sky that has not seen a cloud for months, it scorches, white-hot and annihilating, over every living thing.... Before us lies the mighty plain, surrounded by mountains. The Orontes winds its sluggish, dirty yellow ribbon across it, on its way to the Mediterranean.[209]

In the Amanus Mountains is a group of Armenian villages. During the devastation caused by the Ottomans during the First World War, the inhabitants fled to the top of Musa Dagh mountain and entrenched themselves there for forty days until they were eventually rescued by French naval forces.[210] Now many of them had returned.

Between the lines, we can detect hints of the crime writer in Jonas Lie's description of his meeting with the Armenian chief, Kalustian, in the village of Bitas:

> He was a broad-shouldered, tall, friendly man in his prime, with a powerful, weather-beaten face. Passion, grief and anxiety had chiselled deep furrows. His voice was deep with an undertone of intensity.[211]

Lie, of course, takes the time to inspect the chief's bookshelves. He's impressed: 'Neither Hitler's *Mein Kampf* nor Mussolini's war journal were missing from this Armenian leader's collection.'[212]

In the election, the ethnic Turks win a parliamentary majority. They immediately introduce Turkish laws, Turkish currency and Turkish as the main language. In Turkey, President Kemal Atatürk has already finished his sketch of the national flag and he orders the newly formed republic to adopt a series of stamps with himself as their motif. Turkey is a secular state, and Atatürk appears in refined European clothing, with a pale bow tie over a modest shirt collar. At first glance, he looks surprisingly mild. He positively oozes democracy. But at the same time, there is something glassy and cold about it all.

The election result terrifies the Armenians. Along with large groups of Arabs, Greeks, Jews and Kurds, many of them flee across the borders, to the south and east. This exodus is hastened by the large Turkish forces that are sent in to uphold law and order.

Eventually, compelling proof emerges that the election was fixed through the use of falsified polling lists, the bribery of Alawites and the systematic exclusion of both Arabs and Armenians.[213] But none of this receives the attention of the representatives of the League of Nations, and the Turks win the day. Later that same autumn, they win another plebiscite, this time on whether Hatay should permanently become part of Turkey. France has few objections, but takes the opportunity to ensure that Turkey

1939: Overprint on a Turkish stamp from 1931 bearing a portrait of President Kemal Atatürk.

signs a treaty guaranteeing its neutrality in the event that war breaks out again in Europe.[214] On 29 June 1939, the parliament in Hatay is formally dissolved and the country is placed under Turkish rule. Here, it soon acquires the status of a separate province.

Back home in Norway, Jonas Lie eventually abandoned his crime-writing career. He became a member of Nasjonal

Samling, Norway's national socialist party, and later became a cabinet minister in Quisling's government.

In the Province of Hatay, severe restrictions were imposed to reinforce the position of Turkish culture and language. For a long time, Turkish was mandatory even in private conversations. There has been some softening over the years, but Turkish is still the only language used in schools.

BOOKS

Franz Werfel (1934)
The Forty Days of Musa Dagh

Jonas Lie (1940)
I 'fred' og ufred ('In Peace and Strife')

///

**The landscape lies exhausted
in the oppressive heat, the sun
burns from a sky that has not seen
a cloud for months, it scorches,
white-hot and annihilating,
over every living thing**

JONAS LIE

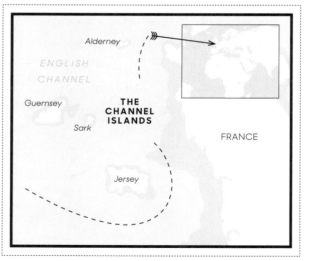

Sabotage with stamps

....

For the German parachutists slowly descending through the light cloud in summer 1940, the Channel Islands must have looked like a collection of intensely green grassy hillocks scattered at random across the blue sea. And the further they descended, the clearer it would have become that the main industry here must be agriculture, and that it was an easy business. It was all gentle slopes with no sign of mountains or forest areas. And at the end of the shallow coves lay small, whitewashed villages and the occasional larger harbour town with quays and breakwater.

Julia Tremayne lives on the island of Sark, in the middle of the group of islands. On 3 July 1940, she summarizes the events of recent days in her diary:

> Everybody says they seem very nice and if we keep to all the rules laid down, things will go on much as usual. No-one must be out after 11 p.m., no spirits sold in hotels, only beer, all guns to be given up, the national anthem is not to be sung.... Worst of all the swastika is flying over Bel Air. Who would have thought we would have lived to see that in this beautiful little Island that I have loved for nearly forty years.[215]

After several hundred years of being plundered by Vikings and Norman dukes, the Channel Islands came under British rule in the 1200s. Even so, they retained a degree of autonomy, with two official districts, or bailiwicks, each ruled by a bailiff selected by the British. In the south was Jersey, named after the largest island in the group, and in the north was Guernsey, named for the second largest.

At the outbreak of the Second World War, 92,000 people were living on the Channel Islands. After withdrawing from the European continent, the British declared that the islands played no strategic role one way or another. In June 1940, a mass evacuation took place, in which around twenty-five per cent of the population was transported by ship to England. These were almost all children, as well as young boys and men of conscription age.

The Germans didn't view the Channel Islands as a strategic coup either. For Hitler, it was primarily about the propaganda gain of occupying his first few patches of British soil. So everything proceeded peacefully: not a shot was fired. And the Germans only made changes that were absolutely necessary. In addition to limiting sales of spirits, they changed the time zone from Greenwich Mean Time to Central European Time, and switched driving from the left- to the right-hand side of the road. They also set to work building bunkers and tunnels that were supposed to form part of the so-called Atlantic Wall, a fortification of several hundred coastal forts that was to stretch from the Spanish border in the south to Finnmark in the north. The work was done by prisoners-of-war from Eastern Europe and North Africa, who were kept in several large camps.

The Germans felt secure. Most of the young men had left the island, and the landscape was easy to keep under surveillance and ill-suited to resistance fighting. Their main problem was all the V-signs painted on the walls and lampposts under the cover of darkness. The Germans dealt with this by appealing for informers, putting up posters on all public buildings:

> A reward will be given to any person giving information about anyone who marks on any visible place the letter V or any other words or signs calculated to offend the German Authorities.[216]

Like rulers elsewhere, they also started issuing stamps. To avoid provoking the inhabitants unnecessarily, they dropped the most obvious solution of using German stamps with portraits of Hindenburg, Mutter Germania or even Hitler himself. Instead, they turned to local designers.

On Guernsey, Edward William Vaudin was given the job. He was probably a patriot, because we can see that he exploited the situation to start his own small and very private resistance effort. If we magnify the stamps, we can just about see a microscopic V in each of the corners. Still, they were so small that the Germans either didn't see them or chose to overlook the matter. And it's uncertain whether other people noticed the sabotage, since the design, paper quality and perforations were so shoddy.

The greatest provocation, though, was the central motif of three lions. The Germans assumed this was a reference to the local bailiff's family coat of arms and let it pass. In fact, it was a direct copy of the coat of arms of the British king, George VI, which had been handed down since the times of Richard the Lionheart.

On Jersey, the designer Edmund Blampied was even more cryptic when he set to work after Field Commander Knackfuss gave him the job of producing a series of stamps with illustrations of local landscapes. One motif of seaweed gatherers on the threepenny stamp incorporated an inverted V over the value, as well as a pair of flourishes that could be read as the initials GR for George Rex, in other words probably a tribute to the king.

At home on Sark, Julia Tremayne continues to jot down her impressions from the island, where the large German contingent have now taken lodgings in many private homes. 'I expect the German troops are revelling in the luxury – plenty of good Sark butter, home-killed meat, home-made bread, gallons of milk and the shops well-stocked.'[217]

The island's aristocratic leader, the Dame of Sark, had run it like her own little feudal society for many years. She didn't like drunkenness and had banned it long before. At the same time, she was working to transform the island into an exclusive tourist destination, and had also placed a prohibition on the use of noisy vehicles. All travel should be by foot or if necessary by horse and cart. The Germans largely accepted her decrees. They even agreed to bow, kiss her hand and then bow again when they visited her. And the Dame of Sark was pleased, especially because several of the German officers were of noble extraction. The level of refinement on the island had never been higher.

1941: Local issue from Guernsey with the coat of arms of the British king, George VI.

1943: Local issue from Jersey featuring seaweed collectors.

On D-Day, 6 June 1944, the Allied Forces sailed past the Channel Islands on their way to the beaches of the European mainland. And once they had advanced further into France, the island group was pretty much isolated. The supply lines for food and other goods from the continent were broken. Despite strict rationing, both the islands' inhabitants and the German occupiers endured several months of hunger and want.

The Channel Islands were liberated before the Second World War ended in Europe – Sark as late as 10 May 1945. As those who had been evacuated returned over the late summer and autumn, it became clear that much had changed. Property ownership was in a mess and the children had lost their local dialects.

Bit by bit, things sorted themselves out. Between the ruins of the German fortifications, the tourist industry reached new heights while the archipelago established itself as a tax haven along the lines of Bermuda. And on Sark, a handful of tractors received special dispensation to waive the prohibition on motor traffic.

BOOK

Simon Hamon (2015)
Channel Islands Invaded: The German Attack on the British Islands in 1940 Told Through Eye-Witness Accounts, Newspaper Reports, Parliamentary Debates, Memoirs and Diaries

//

Worst of all the swastika is flying over Bel Air. Who would have thought we would have lived to see that in this beautiful little Island that I have loved for nearly forty years

JULIA TREMAYNE

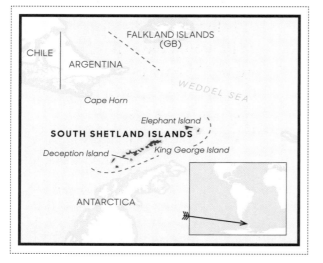

Penguins in the furnace

At first it reminds me of a classic Disney cartoon where the toys in a Christmas present factory are queuing up to be painted by eager elves. In the South Shetland Islands, though, these aren't toys but real penguins – dressed as always in their suits, inquisitive, chattering and erect. Unfortunately they're not waiting in line to be painted, but to serve as fuel in the enormous cod liver oil refinery on Deception Island. They are hoisted up by their wings and heaved in one after the other. The fatty bundles make the bonfires flare.

None of the areas in this book has seen more blood than the South Shetland Islands, if we include animals in the grim calculation. In addition to the penguins, enormous numbers of seals and whales were caught and slaughtered up until the 1960s, to be used as raw material for cod liver oil, margarine and feed concentrate. A single blue whale contains 10,000 litres of blood. Without wishing to draw comparisons, by the way, this corresponds to 2,000 beings; or to put it another way, the combined blood loss of the Norwegian military forces throughout the whole of the Second World War.

Even in the 1914–1915 season, as many as 1,800 blue whales were dragged ashore on the South Shetland Islands.[218]

Towards 1930, the number had doubled, supplemented by the capture of other species, such as finback, humpback and sperm whales.

The South Shetland Islands lie about 100 km (60 miles) off the Antarctic continent and are a continuation of the mountains of the Andes in the north. The archipelago consists of a dozen larger and a number of smaller islands, whose combined area is a little larger than that of Cornwall. Although most of the land is covered with permanent glaciers and the surrounding seas are frozen throughout the winter half of the year, there is plenty of life here, on both land and sea. Through the summer, hundreds of types of lichen colour the mountainsides orange, yellow and rust red, and the numerous cliffs teem with gulls, petrels and storm petrels.

It was the large population of fur seals that first drew British trappers to the islands in the 1820s. Later came the whalers. And it was whaling interests that prompted the Norwegian government to seek a clarification of the legal situation in the area just after the dissolution of the union with Sweden in 1905. Until then, the Antarctic had been treated as ownerless territory, a *terra nullius*. First of all Norway went to its big brother, England, which – after pausing briefly for thought and perhaps from force of habit – declared that the South Shetland Islands should be considered British. But until further notice, the English were not especially particular about international recognition for their claim. And the Norwegian whalers were allowed to continue as before.

A certain Axel F. Mathiesen writes about a morning in the field, whaling. He is standing on the bridge and watching schools of whales blowing: 'Frozen breath! How wonderfully it harmonizes with the white nature out here.'[219]

Once the day's catch of whale carcasses has been made fast alongside, the ship sails to Deception Island in the south of the archipelago. This isn't one of the larger islands, but has the best harbour in the area. It is volcanic in origin: a crater that was flooded and is linked to the sea by a channel wide enough for all ships to pass through. Inside lies the bay, an area of more than 3,000 ha (7,500 acres), sheltered and with first-class harbour conditions. The ash-black mountainsides rise nearly 500 m (1,650 ft) into the air. There's smoke and steam here and there, and the air carries a faint whiff of sulphur.

By the time the first Norwegian factory station, Hektor, was set up on Deception Island in 1913, the beaches were already strewn with white whale skeletons – crania, vertebrae and ribs. They shone in the sun, polished by the ocean and seabirds. The buildings were constructed on a sandy plain in the south of the bay, not far away from a large penguin colony, and consisted of a barracks for the crew, a mess, a pigsty, workshops and factory buildings. And on a hilltop above it all stood a little red house flying the Union Jack. Here, a British inspector dutifully spent the whaling season, from November to the end of February.

There were generally over 2,000 men at work. The whale carcasses were cut up roughly on the flensing deck down by the shore. After that the meat was scraped off and the blubber cooked down to whale oil. The workers waded through bloody water and slipped in fat. The stench was intense and sour.

At home in Norway, the ship owners sat counting their money. And there was more and more of it – right up until the Depression years around 1930, when the price of whale oil gradually began to sink. And suddenly, the whole thing came to a halt. In 1931, the Hektor whaling station was closed and abandoned.

A couple of years later, the Norwegian aviator Bernt Balchen stopped off here to take part in one of Australian Richard E. Byrd's many flying expeditions in the Antarctic. The island was deserted, but most of the buildings were intact, and the sick bay could have reopened at the drop of a hat, since all the equipment had been liberally coated in fat. On the other hand, Balchen found that most of the operating tables and sickbeds were smeared with excrement.[220] He reckoned that somebody had wanted to protest against Norwegian whaling, and thought it must be the English, Chileans or Argentinians, because they were visiting the islands ever more frequently. The ownership dispute over the archipelago had become more intense after research expeditions had indicated that there might be oil, coal and copper deposits.

Chile makes the first move in the battle for sovereignty in 1940, followed by Argentina in 1942. It all starts out in quite civilized fashion. The Chileans issue proclamations, while the Argentineans go to Deception Island and place a metal cylinder there containing a formal claim over all the South Shetland Islands. This is requisitioned by the British

1944: Copy with overprint on a 1938 stamp from the Falkland Islands, which shows the research ship, the William Scoresby.

and sent back. The Argentineans respond by planting the Argentinian flag on the island.

Meanwhile, the Second World War is in full swing and the British are afraid that the German-friendly Argentinians might enable their enemy to establish a naval base in the area.[221] The strategic location close to Cape Horn would make it possible to strike swiftly both in the southern Atlantic Ocean and the Pacific. Therefore, the British themselves station military forces on several of the islands in what is known as Operation Tabarin, in 1944. And then they issue stamps to emphasize the message. They use an overprint of stamps from the Falkland Islands, with a portrait of King

George VI and a selection of artistic motifs. My specimen shows a research ship, the *William Scoresby*, which also played an active role in Operation Tabarin.

After the war, the British continued to patrol the islands and systematically cleared away any huts and equipment that the Argentinians or Chileans might have left behind. They also argued their claim on the basis of historical right, pointing to the seal-hunters of the 1820s. Things took a new turn when Chilean researchers found a couple of arrowheads that appeared to evidence earlier visits from indigenous people living on the South American mainland, although the find proved to have been planted.[222]

The Antarctic Treaty was signed on 1 December 1959 by all twelve states active on the continent. It stipulated that the South Shetland Islands and the rest of the Antarctic could be used by anybody at all in perpetuity, but only for peaceful purposes. Argentina, Chile and Great Britain all signed, but nonetheless maintained their territorial claims over the South Shetland Islands.

Eventually, the islands start to be used as research stations by a number of countries. These stations are most often set up on King George Island, although Deception Island was also used until a fairly large volcanic eruption in 1969. Now that island is almost deserted, although it has become one of the regular stops for the ever-increasing numbers of tourist ships passing through the area. Most of the houses were burnt down or covered in lava. But the huge cod liver oil tanks still tower like rusted knights' helmets above the sloping shore.

BOOK

Peter J. Beck & Clive H. Schofield (1994)
Who Owns Antarctica?
Governing and Managing the Last Continent

//

Frozen breath! How wonderfully it harmonizes with the white nature out here

AXEL F. MATHIESEN

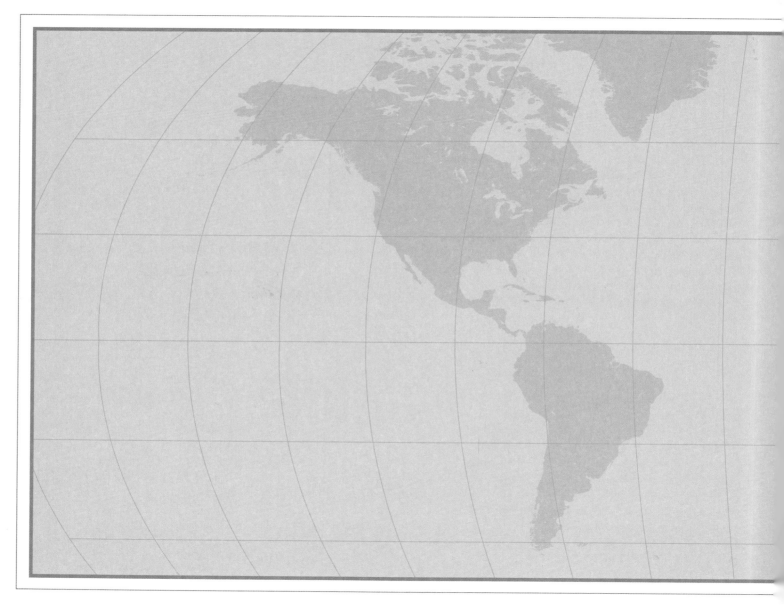

1945 ~to~ 1975

TRIESTE

UPPER YAFA

BIAFRA

SOUTH KASAI

RYUKYU

THE SOUTH MOLUCCAS

PERIOD:

1947–1954

COUNTRY:

TRIESTE

POPULATION: **AREA:**

330,000   738 sq. km

ITALY

Zone A

TRIESTE

• Trieste

YUGOSLAVIA

• Koper

ADRIATIC

Zone B

Rijeka/Fiume •

Istrian Peninsula

A crossroads in history

Nicole, the protagonist of the 1982 erotic film *The Girl from Trieste*,[223] suffers from schizophrenia, making her seem like the incarnation of the city where she lives. Because Trieste, in the far north of the Adriatic, is a place of many faces and with profound internal contradictions, and it has always been this way. The area is a crossroads – no more, no less – where generals and fugitives have flowed back and forth throughout history, just like Danzig in the Baltic Sea and Hatay in the heart of the Mediterranean. This almost suggests empirical grounds for drawing the following conclusion: if you want a quiet life, find a peninsula or a place well inland, but whatever you do, don't live on a bay!

Trieste was founded by the Romans in the second century, ransacked by Huns after the Roman Empire fell, and later ruled in turn by the Byzantines, Carolingians and Venetians, then by Austria and Hungary. Napoleon Bonaparte also dropped in, and then Italy took control after the First World War. These frequent shifts led to a sprawl of cultures and an unusually diverse population. True enough, most were Italians, but there was also a substantial share of Croats, Slovenes and a steadily growing group with no clear ethnicity – as well as a tremendous number of mixed-breed cats.

But on the whole, this was all to the good, according to English travel writer Jan Morris. She lived in Trieste in the 1990s, and tells of a people who are quick to laughter and grateful, without a hint of malice. They have great integrity and are never ruled by changing fashions, public opinion or any form of political correctness.[224]

The author Claudio Magris, who was born and bred in Trieste, describes an absurd atmosphere that is at once proud, splendid and cosmopolitan, blended with melancholy and a slightly resigned atmosphere of the end of days. In his book *Microcosms*, he tells his story from the San Marco café in the centre of town, right beside the park, with 'horse chestnuts, planes and firs – dark waters on which branches and leaves float and into which the birds disappear and sink like stones'.[225] He cites a regular visitor, Austrian author Hermann Bahr, who said he thrived in Trieste because the city gave him the feeling of 'being nowhere'.

According to Magris, the Irish writer James Joyce also feels at home in Trieste, perhaps for the same reason. He lives there for several periods up to 1920 and survives by teaching English to the children of the bourgeoisie. And it is in Trieste that he starts work on his modernistic master-piece, *Ulysses*. The setting is Dublin, but some of the cast of characters are almost certainly drawn from Trieste. The city also left a more personal mark on Joyce, whom Magris quotes as saying: 'And Trieste. Ah, Trieste ate my liver.'[226]

The almost permanent condition of unrest and unpredict-ability left its mark on political relations in the area, too. That is why, after the First World War, the great powers set up the buffer state of Fiume in between the Balkans and Italy, south of the Istrian Peninsula. As we saw earlier, that went awry.

A couple of years after the Second World War, it was Trieste's turn, this time on the north side of Istria. By then, conditions had changed dramatically, both in the area and in the broader political arena. The Prime Minister of Britain, Winston Churchill, had already made his famous Iron Curtain speech at Westminster College in Missouri in 1946: 'From Stettin in the Baltic to Trieste in the Adriatic, an iron curtain has descended across the Continent.'[227]

In January 1947, the UN Security Council announces the creation of the Free Territory of Trieste through Resolution 16, Article 24. The territory comes into being in September of the same year, encompassing an area of 738 sq. km (285 sq. miles) with a total of 330,000 inhabitants. The area is divided into two zones, following the so-called Morgan Line – a line of demarcation drawn after Italy's capitula-tion, which stretched almost to the Austrian border.

Zone A includes the city of Trieste itself, and a narrow strip of coast to the north, while Zone B, more sparsely populated but almost double the area, extends some way out to the northern side of the Istrian Peninsula. Zone A is administered by British and American forces, 10,000 men in all, while Zone B is run by the Yugoslavian army. This implies that the totality is not, in practice, an autonomous country with its own state apparatus.

But Trieste does get its own stamps, albeit still split into zones. Zone B was first up with specially designed May Day stamps that show a robust, jubilant female figure beside the official state symbol, the halberd, against a background of an anchor with a chain. This is issued in three versions, with the text, 'War Government of the Free Territory of Trieste', beneath the image in either Italian, Slovenian or Croatian. Mine is the Slovenian issue, and is postmarked Koper, just south of the border between the zones; the 10,000-strong population of the town is mostly Italian.

Zone A adopts Italian stamps, overprinted with AMG–FTT, which stands for 'Allied Military Government–Free Territory of Trieste'. Mine was originally an Italian stamp from 1945. It depicts Turrita, the personification of Italy, growing from the trunk of an oak tree – an undeniably relevant signal so soon after the collapse of fascism.

The attempt to uphold the free state of Trieste is soon abandoned. The territory is divided up according to an internal agreement between Yugoslavia and Italy in 1954, although this is only formalized long afterwards, through the Osimo Treaty of 1975. Naturally enough, Italy takes over Zone A, which is still called Trieste today, while Zone B goes to Yugoslavia. After Yugoslavia collapses in the 1990s, the zone is divided between Slovenia and Croatia.

On the Italian side, Trieste has gained the status of a free port within the EU system, with lower customs tariffs. The city, still very multicultural, also continues to function smoothly according to Jan Morris:

I have tried to get the hang of many cities, during a lifetime writing about them, and I have reached the conclusion that a particular history and a precarious

1948: Zone A issue, an overprint on an Italian stamp from 1945, which marks the post-war reconstruction.

1948: Zone B issue celebrating May Day.

geographical situation have made Trieste as near to a decent city as you can find, at the start of the twenty-first century. Honesty is still the norm here, manners are generally courteous, bigotries are usually held in check, people are generally good to each other, at least on the surface.[228]

BOOKS

Claudio Magris (2001)
Microcosms

Jan Morris (2001)
Trieste and the Meaning of Nowhere

FILM

La Ragazza di Trieste / The Girl from Trieste (1982)
Directed by Pasquale Festa Campanile

//

Horse chestnuts, planes and firs – dark waters on which branches and leaves float and into which the birds disappear and sink like stones

CLAUDIO MAGRIS, ABOUT THE CITY PARK

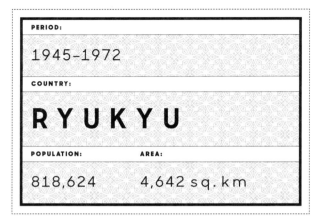

PERIOD:
1945–1972

COUNTRY:
RYUKYU

POPULATION:	AREA:
818,624	4,642 sq. km

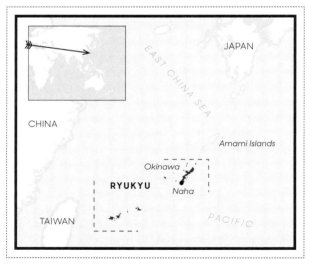

JAPAN

EAST CHINA SEA

CHINA

Amami Islands

Okinawa

RYUKYU   Naha

TAIWAN

PACIFIC

Systemic suicide

A visitor to the island realm of Ryukyu[229] will be astonished by all the languages. There are at least six of them, and they are barely intelligible among themselves, let alone to the Japanese in the north. He will also hear about life in the villages through mild winters and hot, humid summers. And he will be led from the beach up to the terraces of sugar cane, sweet potato and tobacco, and be shown huge camphor trees and, a little further off, the mulberry trees that are the silkworms' grazing grounds. On a fine day, it is difficult to imagine the tropical cyclones that can appear without warning, laying waste to whole islands. And it is quite impossible to tell that it was right here that the Japanese built suicide into the system during the Second World War – it catches you quite off guard.

Ryukyu spans several degrees of latitude, from Japan in the north to Taiwan in the south, forming a chain of more than a hundred volcanic islands on an arc between the shallow East China Sea in the west and the much deeper Philippine Sea, out towards the Mariana Trench in the east.

For several hundred years, the archipelago was an independent kingdom. In the 1800s, China and Japan battled for control, which ultimately went to Japan in 1879.

The Japanese divided Ryukyu into the prefectures of Kagoshima and Oshima in the north and Okinawa in the south. The border was placed between the Amami Islands and Okinawa, the largest island in the whole archipelago. This takeover marked the beginning of a brutal regime.

The Japanese aimed to sweep aside all that remained of local culture, and Japanese was imposed as the sole language in the schools. But they also cleared up in a more practical sense. Among other animals, they introduced the Indian mongoose – a feline bundle of fur with razor-sharp teeth – to control the massive snake population. However, the plan went awry when the mongooses turned out to be almost as keen on other species. And since they themselves had no natural enemies on the island, they rapidly became pests themselves.

Japan maintained its position on Ryukyu right up to the end of the Second World War. On 23 March 1945, the USA launched an attack on the smaller Kerama Islands, 25 km (15 miles) west of Okinawa. After securing positions there, they continued towards the main island. Their mission had been given the slightly odd name of Operation Iceberg and was planned as a final offensive before the attack on Japan itself.

The Americans had counted on the people of Ryukyu welcoming them as liberators. Instead, they met with civil resistance that was greater and more entrenched than at any other place in the war to date. It turned out that Japan's epic indoctrination campaign had succeeded: the islanders now felt they were Japanese and acted accordingly.

Others claim the whole thing was the result of alarmist propaganda. Over a prolonged period, Japanese pamphlets, newspapers and radio broadcasts had presented the Americans as barbarians. They were – according to these reports – utterly merciless. They raped first and killed afterwards, almost by nature.

On one of the mangrove-covered Yaeyama Islands in the south, whole populations flee up into the mountains. After several weeks more than half of them are dead from starvation and sickness. And on Zamami, one of the Kerama Islands, almost an entire village commits collective suicide after just two days. On Okinawa, young women throw themselves off the black cliffs on the south of the island.

Others go actively into battle. These include several hundred schoolgirls as young as fifteen. They call themselves the princess lilies (*hime-yuri*) and work as field nurses. On Okinawa, almost all of them die. And those who are not killed in battle also commit suicide, generally in groups. One of the princess lilies later described her experiences:

> We had undergone strict Japanese education, so being taken prisoner was the same as being a traitor. We were taught to prefer suicide to being taken prisoner.[230]

The mass suicides are generally carried out using hand grenades and, with a few exceptions, they are ordered by Japanese officers. This is comprehensively documented by Kenzaburō Ōe, later a winner of the Nobel Prize for Literature, in his essay *Okinawa Notes*.[331] In 2005, two Japanese war veterans tried to have Ōe's claims dismissed as fabrications, but lost their case.

To some extent, it was true that the Americans could behave badly. Rapes did happen and many civilians were killed in the battles. The American soldiers excused themselves by saying that the civilians were fighting out of uniform, an argument that would later be repeated during the protracted Vietnam War.

By the time the battle for Okinawa was over in summer 1945, more than 150,000 of the island's civilians had lost their lives. That is equivalent to one-third of the island's original population.

When Japan capitulated shortly afterwards, it became necessarily to clarify the future administration of Ryukyu. The USA had already raised the problem a couple of years earlier with the Chinese, who envisaged a solution that would involve them as well. However, any such arrangement didn't get beyond the talking stage. The USA decided to keep the original prefecture of Okinawa for itself. This was eventually formalized in the peace treaty between Japan and the Allies in 1952.

The American dollar is introduced as the monetary unit, and cars have to drive on the right-hand side. Stamps are also issued – the first in 1948 – but the motifs and text have clear local associations. My stamp from 1957 portrays a flying goddess, an *apsara*, who, according to Buddhist mythology, entertains humans with beauty and

1957: Issue featuring an apsara, a flying goddess from Buddhist mythology.

flute music. It is postmarked Naha, which was the largest city on Okinawa for several centuries before being blown to bits in the final phase of the Second World War.

After a rapid reconstruction, Naha now looks like the spitting image of a town in the American Midwest, with a sprawling mix of building styles and shrieking billboards along a wide main street with a tangle of telephone wires dangling on either side – while an almost continuous cortege of shining, oversized vehicles roars back and forth.

The Americans quickly established military bases on Okinawa, for both air force and navy. These remained when Japan regained formal ownership of the archipelago in 1972.

Today, the Americans have 30,000 men on the island, and have nineteen per cent of the surface area at their disposal. The Japanese went back to driving on the left in 1978. Otherwise, little has happened. Anti-American attitudes are on the rise throughout Ryukyu, and at the same time the Chinese have entered the arena, staking a claim on the Senkaku Islands in the far south. This has stirred up nationalistic feelings on both sides. The islands themselves may look like lifeless, useless cliffs, but there is much to indicate that the surrounding seas are rich in gas and oil deposits.

BOOKS

Kenzaburō Ōe (1970)
Okinawa Notes

Gregory Smits (1999)
Visions of Ryukyu: Identity and Ideology in Early-Modern Thought and Politics

Arne Røkkum (2006)
Nature, Ritual and Society in Japan's Ryukyu Islands

//

We had undergone strict Japanese education, so being taken prisoner was the same as being a traitor. We were taught to prefer suicide to being taken prisoner

ANONYMOUS WOMAN

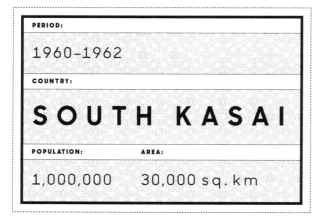

PERIOD:

1960-1962

COUNTRY:

SOUTH KASAI

POPULATION:	AREA:
1,000,000	30,000 sq. km

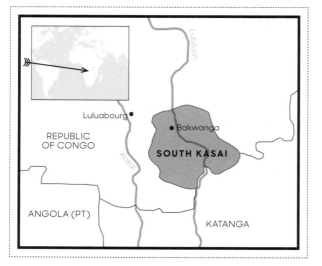

Miserable Balubas and precious minerals

When Belgium's King Baudouin drove an open-topped limousine from the airport to the ceremony that would formally dissolve the Congo as a Belgian colony, he had his elegant if useless ceremonial sword stolen. The thief seized it right out of his lap then leapt proudly over the car bonnet and ran away. The king was irritated and wanted to get the whole thing over and done with as quickly as possible. Even so, he couldn't resist the temptation of praising his uncle King Leopold II, who had ruled what was known as the Free State of Congo with legendary brutality in the 1800s. Patrice Lumumba, later president of the Congo, was enormously provoked and is said to have responded brusquely: 'We are no longer your monkeys.'[232]

In 1959, the Belgian Congo provided ten per cent of the world's copper, fifty per cent of its cobalt and seventy per cent of all its industrial diamonds. No wonder, then, that Belgium fought back when the Congolese elite united to demand national sovereignty with immediate effect in spring 1960. But since Belgium had signed a UN treaty some years before that clearly stated the principles of independence and self-determination, there was simply no way out of it.

In the weeks that followed, the new country was to be consolidated. The Congo was huge, and much of it was impenetrable jungle. More than 200 languages were spoken within its borders, and there were at least as many ethnic groups. None of this was reflected in the way the previous colonial government had divided up districts and power structures. Trouble was inevitable.

Katanga Province quickly breaks away, declaring itself autonomous, and is followed by South Kasai on 8 August 1960, led by Albert Kalonji. He is the chief of the powerful Baluba tribe and calls himself a king, *mulopwe*. His administration is militaristic and authoritarian: members of other tribes are frozen out, and opposition politicians are assassinated or sent into exile. The capital of South Kasai is established in Bakwanga, today's Mbuji-Mayi, close to some large diamond deposits that were discovered around the turn of the century. Over the following weeks, Balubas from the whole region come flooding in, often forced to flee by vengeful members of the Lula tribe.

Until as late as the 1800s, the Balubas had ruled their own tribal area between the Lualaba and Lubilash Rivers, but had been split up by Leopold II's soldiers and colonial bureaucrats at the beginning of the 1900s. So by the beginning of the 1960s, the Balubas are living in widely scattered villages, although they still keep things running smoothly and are astonishingly well organized. There is nothing here to justify the Scandinavian use of the term '*full baluba*' (whose rough meaning in English is 'total chaos'), although it undoubtedly originated from the name

of this ethnic group.[233] Everything revolves around a single village street lined on either side by rectangular houses made of compressed mud bricks. The roofs are made of corrugated metal to keep out the tropical rain. And in front of the entrances hang colourful pieces of fabric that not only evidence surplus income and hospitality but also distinguish different houses. The children play together in the village street – remarkably quietly. The girls practise carrying things on their heads and play families. The boys make bows and go hunting in the back gardens. The air is fresh with the smell of foliage and herbs.

What they encounter in Bakwanga is water shortages and crumbling buildings. The city has no roads, electricity or sewage system. And the soil is barren, at best good for eking out some cassava root. The result is severe outbreaks of *kwashiorkor*, a deficiency disease whose familiar symptoms are swollen faces and bloated bellies. Children are the hardest hit and they die in large numbers.

Christian missionaries had been active in the Kasai area since the turn of the century. Norwegian Gunnerius Tollefsen had travelled into the area in a flat-bottomed riverboat with a Danish skipper. It had taken a strong man in the prow with a bamboo pole to find a route between the treacherous sandbanks.

Now, Tollefsen was despairing over descriptions of the Balubas as a violent people, and insisted on giving his own view: 'In fact, the Balubas are a peaceful people, more open to the evangelical message than many other tribes in the Congo.'[234]

Together with his fellow-missionaries, he was instrumental in having a planeload of Norwegian dried cod sent to the people of the Kasai region at Christmas in 1960.

The regime in South Kasai received some financial support from Belgian companies in return for mining concessions. More of this went on weapons than on food and medicine. Some of it also went on stamp issues, initially Belgian colonial stamps overprinted with *Etat Autonome du Sud Kasai* ('Autonomous State of South Kasai'). Later the country produced its own series bearing a snarling leopard head, which speaks for itself. The work was outsourced to the Swiss printers, Courvoisier, and at the last minute the motifs were supplemented with a V for Victory. This had proven to be an effective symbol for the Allies during the Second World War; perhaps it would work here too.

In the meantime the central government in the Congo, with President Lumumba at its head, decided to destroy the breakaway state of South Kasai once and for all. They asked the UN to help out. The organization was already on hand in the area with peacekeeping forces, but drew the line at the use of active firepower. Next, the Soviet Union was contacted, and proved more than willing to provide air transport for the Congolese government troops in autumn 1961.

During the battles that followed, 3,000 Balubas were killed and several hundred thousand put to flight. Kalonji was taken prisoner, but later managed to escape and re-establish a provisional administration. He eventually gave up in October 1962.

1961: Leopard head with V sign.

Eric Packham, who worked from 1961 to 1962 as the UN's Chief Civilian Affairs Officer in Luluabourg on the border of South Kasai, later wrote about his experience of this time:

What I found fascinating in the Congo was the mix of the absurd and the deadly serious, the horrific and the beautiful, the innocent and the evil, the mean and cowardly and the generous and noble, the terrifying and the hilarious. There was never a dull moment because one never quite knew what would happen next: the mood could change as quickly as the expression on the face of a baby.[235]

South Kasai returned to the Republic of Congo as one of the country's twenty-one provinces, but was later restructured and renamed East Kasai, after unrest in 1965. And thus it has continued in the whole Congo area, with profound internal differences that have never been resolved. Again and again, they have flared up into bloody clashes.

At the same time, slowly but surely, the country is being emptied of gold, diamonds and other valuable minerals. From the edges of the forests around the many remote airstrips, the local people observe quiet negotiations between strangers before small white planes are quickly emptied of packages containing clothes, medicine and money. They take off again for Dubai, Brussels, Hong Kong and London, heavily laden with less practical treasures.[236]

BOOKS

Eric Packham (1996)
Freedom and Anarchy

M. W. Hilton-Simpson (1912)
Land and the Peoples of the Kasai

//

What I found fascinating in the Congo was the mix of the absurd and the deadly serious, the horrific and the beautiful, the innocent and the evil, the mean and cowardly and the generous and noble, the terrifying and the hilarious

ERIC PACKHAM

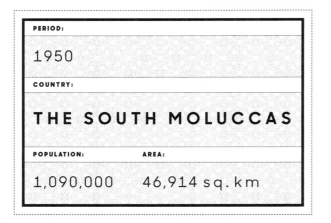

PERIOD:

1950

COUNTRY:

THE SOUTH MOLUCCAS

POPULATION: AREA:

1,090,000   46,914 sq. km

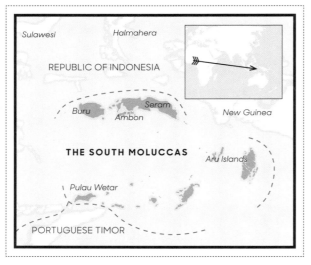

Sulawesi   Halmahera

REPUBLIC OF INDONESIA

Buru   Seram
Ambon   New Guinea

THE SOUTH MOLUCCAS

Aru Islands

Pulau Wetar

PORTUGUESE TIMOR

Spices and terrorism

It's the crack of dawn in the Netherlands on 2 December 1975. A small group of men has boarded a packed passenger train, each carrying a long package wrapped in colourful festive wrapping paper. Just after the village of Wijster, they unwrap their weapons and pull the emergency brake. The train stops in the middle of a field. The engine driver is shot at once. And over the days that follow, several hostages are killed, then thrown out and left lying on the ground. It is unclear at first what the kidnappers want, but eventually it emerges that the aim of the action is to raise awareness about the situation in the South Moluccas.[237]

The South Moluccas is a group of islands in the Banda Sea between New Guinea and Sulawesi. Because they were the only source of certain spices, mainly nutmeg and cloves, they have a history of being the most coveted islands in the area. Once the spices arrived in the European market, they were worth their weight in gold. The Portuguese, who were the first Europeans to arrive in the 1500s, faced constant challenges from the other colonial powers. Through a combination of diplomacy and raw might, the Dutch East India Company eventually came out on top, and gained a monopoly on all spice exports from the archipelago.

The Dutch went to work methodically, streamlining and controlling spice cultivation. Some islands were only for nutmeg, while others were reserved for cloves. The locals were chased off the land, which was taken over by officials from the Dutch company who ran the business using imported slaves. The market only began to shrink in the mid-1800s – plants and seeds had been smuggled out, resulting in competing plantations on the Seychelles and Madagascar. In addition, the Europeans had developed a taste for other types of spices from India and Africa.

After the company went bankrupt, the Dutch state took over the area as a colony. It was merged with the rest of the large archipelago known as Dutch India, which stretched from the Malacca Strait to Australia. After an interlude under Japan, which occupied the area during the Second World War, the Dutch took over again in 1945, aiming to continue with business as usual.

They were quickly challenged by local leaders, who demanded full autonomy and launched a war of liberation. After international pressure, the Netherlands gave up in 1949. The peace treaty stated that the whole archipelago should be organized as a federation of autonomous states. This was the profound wish of many of the regions, including the South Moluccas.

The powerful leaders on the large island of Java, in the far west, saw things differently. They had no intention of complying with the treaty; instead, they established the Republic of Indonesia as a centralist model for the whole area. Until further notice, they would take charge of all positions of leadership. But the fact that they were also Muslims was the main reason why the South Moluccas declared full independence as the autonomous republic of Maluku Selatan on 25 April 1950. Despite the brutal excesses of the Dutch in the area, large numbers of the indigenous population had been Christianized over several centuries during which the region had been a successful mission field for Dutch Calvinists. In addition, the Netherlands had been careful to conscript large sections of the male population into its colonial army. Now those soldiers had been demobilized overnight, but they still felt loyal to the Dutch throne. The same went for their leader, Chris Soumokil, who had trained as a lawyer in the Netherlands. But he and his colleagues lacked any underlying expertise in state administration. Moreover, the soldiers' discipline had rapidly evaporated after the Dutch officers went home. 'There were three adjutants, Sopacua, Tahapary and Siwabessy, the rest were sergeant-majors, sergeants and corporals. None of them wanted to serve under another, each of them thought they were better.'[238]

Despite the difficulties, a functioning administrative centre is established on Ambon, a little island in the north of the archipelago, due south of the much bigger and mostly deserted island of Seram. Both are densely overgrown right down to the shoreline and on Seram the mountains tower to heights of 3,000 m (10,000 ft).

They issue their own stamps: overprints on 1949 stamps from the Dutch colonial administration. The motif on my stamp, a solid house with several gables, is from Sumatra and has little to do with the South Moluccas. Here, the houses are built of bamboo and palm leaves, and look much more temporary. This is because the soil on the islands is so poor that the villages have to be moved constantly. This is embedded in the culture: it is time to move when a given number of the village's inhabitants have died of old age or other causes. It is rare for more than twenty years to pass between each move, and after this period, a curse of equivalent duration is placed on the site. This is why the Dutch have always failed in their efforts to establish more permanent housing in the area.

President Sukarno in the Republic of Indonesia did not recognize the breakaway state and sent large naval forces to Ambon. Although the South Moluccan soldiers were well trained, they had to admit defeat on 28 September 1950. By then, the little island state had existed for six months.

The Dutch, who had supported the federal model, offered the soldiers and their families temporary refuge in the Netherlands. In all, 12,500 South Moluccans took them up on the offer. All were convinced that this was a provisional solution and that they would eventually return.

Once in the Netherlands, the South Moluccans were installed in remote camps that had previously been used to imprison Nazis. Here they lived cut off from Dutch society – they had their own schools, and no efforts whatsoever were made to integrate them. There was no question of Dutch citizenship, either. Because the Dutch also took it for granted that the South Moluccans would go home, one way or another, although it was quite out of the question that this would involve any reconquest of the islands.[239]

1950: Overprint on a stamp from Indonesia under Dutch administration, 1949, showing a Minangkabau house from Sumatra.

In the meantime, Chris Soumokil fought on with a thousand-strong guerrilla army in the jungle on Seram, until he, too, had to surrender to the Indonesian forces in December 1963. After three years in prison, he was executed. The South Moluccans in the Netherlands responded by establishing their own government in exile. Nonetheless, increasing numbers of them were also beginning to doubt the likelihood of reconquering the South Moluccas. Slowly the frustration grew, along with a sense of being locked into an unbearable situation.

After 1970, the Netherlands experiences a number of more or less savage terror actions. It starts with an attack on the home of the Indonesian ambassador and continues with the hijacking of the train in Wijster. Here, the terrorists give up after twelve days, in part because of some nights of severe frost and in part because it is rumoured that the Indonesians have started exacting reprisals on the Moluccans. Later, a further attempt is made on another train, this time in May. In addition, a school and a town hall are attacked, and several people are killed. The terrorists achieve nothing whatsoever, moving only from one fiasco to the next.

It eventually becomes clear to the Dutch authorities that there is no avoiding integration. The internment camps are closed. Most of the South Moluccans are given Dutch citizenship and the terror attacks fade away.

The government in exile remains intact to this day, and regularly elects new presidents. Although nobody now believes there is any chance of a return to the South Moluccas, there is always a bit of sabre-rattling when the opportunity arises. When the Indonesian president was scheduled to travel to the Netherlands on a state visit in 2010, the president in exile, John Wattilete, issued a demand that he should be imprisoned for war crimes. This was, of course, refused by the Dutch authorities, but the Indonesian president got cold feet and called off the visit.

BOOK

Wim Manuhutu (1991)
Moluccans in the Netherlands: A Political Minority?

//

There were three adjutants, Sopacua, Tahapary and Siwabessy. None of them wanted to serve under another, each of them thought they were better

J.A. MANUSAMA OF THE STATE ADMINISTRATION

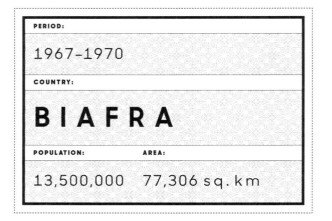

PERIOD:
1967–1970

COUNTRY:
BIAFRA

POPULATION:	AREA:
13,500,000	77,306 sq. km

NIGERIA

Enugu

BIAFRA

Umuahia

CAMEROON

ATLANTIC

BIGHT OF BIAFRA

Famine and proxy war

The health workers find the child emaciated, wide-eyed and swollen-bellied. Swarms of flies jostle for position around her mouth and eyes. The little girl uses the last of her strength to fight off these tormentors – she bites and scratches, but soon she can't take any more. The needle is inserted and the sugar solution flows into her feeble bloodstream. In the first few days, calories are added in the form of finely ground cereal products and protein in the form of bean paste. The treatment takes four to eight weeks – if it's successful.

This is a Biafran baby, a term from times past that is embedded permanently in our language. Everybody of a certain age knows what a Biafran baby is: it is a child suffering from *kwashiorkor*, an illness caused by a prolonged lack of protein.

The sickness had long gone hand in hand with wars on the African continent, well before French doctors had made the West aware of Biafran babies in 1968. Soon after the civil war in Nigeria got under way, the area was hit by famine, and the French medics' efforts to get the Red Cross involved were all in vain. So they formed the organization Médecins Sans Frontières, and followed up with shocking pictures of sick children in an intensive awareness-raising campaign in Europe and North America. Millions of us were deeply affected.

Nigeria gained independence from the colonial power of Great Britain in 1960. There had long been tension between the different ethnic groups in the country, stemming from conflicts not only over resources but also over religion. While the tribal areas in the north had a clear Muslim majority, the populations along the coast were Christian or animist. It all culminated in a *coup d'état* by the Christian Igbo people in the southeast, rapidly followed by a counter-coup in the north, where several thousand Igbos were killed.

In a radio broadcast at 6 a.m. on 30 May 1967, the military governor of the Eastern Region of Nigeria, Chukwuemeka Odumegwu Ojukwu, announced the establishment of Biafra as an independent and sovereign state for the Igbo people. It takes its name from the Bight of Biafra, and stretches from the River Niger in the west to the mountain chain that today serves as the border between Nigeria and Cameroon in the east. It is stipulated that the territory will also include the continental shelf in the sea off the coastline. The background to this is that British companies have found oil in the area. Extraction has already been under way for several years, and has rapidly become Nigeria's main source of revenue.

The Biafran climate was characterized by heavy rain in the summer months and drought throughout the winter. The country was the size of Ireland and had 13.5 million inhabitants at its peak. The majority were farmers, who had traditionally lived in low, square mud huts thatched with palm leaves. The society had previously been organized into small villages, the system of government of which followed democratic principles, with an assembly of representatives from the different families taking joint decisions. This all changed after colonization in the 1800s, when the British introduced a feudal model headed by warrant chiefs, de facto local rulers, a move that also hastened the growth of larger towns in the area.

Biafra quickly produced its own national anthem. It was in English and was called 'Land of the Rising Sun':

> Land of rising sun, we love and cherish,
> Beloved homeland of our brave heroes;
> We must defend our lives or we shall perish,
> We shall protect our hearts from all our foes;
> But if the price is death for all we hold dear,
> Then let us die without a shred of fear.[240]

Japan had also long called itself the Land of the Rising Sun, and with more reason, seeing as Biafra was clearly on the sunset side of the African continent. But perhaps we have to accept that the symbolic aspect was what mattered here. That said, the decision to set the anthem to a high-flown section of Sibelius's *Finlandia Suite* makes it difficult to ignore that the newly established state must have been in a serious hurry to get things done.

The stamps took a bit longer. The first set came out in April 1968: Nigerian stamps overprinted with 'Sovereign

Biafra'. Eventually, the country got its very own stamps, printed with the help of the Portuguese.

My stamp was issued on the first anniversary of independence. It is difficult to make out the postmark, but based on three other stamps that appear to have been placed on the same envelope, I can work out that it is Umuahia, Biafra's second capital after Enugu. The motif is reminiscent of the chaotic kid's room in *Calvin and Hobbes*.[241] And the overprint 'Help Biafran Children' does nothing to lessen the absurdity of the message.

But of course this is no laughing matter. Civil war was inevitable, because the rest of Nigeria could not let Biafra walk off with such immense oil wealth. And after the front had moved back and forth for a while, things started going downhill for the breakaway state and Biafra had to ask the Nigerian government for a ceasefire.

Ojukwu fled to Ivory Coast and on 15 January 1970, Biafra was incorporated into Nigeria again. By then more than a million people had died, most of starvation and sickness.

In the novel *Half of a Yellow Sun*, Chimamanda Ngozi Adichie notes that the Biafran War also had an international dimension, because the major powers were heavily involved on both sides. The Soviet Union, which had gradually got into the habit of exploiting international crises to increase its own influence, put its money on Nigeria. It quickly entered the fray with weapons experts, fighter planes and bombs. The old colonial power of Great Britain, meanwhile, feared that the Soviets would gain a foothold in the region and therefore also opted to deliver arms to

1968: Stamp with flag and researchers, issued on the first anniversary of Biafra's independence.

the Nigerian side. But Prime Minister Harold Wilson said these should only be for self-defence: no aircraft bombs or more sophisticated weapons.[242]

The British government was struggling with another dilemma too. As so many times before – and after – it was all a question of oil. France had already sided with Biafra, and the British were afraid that British Petroleum and Shell would lose their concessions to French competitors if Biafra won. And it didn't help matters when China also turned up in Biafra with military experts and weapons.

While Great Britain vacillated, people elsewhere in Europe sided with Biafra, especially Christian organizations. Airdrops delivering aid were organized to mitigate the impact of the famine.

It also became acceptable for European military officers and others to offer their expertise to the fairly modest army, which initially consisted of only 3,000 men with little weapons training. One of these was Carl Gustav von Rosen, a Swede who started up his own little air force, 'Biafra Babies'. It consisted of Swedish training planes flown in via France, where they were given a coat of camouflage paint and fitted out with anti-armour rockets.

At worst, all this assistance simply helped prolong the war, which ended without having resolved any problems. On the other hand, the whole business had exposed the old colonial powers' enduring interest in the area. And one may hope that it taught the Africans yet another lesson about what can be expected from that quarter, good and bad – and generally the latter.

BOOKS

Chinua Achebe (1958)
Things Fall Apart

Carl Gustaf von Rosen (1969)
Biafra: som jeg ser det ('Biafra: As I See It')

Chimamanda Ngozi Adichie (2006)
Half of a Yellow Sun

//

Only for self-defence: no aircraft bombs or more sophisticated weapons

HAROLD WILSON, BRITISH PRIME MINISTER, ON ARMS DELIVERIES TO THE NIGERIAN SIDE

PERIOD:

1800–1967

COUNTRY:

UPPER YAFA

POPULATION: **AREA:**

35,000   1,600 sq. km

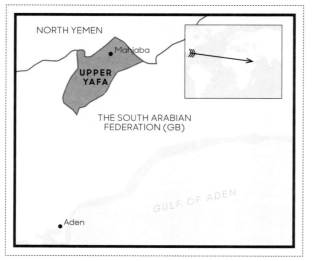

NORTH YEMEN

Mahjaba

UPPER
YAFA

THE SOUTH ARABIAN
FEDERATION (GB)

GULF OF ADEN

Aden

Mud houses and gaudy stamps

Some 120 km (75 miles) inland from the coast of the Gulf of Aden in a narrow mountain gorge 2,000 m (6,500 ft) above sea level lies the village of Mahjaba. Only rarely is it mentioned on modern maps and in statistics, and it's a matter of pure guesswork how many people live there – perhaps a few hundred. From the early 1800s, it was the capital of the Upper Yafa Sultanate, which united the northern Yafa tribes.

Mahjaba consists of a couple of dozen tower-like buildings, tightly packed together and up to seven storeys high, like a miniature Manhattan. It is built on stone foundations topped by walls of compressed mud bricks that are 80 cm (30 in.) thick at the bottom and 15 cm (6 in.) by the roof ridge. The whole thing is built and then rendered with local clay mortar, making the buildings look like a natural part of their scorched surroundings. Concrete has never found its way here. And that's a good thing, because, with its high thermal capacity and good moisture-regulating properties, no other material can compete with mud when it comes to cooling and stabilizing the room temperature during the area's hot summers, when daytime temperatures can climb as high as 50 °C (122 °F). The women are the ones who build the houses in Mahjaba, and the interior staircase is known as an *arus* or bride.[243] The window frames are decorated in bright manganese blue, while the divisions between the floors are indicated on the facade with chalk-white horizontal stripes. In the shadow-filled, hilly landscape between the buildings, paths run amid terraces of acacia trees and tamarind bushes, and here and there a tilled patch of millet.

Upper Yafa covered 1,600 sq. km (615 sq. miles) – about the same area as Greater London – and had between 30,000 and 40,000 inhabitants. Although they were all orthodox Muslims, they had a surprising penchant for old superstitions and mysticism, from magic drums to rain dances.

After colonizing Aden at the beginning of the 1800s under the pretence of combating piracy in the area, the English helped themselves to the adjacent sultanates further into the interior, too. The sultan of Upper Yafa, Qahtan ibn 'Umar ibn al-Husayn Al Harhara, signed a mutual defence treaty in 1903, and the tribal area thereby became part of the British Protectorate of Aden, on paper at least. Up until 1960, the district was only visited by a handful of Europeans. They told of hostile inhabitants and roads passable only by donkey and camel. And they complained about constant harassment from the sultan's soldiers.

Within the tribal area, there were also clashes. In the 1950s, a series of feuds broke out and, ultimately, a stormy rebellion against the sultan himself, Muhammad ibn Salih ibn 'Umar Al Harhara, who had taken over the Harhara dynasty in 1948. In the end, the sultan asked the British for help, and they sent in their Hawker Hunter bombers to make repeated raids on the rebels. Many villages were reduced to dust. A British officer who helped coordinate the attacks summed up the outcome: '[The territory] remained unconquered and hostile, its valleys alive with vigorous, arrogant Yafais.'[244]

When the British merged the sultanates in the area to form the South Arabian Federation in 1963, the sultan of Upper Yafa opted to become part of the less binding Protectorate of South Arabia, along with some small states further east. Although this still meant being merged under British authority, the country now felt it was almost sovereign. And on 30 September 1967, it celebrated its independence by issuing ten stamps bearing fluttering national flags in red and green, decorated with a crescent moon and scimitar. The initiative appears slightly odd, considering that actual mail delivery, both internally and in and out of the realm, was almost non-existent. Upper Yafa had absolutely no functioning postal system, and there has never, before or since, been so much as a single postbox to be seen in Mahjaba. In fact, the whole thing was instigated by the British stamp firm, Harrison & Sons. They had tempted the sultan with the prospect of huge sales to the stamp collectors of the world, and money straight into the state coffers. He'd taken the bait.

The absurdity reaches its height some weeks later when the flag series is followed up with some larger formats bearing images of world-famous artworks. One of the motifs marks the fifth anniversary of the death of America's President Kennedy, while another shows a Dutch windmill. My specimen is the famous painting of dancers by the

French Impressionist Edgar Degas, in which the women's dress code is anything but Islamic. The sultan should be pleased it never made its way to Upper Yafa. The closest it got was probably an office shelf in Aden, where Upper Yafa eventually had its own stamp office.

The brutal behaviour of the British in the region had gradually bolstered the anticolonial and nationalistic currents that were spreading throughout the Middle East at that time. The hero was Gamal Abdel Nasser. After coming to power in Egypt, he had repelled an attempted invasion by an alliance of Israel, England and France in 1956. Nothing like this had ever happened before. The atmosphere eventually spread throughout the Aden region. It didn't help much that the British responded by systematically liquidating their opponents. When the once-loyal colonial army mutinied in November 1967, that was the end of that. The British withdrew overnight.

All the British-friendly monarchs in the area were overthrown and the sultan of Upper Yafa was assassinated on 29 November 1967. After that, the mini-state was quickly dissolved and brought under the authority of the newly established People's Republic of South Yemen, renamed the Democratic People's Republic of Yemen a couple of years later. With solid backing from the Soviets, it became the Middle East's first and last Marxist state.

Its ideological power gradually waned until in 1990 the People's Republic was merged with North Yemen to form Yemen. Since that time, the area has been continuously ravaged by bloody internal conflicts and civil war.

1967: Stamp with motif from Edgar Degas's painting 'The Ballet Dancers' (1874).

The Yafa tribe has also been involved. And as American drones have buzzed across the skies, control has constantly shifted between sporadic emirates established by different Islamist groupings.

Time after time, there has been enormous material destruction, to the great frustration of the local population.

But at least they have been able to console themselves with the thought that their elaborate mud houses are relatively easy to repair and rebuild. A pile of earth is a pile of earth. Its quality is the same whether it has been bombed into dust or produced through a thousand-year process of natural erosion.

BOOKS

Steven W. Day (2012)
Regionalism and Rebellion in Yemen: A Troubled Nation

Salma Samar Damluji (2007)
The Architecture of Yemen: From Yafi to Hadramut

//

[The territory] remained unconquered and hostile, its valleys alive with vigorous, arrogant Yafais

DONALD S. FOSTER, BRITISH SOLDIER

Notes

FOREWORD

1   Jared Diamond (2012): *Collapse: How Societies Choose to Fail or Succeed.*

2   Terje Bongard & Eivin Røskaft (2010): *Det biologiske mennesket.*

3   Steven Pinker quoted by Harald Høiback (2014): *Krigskunstens historie fra 1500 til i dag.*

1840–1860

4   Susan Sontag (1992): *Volcano Lover: A Romance.*

5   Julia Kavanagh (1858): *A Summer and Winter in the Two Sicilies.*

6   Giuseppe Tomasi de Lampedusa (2007): *The Leopard* (trans. Archibald Colquhoun).

7   Ibid.

8   Tacitus (98): *Germania.*

9   M. L'Estrange & Anna Maria Wells (1850): *Heligoland Or Reminiscences of Childhood: A Genuine Narrative of Facts.*

10 Ibid.

11 From a poem on a postcard from L. Von Sacher-Masoch: 'Grün ist das Land. Roth ist die Kant. Weiss ist der Sand. Das sind die Farben von Heligoland.'

12 John Gribbin (1985), 'Uncertainty that settled many a doubt', *New Scientist 6.*

13 Stuart Cameron & Bruce Biddulph (2015): *SS Hungarian.*

14 M. H. Perley (1857): *A Hand-Book of Information for Emigrants to New-Brunswick.*

15 Ibid.

16 Alexander Monro (1855): *New Brunswick: With a Brief Outline of Nova Scotia and Prince Edward Island. Their History, Civil Divisions, Geography and Productions.*

17 Ibid.

18 Øvre Richter Frich (1912): *Kondoren: en Landflygtigs roman.*

19 Georg Wedel-Jarlsberg (1913): *Da jeg var cowboy.*

20 Jack Child (2008): *Miniature Messages: The Semiotics and Politics of Latin American Postage Stamps.*

21 Patricia Fernández-Kelly & Jon Shefner (2006): *Out of the Shadows: Political Action and the Informal Economy in Latin America.*

22 Captain Keppel, cited in St John, Spenser, *The Life of Sir James Brooke, Rajah of Sarawak,* 1879.

23 Adolf Erik Nordenskiöld (1881): *Vegas färd kring Asien och Europa.*

24 Ibid.

25 Emilio Salgari (1900): *Sandokan: Le Tigri de Mompracem,* trans. Anna Cancogni in Umberto Eco's *Open Work* (1989).

26 Umberto Eco (1989): *Open Work* (trans. Anna Cancogni).

27 Section from Verse Four.

28 Arne Lochen (1900): *J. S. Welhaven: liv og skrifter.*

29 Christopher Bruun (1964): *Soldat for sanning og rett. Brev frå den dansk-tyske krigen 1864.*

30 Joachim Toeche-Mittler (1971): *Die Armeemarschsammlung.*

31 Christopher Bruun (1964): *Soldat for sanning og rett. Brev frå den dansk-tyske krigen 1864.*

32 Thorkild Hansen (1969): *Slavenes skip.*

33 Anonymous (1792): *Om livet på plantagerne.*

34 Thorkild Hansen (1970): *Slavenes øyer.*

35 Ibid.

36 Jonathan Swift (1726): *Gulliver's Travels.*

37 Sidsel Wold (1999): *Warra! Warra! Da de hvite kom til Australia.*

38 Ibid.
39 Basset Hull (1890): *The Stamps of Tasmania.*
40 James Boyce (2010): *Van Diemen's Land.*
41 Mary Henrietta Kingsley (1897): *Travels in West Africa. Congo Français, Corisco and Cameroons.*
42 Per Arne Aasen (1954): *Alfred Saker: Bantu-Afrikas Apostel.*
43 Mary Henrietta Kingsley (1897): *Travels in West Africa. Congo Français, Corisco and Cameroons.*
44 Ibid.
45 Benita Sampedro Vizcaya (2012), 'Routes to Ruin', Article in *LL Journal*, Vol. 7, No. 2.
46 Ibid.
47 *Der Spiegel* (28 August 2006).
48 Charles Edward Barrett-Lennard (1862): *Travels in British Columbia: with a narrative of a yacht voyage round Vancouver's Island.*
49 Ibid.
50 Robin Fisher (1992): *Contact and Conflict: Indian-European Relations in British Columbia.*
51 Ibid.
52 Edwin Ernest Rich (1959): *The History of the Hudson's Bay Company.*
53 Robin Fisher (1992): *Contact and Conflict: Indian-European Relations in British Columbia.*

1860–1890

54 Equivalent to 230 kg (500 lb) of silver at that time.
55 Danikil is the name of the desert region.
56 Wyatt Alexander Mason (2003): *I Promise to be Good: the Letters of Arthur Rimbaud.*
57 Ibid.
58 Ibid.
59 Per Buvik, *Dekadanse* (2001).
60 Luisa María Mora, cited in Juan Salamanca Uribe (2007): *La Gruta Simbólica: Una anécdota en sí misma.*
61 Julio Floréz, 'Mis flores negras', first of five verses.
62 For example, Carlos Gardel, 'Mis flores negras', new recording, 1999.
63 G. B. Malleson (1875): *A Historical Sketch of the Native States of India.*
64 Eliza Ruhamah Scidmore (1903): *Winter India.*
65 Ibid.
66 Olle Strandberg, (1961): *Tigerland og sydlig hav.*
67 Margaret Bourke-White (1949): *Halfway to Freedom.*
68 Erling Bjol (1986): *Imperialismen.*
69 A. J. P. Taylor (1972): *The Struggle for Mastery in Europe 1848–1918.*
70 Ingvald Schrøder-Nilsen (1925): *Blant boerne i fred og krig.*
71 Ibid.
72 Ibid.
73 Ibid.
74 Andrea Lollini (2011): *Constitutionalism and Transitional Justice in South Africa.*
75 Ingvald Schrøder-Nilsen (1925): *Blant boerne i fred og krig.*
76 Martin Meredith (2008): *Diamonds, Gold and War: The British.*
77 Robin Clarke (1991): *Water: The International Crisis.*
78 William Edmundson (2011): *The Nitrate King: A Biography of 'Colonel' John Thomas North.*
79 Ibid.
80 Ibid.
81 Eduardo Galeano (2009) *Open Veins of Latin America*, trans. Cedric Belfrage.
82 Eduardo Galeano (1985): *Memory of Fire 3: Century of the Wind*, trans. Cedric Belfrage.

83 Carsten Jensen (1999): *Jeg har hørt et stjerneskud.*

84 Tariq Ali (1985): *An Indian Dynasty: the Story of the Nehru-Gandhi Family.*

85 Anne-Marie Schimmel (1980): *Islam in the Indian Subcontinent.*

86 Iqubal A. Nanjee & Shaid Zaki (year of publication unknown): 'Bhopal Puzzle'.

87 Nawab Sultan Jahan Begam (1912): *An Account of My Life,* trans. C. H. Payne.

88 Ibid.

89 Hugh Clifford (1906): *Heroes in Exile.*

90 Ibid.

91 Jan Dodd & Mark Lewis (2008): *Rough Guide to Vietnam.*

92 According to the miasma theory, popular at the end of 1800s, diseases such as cholera, chlamydia and the Black Death were caused by a kind of nauseating, unhealthy air that stemmed from rotting matter.

93 Isabella L. Bird (1883), *The Golden Chersonese.*

94 Now the Malay Peninsula.

95 H. Conway Belfield (1902): *Handbook of the Federated Malay States.*

96 Isabella L. Bird (1883), *The Golden Chersonese.*

97 Ibid.

1890–1915

98 Bjarte Breiteig (2013): *Ile Sainte-Marie.*

99 Charles Johnson (1724): *A General History of the Pyrates.*

100 Peter Hawkins (2007): *The Other Hybrid Archipelago: Introduction to the Literatures and Cultures of the Francophone Indian Ocean.*

101 R. V. Russell (1916): *The Tribes and Castes of the Central Provinces of India.*

102 *American Journal of Philately* (1891).

103 Laxmibai Tilak (2007): *Sketches from Memory.*

104 Ibid.

105 Ernest F. Ward & Phebe E. Ward (1908): *Echoes from Bharatkhand.*

106 Laxmibai Tilak (2007): *Sketches from Memory.*

107 From a parliamentary debate on 6 December 1897, cited in Gilbert Krebs and Bernard Poloni (1994): *Volk, Reich und Nation: Texte zur Einheit Deutschlands in Staat, Wirtschaft und Gesellschaft 1806–1919 .*

108 Philip Alcabes (2010): *Dread: How Fear and Fantasy Have Fuelled Epidemics from the Black Death to Avian Flu.*

109 S. C. Hammer (1915): *Wilhelm II.*

110 Ibid.

111 From the so-called Hun Speech, trans. S. C. Hammer (1915): *Wilhelm II.*

112 Joachim Schultz-Naumann (1985): *Unter Kaisers Flagge, Deutschlands Schutzgebieteim Pazifik und in China einst und heute.*

113 Otto Hornung (1982): *The Man from Tierra del Fuego.*

114 Captain Cook 1769, quoted in John C. Beaglehole (1961): *The Journals of Captain James Cook: The Voyage of the Endeavour 1768–1771.*

115 Patricio Manns (1996): *Cavalier seul.*

116 Robert Baden-Powell (1933): *Lessons from the Varsity of Life.*

117 Solomon Plaatje (1990): *The Mafeking Diary.*

118 Hope Hay Hewison (1989): *Hedge of Wild Almonds: South Africa, the Pro-Boers & the Quaker Conscience, 1890–1910.*

119 Sarah Isabella Augusta Wilson (1909): *South African Memories. Social Warlike & Sporting, from diaries written at the time.*

120 William Hillcourt (1964): *Baden-Powell: Two Lives of a Hero.*

121 James Lawrence (2006): *The Middle Class: A History.*

122 William Furness (1910): *The Island of Stone Money.*

123 Paul Rainbird (2003): *The Archaeology of Micronesia.*

124 Lawrence Klingman & Gerald Green (1952): *His Majesty O'Keefe*.

125 Dennis M. Powers (2010): *Tales of the Seven Seas: The Escapades of Captain Dynamite Johnny O'Brien*.

126 Joe Race (2010): *The Royal Headley of Pohnpei: Upon a Stone Altar*.

127 *The Canal Record* (6 December 1911): 'Villages Antedating Settlement of US Lie Buried Under Waters of Gatun Lake'.

128 Now the Culebra Cut.

129 David du Bose Gaillard. In a collection of letters published by the 3rd United States Volunteer Engineers (1916).

130 Noel Maurer & Carlos Yu (2010): *The Big Ditch: How America Took, Built, Ran, and Ultimately Gave Away the Panama Canal*.

1915–1925

131 T. E. Lawrence (1927): *Revolt in the Desert*.

132 *Makkah al-Mukarramah* is also the full official name of Mecca.

133 Philip Knightly & Colin Simpson (1969): *The Secret Lives of Lawrence of Arabia*.

134 Alexander Solzhenitsyn (1972): *August 1914*.

135 From the Treaty of Peace between the Allied and Associated Powers and Germany, 28 June 1919.

136 Now Lubów.

137 Reha Sokolow, Al Sokolow & Debra Galant (2003): *Defying the Tide: An Account of Authentic Compassion During the Holocaust*.

138 From 1999, the Warmia-Masurian voivodeship.

139 Thor Heyerdahl (1970): *Ra*.

140 Arthur Cotton (1894/2012): *The Story of Cape Juby*.

141 Antoine de Saint-Exupéry (1929): *Courrier Sud*.

142 Antoine de Saint-Exupéry (1939): *Terres des Hommes*.

143 Ibid.

144 Ibid.

145 Ibid.

146 Carl Eric Bechhofer (1923): *In Denikin's Russia and the Caucasus, 1919–1920*.

147 Chris Wrigley (2002): *Winston Churchill: A Biographical Companion*.

148 Gwyneth Hughes (1991): *Red Empire: The Forbidden History of the USSR*.

149 Carl Eric Bechhofer (1923): *In Denikin's Russia and the Caucasus, 1919–1920*.

150 Ibid.

151 Gwyneth Hughes (1991): *Red Empire: The Forbidden History of the USSR*.

152 A. I. Denikin (1920): *The Russian Turmoil, Memoirs, Military, Social and Political*.

153 Knut Hamsun (1903): *I Æventyrland. Opplevet og drømt i Kaukasien*.

154 Eric Linklater (1941): *The Man on my Back*.

155 Fridtjof Nansen (1927): *Gjennom Armenia*.

156 Ibid.

157 Brita Asbrink (2010): *Ludvig Nobel: 'Petroleum har en lysande framtid': En historia om eldfängd och olja och revolution I Baku*.

158 Anthony Sampson (1975): *The Seven Sisters*.

159 Hermann Rauschning (1939): *Hitler Speaks*.

160 Günter Grass (2009): *The Tin Drum*, trans. Breon Mitchell.

161 Hermann Rauschning (1939): *Hitler Speaks*.

162 Jan H. Landro (1998): *Günter Grass*.

163 Boris Pasternak (1959): *Doctor Zhivago* (trans. Max Hayward & Manya Harari).

164 Roman Brackman (2001): *The Secret File of Joseph Stalin: A Hidden Life*.

165 Nicholas Griffin (Ed.) (2002): *The Selected letters of Bertrand Russell, Volume 2: The Public Years 1914–1970*.

166 Roman Brackman (2001): *The Secret File of Joseph Stalin: A Hidden Life*.

167 Michael Scammell (2014): *The CIA's: 'Zhivago'.*

168 Lisa Anderson (1982): *The Tripoli Republic.*

169 Anna Baldinetti (2014): *The Origins of the Libyan Nation.*

170 Ali Abdullatif Ahmida (2011): *Making of Modern Libya: State Formation, Colonization and Resistance.*

171 Anna Baldinetti (2014): *The Origins of the Libyan Nation.*

172 Khalid I. El Fadli et al. (2013): 'World Meteorological Organization Assessment of the Purported World Record 58°C Temperature Extreme at El Azizia, Libya (13 September 1922)'.

173 *Kalevala*, after a Swedish rendering by Lars and Mats Huldén.

174 Jussi Niinistö (2001): *Bobi Sivén – Karjalan puolesta.*

175 Kim Leine (2015): *Avgrunnen.*

176 Now Kuyto.

177 D'Annunzio, in a speech in 1919, quoted in Lucy Hughes-Hallett (2013): *The Pike: Gabriele D'Annunzio, Poet, Seducer and Preacher of War.*

178 Italian prime minister Francesco Nitti, in a 1919 speech, quoted in Enzo Biagi (1964): *Storia del fascismo, Volum 1.*

179 Edvard Nilsen & Hans Vatne, Ed. (1955): *Verden i bilder.*

180 Fred Licht (1982): *The Vittoriale degli Italiani.*

181 Rebecca West (1941): *Black Lamb and Grey Falcon.*

1925–1945

182 Simon Winchester & Aisin-Gioro Pu Yi (1987): *From Emperor to Citizen. The Autobiography of Aisin-Gioro Pu Yi.*

183 Gregory Dean Byrd, (2005): General Ishii Shiro: 'His Legacy Is that of Genius and Madman', Electronic Theses and Dissertations. Paper 1010. http://dc.etsu.edu/etd/1010

184 Ibid.

185 Now Nanjing.

186 Hassoldt Davis (1952): *The Jungle and the Damned.*

187 Henri Charrière (1970): *Papillon.*

188 From Annam Province in Vietnam.

189 Hy V. Luong (1992): *Revolution in the Village.*

190 Comité Français de L'Union Internationale pour la Conservation de la Nature (2003): *Guyane.*

191 Tim Severin (1987): *The Ulysses Voyage.*

192 David Abulafia (2011): *The Great Sea: A Human History of the Mediterranean.*

193 Cited in Caterina Gerardi (2013): *L'Isola di Rina: Ritorno a Saseno.*

194 Otto Mänchen-Helfen (1931): *Reise ins asiatische Tuwa.*

195 Ibid.

196 Samuel M. Blekhman (1997): *The Postal History and Stamps of Tuva.*

197 Johnny Haglund (2003): *Forunderlige steder.*

198 Graham Stuart (1931): *The International City of Tangier.*

199 Paul Bowles (1958): *The World of Tangier.*

200 Greg Mullins (2002): *Colonial Affairs: Bowles, Burroughs and Chester Write Tangier.*

201 Paul Bowles (1958): *The Worlds of Tangier.*

202 Ibid.

203 Stacey A. Suver (2012): *A Dream of Tangier: Revolution and Identity in Post-War Expatriate Literature.*

204 Michael K. Walonen (2010): *Lamenting Culture and Coke: Paul Bowles and Brian Gysin on the Changing Spaces of Postcolonial Morocco.*

205 Paul Bowles (1958): *The Worlds of Tangier.*

206 Franz Werfel (1934): *The Forty Days of Musa Dagh.*

207 Hans-Lukas Kieser (2006): *Turkey Beyond Nationalism: towards Post-Nationalist Identities.*

208 Sverre Rødder (1990): *Min ære er troskap: om politiminister Jonas Lie.*

209 Jonas Lie (1940): *I 'fred' og ufred.*

210 Franz Werfel (1934): *The Forty Days of Musa Dagh.*

211 Jonas Lie (1940): *I 'fred' og ufred*.

212 Ibid.

213 Robert D. Kaplan (1996): *The Ends of the Earth. A Journey at the Dawn of the 21st Century*.

214 *Ewan W. Anderson (2014): Global Geopolitical Flashpoints: An Atlas of Conflict*.

215 Simon Hamon (2015): *Channel Islands Invaded: The German Attack on the British Islands in 1940 Told Through Eye-Witness Accounts, Newspaper Reports, Parliamentary Debates, Memoirs and Diaries*.

216 Robert Fisher (2013): *German Occupation of British Channel Islands*.

217 Simon Hamon (2015): *Channel Islands Invaded*.

218 Dan Bortolotti (2008): *Wild Blue: A Natural History of the World's Largest Animal*.

219 *Aftenposten* (30 July 1919).

220 Leo Oterhals (2000): *Hvite horisonter*.

221 Erland Kolding Nielsen, Arild Hvidtfeldt, Axel Andersen & Tim Greve (1982): *Australia, Oceania og Antarktis*.

222 Ruben Stehberg & Liliana Nilo (1983): 'Procedencia Antarctica inexacta de dos puntas de proyectil'

1945–1975

223 *La Ragazza di trieste* (1982).

224 Jan Morris (2001): *Trieste and the Meaning of Nowhere*.

225 Claudio Magris (2001): *Microcosms* (trans. Iain Halliday)

226 Ibid.

227 Winston Churchill (1946): *The Sinews of Peace*.

228 Jan Morris (2001): *Trieste and the Meaning of Nowhere*.

229 Nansei Islands in Japanese.

230 Katsu Moriguchi (1992): *Fukki ganbo*.

231 Kenzaburō Ōe (1970): *Okinawa Notes*.

232 Leo Zelig (2008): *Lumumba: Africa's Last Leader*.

233 Toril Opsahl, University of Oslo.

234 Gunnerius Tollefsen (1963): *Men Gud gav vekst. En pioner-misjonær ser seg tilbake*.

235 Eric Packham (1996): *Freedom and Anarchy*.

236 Juakali Kambale (2011): *Who is stealing DRC's gold?*

237 Antoine M. Hol & John A. E .Vervaele (2005): *Security and Civil Liberties: The Case of Terrorism*.

238 J. A. Manusama of Soumokil's group of leaders, cited in Richard Chauvel (2008): *Nationalists, Soldiers and Separatists: The Ambonese Islands from Colonialism to Revolt, 1880–1950*.

239 Wim Manuhutu (1991): *Moluccans in the Netherlands: A Political Minority?*

240 First verse of Biafra's national anthem, 'Land of the Rising Sun'; lyrics by Nnam di Azikiwe.

241 By Bill Waterson, 1985–1995.

242 Kwasi Kwarteng (2011): *Ghosts of Empire: Britain's Legacies in the Modern World*.

243 Salma Samar Damluji (2007): *The Architecture of Yemen: From Yafi to Hadramut*.

244 Donald S. Foster (1969): *Landscape with Arabs*.

Bibliography

Aasen, Per Arne (1954): *Alfred Saker: Bantu-Afrikas apostel.* Stavanger, Misjonsselskapets forlag.

Abulafia, David (2011): *The Great Sea: A Human History of the Mediterranean.* Oxford, Oxford University Press.

Achebe, Chinua (1958): *Things Fall Apart.* New York, Anchor Press.

Adichie, Chimamanda Ngozi (2006): *Half of a Yellow Sun.* New York, Anchor Books.

Ahmida, Ali Abdullatif (2011): *Making of Modern Libya: State Formation, Colonization and Resistance.* New York, State University of New York Press.

Alcabes, Philip (2010): *Dread: How Fear and Fantasy Have Fueled Epidemics from the Black Death to Avian Flu.* ReadHowYouWant.com.

Ali, Tariq (1985): *The Nehrus and the Gandhis, An Indian Dynasty.* London, Chatto & Windus.

Andelman, David A. (2014): *A Shattered Peace: Versailles 1919 and the Price We Pay Today.* Hoboken, John Wiley & Sons, Inc.

Anderson, Ewan W. (2014): *Global Geopolitical Flashpoints: An Atlas of Conflict.* New York, Routledge.

Anderson, Lisa (1982): *The Tripoli Republic.* Wisbeck, Menas Press.

Anderssen, Justus & Henrik Dethloff (1915): *Frimerkesamlerens ABC.* Kristiania, Aschehoug.

Anonymous (1792): 'Om livet på plantagerne'. *Minerva* magazine, Copenhagen.

Anonymous (1875): *Sketch of the Orange Free State.* Bloemfontein, Brooks & Fell, Printers.

Åsbrink, Brita (2010): *Ludvig Nobel: "Petroleum har en lysande framtid": En historia om eldfängd olja och revolution i Baku.* Stockholm, Wahlström & Widstrand.

Awa, Okonkwo Okuji (2009): *My Journey from Stamp Collecting to Philately.* Lulu.com.

Baden-Powell, Robert (1933): *Lessons from the Varsity of Life.* London, C. A. Pearson.

Baldinetti, Anna (2014): *The Origins of the Libyan Nation.* New York, Routledge.

Baldus, Wolfgang (1970): *The Postage Stamps of the Kingdom of Sedang. History and Background Stories of Unusual Stamps, No. 4.*

Barrett-Lennard, Charles Edward (1862): *Travels in British Columbia: With a Narrative of a Yacht Voyage Round Vancouver's Island.* London, Hurst and Blackett, Publishers.

Beaglehole, John C. (1961): *The Journals of Captain James Cook: The Voyage of the Endeavour 1768–1771*, Cambridge, Hakluyt Society.

Bechhofer, Carl Eric (1923): *In Denikin's Russia and the Caucasus 1919–1920.* London, W. Collins Sons & Co, Ltd.

Beck, Peter J. & Clive H. Schofield (1994): *Who Owns Antarctica? Governing and Managing the Last Continent.* Durham, University of Durham.

Begum, Nawab Sultan Jahan (1912): *An Account of My Life*, trans. C. H. Payne. London, John Murray.

Belfield, H. Conway (1902): *Handbook of the Federated Malay States.* London, Edward Stanford.

Berrichon, Paterne (1899): *Lettres de Jean-Arthur Rimbaud – Égypte, Arabie, Éthiopie.* Paris, Société du Mercure de France.

Biagi, Enzo (1964): *Storia del fascismo*, Vol. 1. Rome, Sadea della Volpe Editori.

Bird, Isabella Lucy (1883): *The Golden Chersonese.* New York: G. P. Putnam's Sons.

Bjøl, Erling (1986): *Imperialismen*. Oslo, Cappelen.

Blekhman, Samuel Markovich (1997): *The Postal History and Stamps of Tuva*. Woodbridge, Scientific Consulting Services International.

Bongard, Terje & Eivin Røskaft (2010): *Det biologiske mennesket*. Trondheim, Tapir forlag.

Bortolotti, Dan (2008): *Wild Blue: A Natural History of the World's Largest Animal*. Toronto, Thomas Allen Publishers.

Bourke-White, Margaret (1949): *Halfway to Freedom*. New York, Simon & Schuster.

Bowles, Paul (1958): 'The Worlds of Tangier'. *Holiday* 23, no. 3.

Boyce, James (2010): *Van Diemen's Land*. Melbourne, Black Inc.

Brackman, Roman (2001): *The Secret File of Joseph Stalin: A Hidden Life*. London, Frank Cass.

Brebbia, Carlos A. (2006): *Patagonia, a Forgotten Land*. Southampton, WIT Press.

Breiteig, Bjarte (2013): *Ile Sainte-Marie*. Oslo, Flamme forlag.

Brochmann, Georg (1948): *Panamakanalen*. Oslo, Dreyers forlag.

Bruun, Christopher (1964): *Soldat for sanning og rett. Brev frå den dansk-tyske krigen 1864*. Oslo, Samlaget.

Buvik, Per (2001): *Dekadanse*. Oslo, Pax.

Cameron, Stuart & Bruce Biddulph (2015): *SS Hungarian*. The Clyde built ships database.

Caulk, Richard Alan (2002): *Between the Jaws of Hyenas: A Diplomatic History of Ethiopia*. Wiesbaden, Harrassowitz Verlag.

Cavling, Henrik (1894): *Det danske Vestindien*. Copenhagen, Reitzel.

Charrière, Henri (1970): *Papillon*, trans. Patrick O'Brian. London, Hart-Davis.

Chauvel, Richard (2008): *Nationalists, Soldiers and Separatists: The Ambonese Islands from Colonialism to Revolt, 1880–1950*. Leiden, KITLV Press.

Child, Jack (2008): *Miniature Messages: The Semiotics and Politics of Latin American Postage Stamps*. Durham, Duke University Press.

Churchill, Winston (2014/1946): *The Sinews of Peace*, e-book. Rosetta Books.

Clarke, Robin (1993): *Water, The International Crisis*. Cambridge, MIT Press.

Clifford, Hugh (1906): *Heroes in Exile*. London, Smith, Elder & Co.

Cotton, Arthur (1894/1912): *The Story of Cape Juby*. London, Waterlow & Sons.

Criscenti, Joseph (1993): *Sarmiento and His Argentina*. Boulder, Lynne Rienner Publishers.

Damluji, Salma Samar (2007): *The Architecture of Yemen: From Yafi to Hadramut*. London, Laurence King Publishing.

Davis, Hassoldt (1952): *The Jungle and The Damned*. New York, MA Duell/Sloan/Pearce/Little B.

Day, Steven W. (2012): *Regionalism and Rebellion in Yemen: A Troubled Nation*. Cambridge, Cambridge University Press.

Debo, Richard K. (1992): *Survival and Consolidation: The Foreign Policy of Soviet Russia 1918–1921*. Montreal, McGill-Queen's University Press.

Denikin, Anton I. (1922): *The Russian Turmoil, Memoirs, Military, Social and Political*. London, Hutchinson.

Denikin, Anton I. (1975): *The Career of a Tsarist Officer: Memoirs 1872–1916*. Minneapolis, University of Minnesota Press.

Diamond, Jared (2005): *Collapse: How Societies Choose to Fail or Succeed*. New York, Viking.

Dodd, Jan & Mark Lewis (2008): *Rough Guide to Vietnam*. Rough Guides UK.

Dowson, E. M. (1918): *A Short Note on the Design and Issue of Postage Stamps Prepared by the Survey of Egypt for His Highness Husein Emir & Sherif of Macca & King of the Hejaz*. Survey of Egypt.

Duly, Colin (1979): *The Houses of Mankind*. London, Thames & Hudson.

Eco, Umberto (1962): *Opera aperta*. Milan, Bompiani.

Edmundson, William (2011): *The Nitrate King: A Biography of 'Colonel' John Thomas North*. New York, Palgrave Macmillan.

Evans, Stephen R., Abdul Rahman Zainal & Rod Wong Khet Ngee (1996): *The History of Labuan Island*. Singapore, Calender Print.

Falk-Rønne, Arne (1975): *Reisen til verdens ende*. Oslo, Luther.

Fernández-Kelly, Patricia & Jon Shefner (2006): *Out of the Shadows: Political Action and the Informal Economy in Latin America*. Pennsylvania, Pennsylvania State University Press.

Fisher, Robert (2013): *German Occupation of British Channel Islands*. Stamps.org.

Fisher, Robin (1992): *Contact and Conflict: Indian-European Relations in British Columbia*. Vancouver, UBC Press.

Foster, Donald S., *Landscape with Arabs*, London, Clifton Books, 1969.

Friberg, Eino (1989): *The Kalevala*. Helsinki, Otava.

Frich, Øvre Richter (1912): *Kondoren, En Landflygtigs roman*. Kristiania, Narvesen.

Furness, William (1910): *The Island of Stone Money*. Philadelphia, J. B. Lippincott Company.

Galeano, Eduardo (1973): *Open Veins of Latin America*, trans. Cedric Belfrage. Monthly Review Press.

Galeano, Eduardo (1999): *Memory of Fire III: Century of the Wind*, trans. Cecil Belfrage. New York, Pantheon.

Gerardi, Caterina (2013): *L'Isola di Rina. Ritorno a Saseno*. Roma, Milella.

Gold, Hal (2004): *Unit 731: Testimony*. Boston, Tuttle Publishing.

Grannes, Alf, Kjetil Rå Hauge & Siri Sverdrup Lunden (1981): *Som fugl Føniks, Bulgaria gjennom 1300 år*. Lysaker, Solum.

Grass, Günter (2009): *The Tin Drum*, trans. Breon Mitchell. Boston, New York, Houghton Mifflin Harcourt.

Gribbin, John (1985): 'Uncertainty that settled many a doubt'. *New Scientist 6*.

Griffin, Nicholas, ed. (2002): *The Selected Letters of Bertrand Russell, Volume 2: The Public Year 1914–1970*. London, Routledge.

Gusinde, Martin (2015): *The Lost Tribes of Tierra del Fuego*, London, Thames & Hudson.

Haglund, Johnny (2002): *Forunderlige steder*. Oslo, Orion.

Hammer, S. C. (1917): *William the Second as Seen in Contemporary Documents and Judged on Evidence of His Own Speeches*. London, Heinemann.

Hamon, Simon (2015): *Channel Islands Invaded: The German Attack on the British Islands in 1940 Told Through Eye-Witness Accounts, Newspaper Reports, Parliamentary Debates, Memoirs and Diaries*. Barnsley, Frontline Books.

Hamsun, Knut (1903): *I Æventyrland, Oplevet og drømt i Kaukasien*. Copenhagen, Gyldendal.

Hansen, Thorkild (1969): *Slavenes skip*, trans. Harald Sverdrup. Oslo, Gyldendal.

Hansen, Thorkild (1990): *Slavenes øyer*, trans. Georg Stang. Stabekk, Den norske bokklubben.

Harding, Les (1998): *Dead Countries of the Nineteenth and Twentieth Centuries, Aden to Zululand*. Lanham, Scarecrow Press.

Hawkins, Peter (2007): *The Other Hybrid Archipelago: Introduction to the Literatures and Cultures of the Francophone Indian Ocean*. Lanham, Lexington Books.

Hewison, Hope Hay (1989): *Hedge of Wild Almonds: South Africa, the Pro-Boers & the Quaker Conscience, 1990–1910*. London, James Currey.

Heyerdahl, Thor (1970): *Ra*. Oslo, Gyldendal.

Hickey, Gerald Cannon (1988): *Kingdom in the Morning Mist. Mayréna in the Highlands of Vietnam*. Pennsylvania, University of Pennsylvania Press.

Hillcourt, William (1964): *The Two Lives of A Hero*. London, Heinemann.

Hilton-Simpson, M. W. (1912): *Land and the Peoples of the Kasai*. London, Constable.

Høiback, Harald (2014): *Krigskunstens historie fra 1500 til i dag*. Oslo, Cappelen Damm akademisk.

Hol, Antoine M. & John A. E. Vervaele (2005): *Security and Civil Liberties: The Case of Terrorism*. Cambridge, Intersentia.

Hornung, Otto (1982): 'The Man from Tierra del Fuego', *Stamp Collecting*, July.

Horsfield, Margaret & Ian Kennedy (2014): *Tofino and Clayoquot Sound: A History*. Madeira Park, Harbour Publishing.

Hughes, Gwyneth (1990): *Red Empire: The Forbidden History of the USSR*. New York, St. Martin's Press.

Hughes-Hallett, Lucy (2013): *The Pike: Gabriele d'Annunzio, Poet, Seducer and Preacher of War*. London, Fourth Estate.

Hull, Basset (1890): *The Stamps of Tasmania*. London, Philatelic Society.

Idsøe, Olav (1978): *Et folkemord, Tasmanernes undergang*. Oslo, Dreyer.

Jensen, Carsten (1999): *Jeg har hørt et stjerneskud*, trans. Bertil Knudsen. Oslo, Forlaget Geelmuyden Kiese.

Johnson, Charles (1724): *A General History of the Pyrates*. London, T. Warner.

Kamal, Mohammad Arif (2014): 'The Morphology of Traditional Architecture of Jeddah: Climate Design and Environmental Sustainability'. *GBER* 9, no. 1.

Kaplan, Robert D (1996): *The Ends of the Earth: A Journey at the Dawn of the 21st Century*. New York, Random House.

Kavanagh, Julia (1858): *A Summer and Winter in The Two Sicilies*. London, Hurst and Blackett Publishers.

Khan, Shaharyar M. (2000): *The Begums of Bhopal: A History of the Princely State of Bhopal*. London, I. B. Tauris Publishers.

Kieser, Hans-Lukas (2006): *Turkey Beyond Nationalism: Towards Post-Nationalist Identities*. London, I. B. Tauris Publishers.

Kingsley, Mary Henrietta (1897): *Travels in West Africa. Congo Français, Corisco and Cameroons*. London, Macmillan & Co.

Klingman, Lawrence & Gerald Green (1952): *His Majesty O'Keefe*. New York, Scribner.

Knightley, Philip & Colin Simpson (1969): *The Secret Lives of Lawrence of Arabia*. London, Thomas Nelson & Sons.

Krebs, Gilbert & Bernard Poloni (1994): *Volk, Reich und Nation: Texte zur Einheit Deutschlands in Staat, Wirtschaft und Gesellschaft 1806–1918*. Asnières, Presses de la Sorbonne Nouvelle et CID.

Kwarteng, Kwasi (2011): *Ghosts of Empire: Britain's Legacies in the Modern World*. London, Bloomsbury.

Landro, Jan H. (1998): *Günter Grass*. Stabekk, De norske bokklubbene.

Lawrence, James (2006): *The Middle Class: A History*. London, Hachette Digital.

Lawrence, T. E. (1927): *Revolt in the Desert* (abridged version of *The Seven Pillars of Wisdom*). New York, Doran.

Leighton, Ralph (1991): *Tuva or bust!* New York, W. W. Norton.

Leine, Kim (2015): *Avgrunnen*. Oslo, Cappelen Damm.

L'Estrange, M. & Anna Maria Wells (1850): *Heligoland Or Reminiscences Of Childhood: A Genuine Narrative Of Facts*. London, John W. Parker.

Licht, Fred (1982): 'The Vittoriale degli Italiani'. *Journal of the Society of Architectural Historians*, Vol. 41, no. 4.

Lie, Jonas (1940): *I 'fred' og ufred*. Oslo, Steenske Forlag.

Linklater, Eric (1941): *The Man on My Back*. London, Macmillan & Co.

Løchen, Arne (1900): *J. S. Welhaven: liv og skrifter*. Kristiania, Aschehoug.

Lollini, Andrea (2011): *Constitutionalism and Transitional Justice in South Africa*. New York, Berghahn Books.

Luff, John N. (1899): *What Philately Teaches*. New York, A Lecture Delivered in 1899 before the Section on Philately of the Brooklyn Institute of Arts and Sciences, February 24.

Luong, Hy V. (1992): *Revolution in the Village. Tradition and Transformation in North Vietnam 1925–1988*. Honolulu, University of Hawaii Press.

Macfie, Matthew (1865): *Vancouver Island and British Columbia: Their History, Resources and Prospects*. London, Longman, Green, Longman, Roberts & Green.

Magris, Claudio (2001): *Microcosms*, trans. Iain Halliday. London, The Harvill Press.

Malleson, G. B. (1875): *A Historical Sketch of the Native States of India*. London, Longmans, Green & Co.

Malraux, André, *La Voie Royale*, Paris, Grasset, 1930.

Mänchen-Helfen, Otto (1931): *Reise ins asiatische Tuwa*. Berlin, Verlag Der Bücherkreis GmbH.

Manns, Patricio (1996): *Cavalier seul*. Paris, Phébus.

Manuhutu, Wim (1991): 'Moluccans in the Netherlands: A Political Minority?' *Publications de l'École française de Rome* 146, no. 1.

Mason, Francis Van Wyck (1949): *Dardanelles Derelict: A Major North Story*. New York, Doubleday.

Mason, Wyatt (2003): *I Promise to be Good: The Letters of Arthur Rimbaud*. New York, Modern Library, Random House.

Maurer, Noel & Carlos Yu (2010): *The Big Ditch: How America Took, Built, Ran, and Ultimately Gave Away the Panama Canal*. Princeton, Princeton University Press.

Melville, Fred. J. (1923): *Phantom Philately*. London, The Philatelic Institute.

Meredith, Martin (2008): *Diamonds, Gold and War: The British, the Boers, and the Making of South Africa*. New York, Public Affairs.

Monro, Alexander (1855): *New Brunswick; With a Brief Outline of Nova Scotia, Their History, Civil Divisions, Geography, and Production*. Halifax, Richard Nugent.

Morris, Jan (2001): *Trieste And The Meaning Of Nowhere*. New York, Simon & Schuster.

Mullins, Greg (2002): *Colonial Affairs: Bowles, Burroughs and Chester Write Tangier*. Madison, University of Wisconsin Press.

Murakami, Haruki (1998): *The Wind-up Bird Chronicle*, trans. Jay Rubin. New York, Vintage International.

Nanjee, Iqbal A. & Shahid Zaki (year of publication unknown): '*Bhopal Puzzle*'. Karachi, Stamp Society of Pakistan.

Nansen, Fridtjof (1927): *Gjennom Armenia*. Oslo, Jacob Dybwads Forlag.

Nassau, Robert Hamill (1910): *Corisco Days. The First Thirty Years of the West Africa Mission*. Philadelphia, Allen, Lane & Scott.

Nielsen, Erland Kolding, Arild Hvidtfeldt, Axel Andersen & Tim Greve (1982): *Australia, Oceania og Antarktis*, trans. Eldor Martin Breckan. Oslo, Cappelen.

Nielsen, Aage Krarup (1939): *Helvete hinsides havet: En straffanges opptegnelser fra Guyana*, trans. Alf Harbitz. Oslo, Gyldendal.

Niinistö, Jussi (2001): *Bobi Sivén – Karjalan puolesta*. Helsinki, Suomalaisen Kirjallisuuden Seura.

Nilsen, Edvard & Hans Vatne, eds (1955): *Verden i bilder*. Oslo, Norsk faglitteratur.

Nordenskiöld, Adolf Erik (1881): *Vegas färd kring Asien och Europa*, trans. B. Geelmuyden. Kristiania, Mallings boghandel.

Norman, Henry (1895): *The Peoples and Politics of The Far East*. New York, Charles Scribner's Sons.

Ōe, Kenzaburō (1970): *Okinawa Notes*. Tokyo, Iwanami shinsho.

Olsson, Hagar (1965): *The Woodcarver and Death: A Tale from Karelia*, trans. G. C. Schoolfield. Madison, University of Wisconsin Press.

Oterhals, Leo (2000): *Hvite horisonter*. Molde, Lagunen.

Packham, Eric (1996): *Freedom and Anarchy*. New York, Nova Science Publishers.

Pasternak, Boris (1957): *Doctor Zhivago*. New York, Pantheon.

Perley, M. H. (1857): *A Hand-Book of Information for Emigrants to New-Brunswick*. London, Edward Stanford.

Plaatje, Solomon (1990): *The Mafeking Diary*. Cambridge, Meridon.

Powers, Dennis M. (2010): *Tales of the Seven Seas: The Escapades of Dynamite Johnny O'Brien*. Lanham, Taylor Trade Publishing.

Race, Joe (2010): *The Royal Headley of Pohnpei: Upon a Stone Altar*. Bloomington, Trafford Publishing.

Rainbird, Paul (2004): *The Archaeology of Micronesia*. Cambridge, Cambridge University Press.

Rauschning, Hermann (1939): *Hitler Speaks*. London, Butterworth.

Ricaurte, José Vicente Ortega & Antonio Ferro (1981): *La Gruta Simbólica*. Bogotá, Bogotá Banco Popular.

Rich, Edwin Ernest (1959): *The History of the Hudson's Bay Company*. London, Hudson's Bay Record Society.

Ritsema, Alex (2007): *Heligoland, Past and Present*. Lulu.com.

Rødder, Sverre (1990): *Min ære er troskap: om politiminister Jonas Lie*. Oslo, Aschehoug.

Røkkum, Arne (2006): *Nature, Ritual and Society in Japan's Ryukyu Islands*. Abingdon, Routledge.

Rossiter, Stuart & John Flower (1986): *World History Stamp Atlas*. London, Macdonald & Co Publishers.

Russel, R. V. (1916): *The Tribes And Castes Of The Central Provinces Of India*. London, Macmillan & Co.

Saint-Exupéry, Antoine de (2000/1952): *Wind, Sand and Stars*, trans. William Rees. London, Penguin Modern Classics.

Saint-Exupéry, Antoine de (2016/1954): *Night Flight*, trans. David Carter. Richmond, Alma Classics.

Salamanca Uribe, Juana (2007): 'La Gruta Simbólica: Una anécdota en sí misma'. *Revista Credencial Historia* 216.

Salgari, Emilio (2007): *Sandokan: The Tigers of Mompracem*, trans. Nico Lorenzutti. ROH Press, rohpress.com, Genoa, Donath.

Sampson, Anthony (1975): *The Seven Sisters: The Great Oil Companies & the World They Shaped*. New York, Viking Press.

Scammell, Michael (2014): 'The CIA's "Zhivago"'. *New York Review of Books*, 10 July.

Schimmel, Annmarie (1980): *Islam in the Indian Subcontinent*, Leiden, E. J. Brill.

Schrøder-Nilsen, Ingvald (1925): *Blandt boerne i fred og krig*. Oslo, Steenske forlag.

Schultz-Naumann, Joachim (1985): *Unter Kaisers Flagge: Deutschlands Schutzgebiete im Pazifik und in China einst und heute*. München, Universitas.

Scidmore, Eliza Ruhamah (1903): *Winter India*. London, T. F. Unwin.

Severin, Tim (1987): *The Ulysses Voyage*. New York, Dutton Adult.

Smedal, Gustav (1938): *Nordisk samarbeide og Danmarks sydgrense*. Oslo, Fabritius.

Smits, Gregory (1999): *Visions of Ryukyu: Identity and Ideology in Early-Modern Thought and Politics*. Honolulu, University of Hawaii Press.

Sokolow, Reha, Al Sokolow & Debra Galant (2003): *Defying the Tide: An Account of Authentic Compassion During the Holocaust*. Jerusalem, Devora Publishing.

Solzhenitsyn, Aleksander (2000): *August 1914*, trans. H.T. Willetts. New York, Farrar, Straus and Giroux.

Sontag, Susan (1992): *Volcano Lover: A Romance*. New York, Farrar Straus and Giroux.

Stehberg, Ruben & Liliana Nilo (1983): 'Procedencia antartica inexacta de dos puntas de proyectil'. *Serie Científica del Instituto Chileno Antàrtico* 30.

Stiles, Kent B. (1931): *Geography and Stamps*. New York, Whittlesey House.

St. John, Spenser (1879): *The Life of Sir James Brooke, Rajah of Saráwak, From His Personal Papers and Correspondence.* Edinburgh. W. Blackwood & Sons.

Strandberg, Olle (1961): *Tigerland og sydlig hav.* Bergen, Eide.

Stuart, Graham (1931): *The International City of Tangier.* Redwood City, Stanford University Press.

Suver, Stacey A. (2012): *A Dream of Tangier: Revolution and Identity In Post-War Expatriate Literature.* Tallahassee, Florida State University.

Tacitus, Cornelius (1935): *Germania,* trans. Trygve With. Oslo, Johan Grundt Tanum.

Taylor, Alan J. P. (1971): *The Struggle for Mastery in Europe 1848–1918.* Oxford, Oxford University Press.

Tilak, Laxmibai (2007): *Sketches from Memory.* New Delhi, Katha.

Tollefsen, Gunnerius (1963): *Men Gud gav vekst: En pionermisjonær ser seg tilbake.* Oslo, Filadelfiaforlaget.

Tomasi Di Lampedusa, Giuseppe (2007): *The Leopard,* trans. Archibald Colquhoun. London, Vintage.

Vizcaya, Benita Sampedro (2012): 'Routes to ruin'. *LL Journal,* Vol. 7, no. 2.

Von Rosen, Carl Gustav (1969): *Biafra. Some jeg ser det,* trans. Øyvind Norstrøm. Oslo, Cappelen.

Wallis, Wilson D. & Ruth Sawtell Wallis (1955): *The Micmac Indians of Eastern Canada.* Minneapolis, University of Minnesota Press.

Walonen, Michael K. (2010): *Lamenting Concrete and Coke: Paul Bowles and Brion Gysin on the Changing Spaces of Postcolonial Morocco.* Helsinki, University of Helsinki.

Ward, Ernest F. & Phebe E. Ward (1908): *Echoes From Bharatkhand.* Chicago, Free Methodist Pub. House.

Wedel-Jarlsberg, Georg (1913): *Da jeg var cowboy og andre opplevelser.* Kristiania, Norli.

Weicker, Hans (1908): *Kiautschou, Das deutsche Schutzgebiet in Ostasien.* Berlin, A. Schall.

Werfel, Franz (1934): *The Forty Days of Musa Dagh,* trans. G. Dunlop. New York, The Viking Press.

West, Rebecca (1941): *Black Lamb and Grey Falcon.* New York, The Viking Press.

Wilson, Sarah Isabella Augusta (1909): *South African Memories, Social, Warlike & Sporting, From Diaries Written at the Time.* London, E. Arnold.

Winchester, Simon & Aisin-Gioro Pu Yi (1987): *From Emperor to Citizen: The Autobiography of Aisin-Gioro Pu Yi.* Oxford, Oxford University Press.

Wold, Sidsel (1999): *Warra! Warra! Da de hvite kom til Australia.* Oslo, Omnipax.

Wrigley, Chris (2002): *Winston Churchill: A Biographical Companion.* Santa Barbara, ABC-CLIO.

Zelig, Leo (2008): *Lumumba: Africa's Lost Leader.* London: Haus.

Index

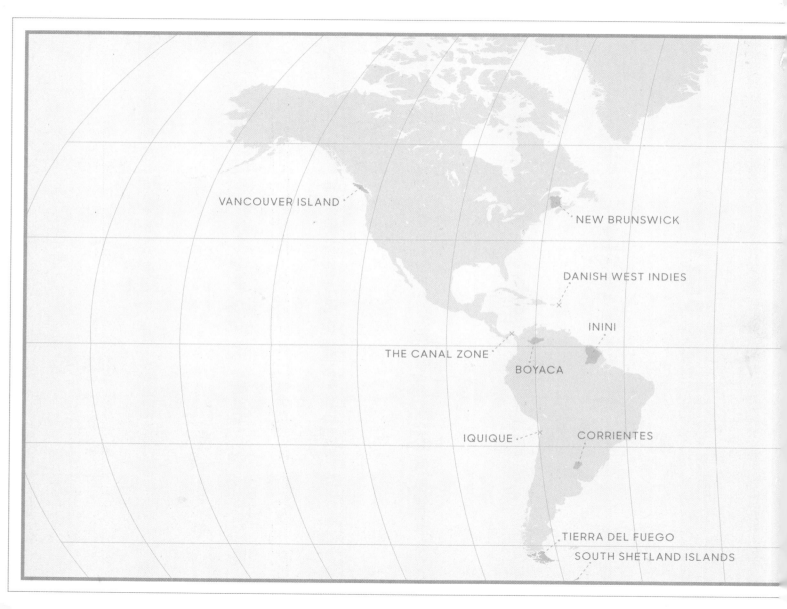

VANCOUVER ISLAND

NEW BRUNSWICK

DANISH WEST INDIES

ININI

THE CANAL ZONE

BOYACA

IQUIQUE

CORRIENTES

TIERRA DEL FUEGO

SOUTH SHETLAND ISLANDS